Land without Masters

Land without Masters

Agrarian Reform and Political Change under Peru's Military Government

ANNA CANT

University of Texas Press *Austin*

Printed in the United States of America
First edition, 2021

Requests for permission to reproduce material from this work should be sent to:
Permissions
University of Texas Press
P.O. Box 7819
Austin, TX 78713-7819
utpress.utexas.edu/rp-form

♾ The paper used in this book meets the minimum requirements of
ANSI/NISO Z39.48-1992 (R1997) (Permanence of Paper).

Library of Congress Cataloging-in-Publication Data

Names: Cant, Anna, author.
Title: Land without masters : agrarian reform and political change under Peru's military government / Anna Cant.
Description: First edition. | Austin : University of Texas Press, 2021. | Includes bibliographical references and index.
Identifiers:
LCCN 2020034689
ISBN 978-1-4773-2202-4 (cloth)
ISBN 978-1-4773-2203-1 (library ebook)
ISBN 978-1-4773-2204-8 (ebook)
Subjects: LCSH: Land reform—Peru—History—20th century. | Peru—Politics and government—20th century.
Classification: LCC HD1333.P4 C354 2021 | DDC 333.3/18509047—dc23
LC record available at https://lccn.loc.gov/2020034689

doi:10.7560/322024

Contents

Acknowledgments

I have many people to thank for their help in writing this book. Special thanks go to all the people who agreed to be interviewed for my research. They gave generously of their time and responded thoughtfully to my many questions.

I am grateful to the Arts and Humanities Research Council for funding my MPhil and PhD research and to Clare College for providing additional funds to support my research in Peru. A year as a fellow in the Department of International History at the London School of Economics and Political Science provided valuable writing time—and support from colleagues—to finish revising the manuscript.

I thank Kerry Webb for her enthusiasm for this project and her help in shepherding it through to publication. The two anonymous readers provided comments and suggestions that have immeasurably improved the end result. I thank them for their time and dedication.

Dr. Gabriela Ramos first inspired me to study Peruvian history and encouraged me to pursue this project. She has taught me never to be satisfied with an easy answer. Her wise words and insightful questions have shaped this book and continue to guide my research.

I am grateful to the staff of Senate House Library in London for facilitating access to the wonderful collection of Latin American pamphlets held in the special collections and for assisting in obtaining scanned images of the Peruvian material.

In Lima, I was assisted by staff at the Biblioteca Nacional del Perú, the Pontificia Universidad Católica del Perú, the Centro de Estudios Histórico Militares del Perú, and the Centro de Estudios para el Desarrollo y la Participación. I thank Ruth Borja for enabling me to access the archives of the

Confederación Campesina del Perú and Víctor Arrambide for his help in navigating the often frustrating world of archival research.

I also thank the staff of regional archives in Tacna, Piura, and Cusco and the Centro Bartolomé de las Casas library in Cusco. Sadly, Bruno Revesz passed away during the writing of the thesis upon which this book is based. I am grateful to him for inviting me to the Centro de Investigación y Promoción del Campesinado as a visiting scholar and to all the staff there for their warm welcome.

Marco Chevarría and Ronald Romero were excellent hosts in Cusco, helping me to enjoy life beyond the archives and keeping me well stocked in Pisco sours. In Lima, the Alvarez family welcomed me with open arms. Their love, support, and laughter kept me sane during some difficult times.

At Cambridge University, I learned a great deal from seminars organized by Professors Joya Chatterji, David Washbrook, and Tim Harper of the history faculty and by Dr. Yael Navaro-Yashin of the Department of Social Anthropology. I also had the good fortune to meet Tara Cookson, Jess Hammett, and Emily Sloan. They walked the often lonely PhD road with me and helped keep my spirits up.

As a doctoral student, I spent six months as a visiting student at Columbia University in New York. I am grateful to Professor Claudio Lomnitz for welcoming me into the anthropology department and for his thoughtful comments on my research. Seminars organized by students of the anthropology and history departments provided a lively, friendly environment in which to exchange ideas.

I thank Matthew Duncombe, Geoff Goodwin, and Jess Hammett for reading and commenting on draft chapters of the book. I am deeply grateful to all my friends and family for supporting me throughout the research and writing process. I especially wish to thank my wonderful mother, sister, and brother for their encouragement and faith in me. Above all, this book would not have been possible without Ramin, whose love and intellectual engagement are a constant source of strength and inspiration.

Abbreviations

Agencies and Organizations

ALFIN	Alfabetización Integral
APRA	Alianza Popular Revolucionaria Americana
CAP	Cooperativa Agraria de Producción
CBC	Centro Bartolomé de las Casas, Cusco
CCP	Confederación Campesina del Perú
CEDEP	Centro de Estudios para el Desarrollo y la Participación
CENCIRA	Centro Nacional de Capacitación y Investigación para la Reforma Agraria
CIPCA	Centro de Investigación y Promoción del Campesinado, Piura
CNA	Confederación Nacional Agraria
CRAV	Comisión para la Reforma Agraria y la Vivienda
DESCO	Centro de Estudios y Promoción del Desarrollo
DGRAAR	Dirección General de Reforma Agraria y Asentamiento Rural
DPDRA	Dirección de Promoción y Difusión de la Reforma Agraria
MIR-CA	Movimiento de Izquierda Revolucionaria-Cuarta Etapa
SINAMOS	Sistema Nacional de Apoyo a la Movilización Social
VR	Vanguardia Revolucionaria
SAIS	Sociedad Agrícola de Interés Social

Land without Masters

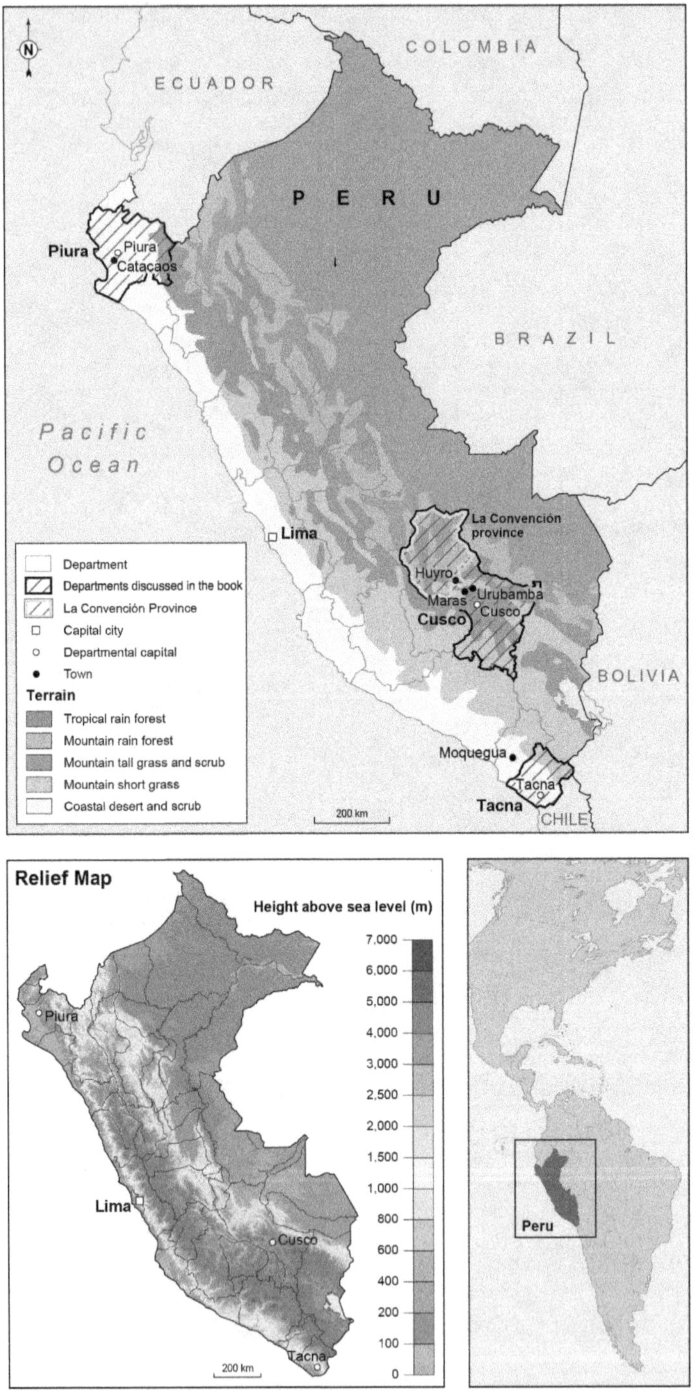

Figure 0.1. Maps of Peru. Produced by Silas Tull, University of Cambridge, 2015.

Introduction

Throughout the twentieth century, unequal access to land and the use of land monopolies to control labor gave rise to intense political struggles across Latin America.[1] In the Mexican Revolution, land reform provided a call to arms among peasants who had been dispossessed during the liberal capitalist government of Porfirio Díaz.[2] Fidel Castro described agrarian reform as "a matter of life and death" and viewed it as essential for solving Cuba's problems of rural poverty, landlessness, and underemployment.[3] In Chile, both the Christian Democrat Eduardo Frei and the socialist Salvador Allende championed agrarian reform as a means to secure greater social equality.[4] Similar reforms took place in Ecuador, Bolivia, Central America, and the Caribbean from the mid-twentieth century onward.[5] In each of these countries, land ownership was viewed as the principal question of wealth distribution and political rights.

When Juan Velasco Alvarado's left-wing military government took power in 1968, land inequality in Peru was amongst the most pronounced across the region. Large amounts of land were concentrated in the hands of a small number of large estates, while huge numbers of peasants survived through subsistence farming of small plots and/or waged labor on large estates.[6] The 1961 census found that the richest 0.2 percent of landowners owned 72.9 percent of agricultural land, while the poorest 34.1 percent owned just 0.7 percent.[7] Previous land reform attempts had faltered due to entrenched elite interests and weak political will. However, the Velasco government placed agrarian reform at the center of its vision for "the new Peru." The 1969 agrarian reform law began an ambitious redistribution of land to peasant cooperatives and set out to abolish land monopolies.

More than 50 years after it was introduced, the agrarian reform remains one of the most controversial issues in Peru's modern history. While right-wing commentators characterize it as a "robolution" that unjustly expropriated land and ruined the Peruvian economy,[8] others emphasize the fact that it brought an end to the semifeudal system of economic exploitation and oppression in the countryside.[9] To some extent these contrasting perspectives reflect the views of the winners and losers in what was a major redistribution of economic and political power (45 percent of Peru's agricultural land was redistributed from large landowners to peasants). But they are also a mark of the intensely ideological terms in which the agrarian reform was justified and carried out.

This was not a neutral process overseen by technocrats in distant government offices but one that was actively promoted through government interventions in local politics, education, and mass communication. Across the country, peasants were encouraged to imagine a more socially just world in which their life chances would not be constrained by the will of the hacendado (landlord). In the words of one of the posters produced at the time, the agrarian reform held the prospect of "land without masters" (*tierra sin patrones*). In a propaganda effort that was unprecedented in Peru's history, the Velasco government hired hundreds of artists, intellectuals, and promoters to articulate its reform agenda. This book takes a fresh look at the political and cultural changes brought by the agrarian reform by moving beyond its success or failure as an agricultural policy and examining its importance as an ideological project. In studying government efforts to promote the agrarian reform at local, regional, and national levels, it shows how the reform process opened new political debates on citizenship, national identity, and the role of the state that in turn transformed Peru's political culture.

Historical Context

On 3 October 1968, General Juan Velasco Alvarado, commander in chief of the Peruvian army, seized control of the government palace. Citing the political instability of the current government and the exposure of a recent corruption scandal as justification, General Velasco ousted the democratically elected President Fernando Belaúnde Terry and installed the Revolutionary Government of the Armed Forces (Gobierno Revolucionario de las Fuerzas Armadas). As the historian Thomas Wright notes, the Velasco coup occurred at the end of a decade that had been marked by revolutionaries' frustrated attempts to replicate the Cuban Revolution across Latin America. Peru's military government "opened a new perspective on revolution in Latin America: the prospect of revolution, or at least structural reform, from above."[10]

Similar kinds of military reformism were seen in the nationalist government of Omar Torrijos in Panama (1970–1971), the leftist military government of Juan José Torres in Bolivia (1970–1981), and the military regime of Guillermo Rodríguez Lara in Ecuador (1972–1976), which explicitly modeled itself on the Peruvian example.[11] In part, the Peruvian military's seizing of power and pursuit of reform from above reflected a region-wide trend toward placing structural change in the hands of the armed forces, viewed as the most capable and trustworthy social sector amidst the political tumult of the Cold War. Yet unlike the military governments in Brazil, Argentina, and Chile, which defended elite privilege and used the threat of communism as moral justification, the Velasco government proclaimed its intention to bring down the oligarchy and introduce major social change to benefit the majority.[12]

The radical nature of the changes proposed by the military government is clear in the language used in its political program, the *Plan Inca*, which begins: "The Revolution of the armed forces will carry out a process of transformation of the economic, social, political and cultural structures, with the aim of achieving a new society, in which the Peruvian man and woman may live with liberty and justice."[13] The plan set out a total of 31 objectives across different policy areas, including the nationalization of the petroleum industry, mining and industrial reform, refinancing the national debt, agrarian reform, a complete overhaul of the education system, and major state investment in health and housing.[14] Following the nationalization of the US-owned International Petroleum Company on 9 October 1968, the agrarian reform was the second major policy to be put into practice by the Velasco government.

The Agrarian Reform Law (Decree Law [D.L.] 17716) was promulgated on 24 June 1969. It aimed to replace the existing agrarian structure of latifundios (large estates) and minifundios (subsistence farms) with "a just system of property, tenancy and exploitation of the land, that will contribute to the social and economic development of the nation, through the creation of an agrarian order that guarantees social justice in the countryside and increases the production and productivity of the agricultural sector."[15] Specifically, the law provided for the expropriation of landholdings that exceeded a maximum number of hectares (150 on the coast and 15–55 in the highlands) and their adjudication to newly established agricultural cooperatives, peasant communities, or individual claimants. It also subjected rural working conditions to state regulation and outlawed practices of neo-feudalism, such as providing access to agricultural land in return for labor.

The national scope of the 1969 agrarian reform gave it much greater weight than previous reform attempts, but the application of a single law across extremely diverse topography, socioeconomic contexts, and agricultural systems also brought great challenges. The production cooperative model envisaged by the reform made a certain amount of sense on the coastal plantations, where industrialized agriculture and a strong trade union history laid the groundwork for collectivized production. Yet such a model was much more difficult to implement among the traditional wool-producing haciendas of the central and southern highlands, which were characterized by highly dispersed populations whose community structures implied a degree of mutual assistance but not collectivized production or land ownership. Cultural differences, such as the predominance of Quechua and the persistence of neo-feudal relations between hacendados and indigenous laborers, also complicated the task of implementing an homogenous, centrally conceived agrarian reform. Aware of the challenges of delivering major reform on a national scale, the Velasco government did not limit itself to passing new legislation but rather created a series of government agencies tasked with promoting and implementing its reforms.

Given that multiple sectors of the population were already demanding land reform by the time the 1968 coup took place, the Velasco government's insistence on promoting and mobilizing support for the agrarian reform in rural areas might seem counterintuitive. However, the government saw the effective promotion of its agrarian reform as vital for a number of reasons. First, it was important to educate hacienda workers about their rights and entitlements so that they might organize and resist landowners' attempts to asset-strip their farms in advance of the reform administrators' arrival. Second, the government wished to disseminate its vision of land reform in place of the more radical approach pursued by peasant communities and guerrilla organizations. Whereas peasant-led land occupations in the early 1960s and the short-lived guerrilla movements of 1965 used direct action to take back land for the landless, the Velasco government, resolute about avoiding capitulation to grassroots actions, was determined that land reform should be led by the state.[16] Third, the Velasco government was keen to link its agrarian reform to a wider vision of social change that included the incorporation of marginalized peasant populations and a more equitable distribution of wealth and political control. In that respect the agrarian reform provided an opportunity not just to redistribute resources but to disseminate new ideas of collectivism and national identity.

All of these tasks required government functionaries to act in a way that was more akin to a political party than a neutral bureaucracy, articulating the ideology that underpinned the agrarian reform and emphasizing its importance within the so-called revolutionary process. To begin with, this state activism was undertaken by ad hoc organizations such as the Dirección de Promoción y Difusión de la Reforma Agraria (Directorate of Promotion and Diffusion of the Agrarian Reform [DPDRA]). In 1971, however, the government created two much larger organizations that adopted a more systematic approach: the Sistema Nacional de Apoyo a la Movilización Social (National System of Support for Social Mobilization [SINAMOS]), whose role spanned the promotion of the government's entire reform program, and the more specific Centro Nacional de Capacitación y Investigación para la Reforma Agraria (National Centre of Training and Research for the Agrarian Reform [CENCIRA]). Through interventions in education, political mobilization, and the mass media, these organizations sought to neutralize political opposition and reinforce the government's ideology. These interventions, and their repercussions in three distinct regions of Peru, are the focus of this book.

Research Themes

Despite the widely recognized significance of the Peruvian agrarian reform, there remain important gaps in knowledge regarding its internal dynamics and long-term effects. The Velasco government came to an abrupt end in 1975, following a coup led by one of Velasco's own cabinet, General Morales Bermúdez. The conservative Morales Bermúdez regime (1975–1980) reversed many of the Velasco government's reforms and began to withdraw state support for the agrarian reform.[17] This change in regime meant that the state had little interest in preserving the history of the agrarian reform. Moreover, the movement away from state-led reform since the 1970s has tended to overshadow the reform's achievements and emphasize its failures.[18]

At the time of the reform, the Peruvian case was the subject of intense scholarly interest from political scientists interested in military reformism and state-led development and from anthropologists and sociologists keen to understand the agrarian reform's impact on community dynamics and regional politics.[19] Researchers who observed the agrarian reform at the local level provided important insights on the heterogeneous contexts in which it was implemented, from large industrialized latifundios on the coast to dispersed rural communities in the highlands, often noting the disconnect between central government policy and local socioeconomic structures.[20] They also highlighted the explosion of political debate that emerged among rural communities.[21] However, these political struggles were analyzed in often rather rigid class terms. For example, Fernando Eguren argued that the intense debates that had emerged in the Chancay Valley (central coastal Peru) were a reflection of the class conflict between the government's "bourgeois" agrarian reform and the "proletarian" vision of the former hacienda workers.[22] David Chaplin claimed that the government's system of cooperatives would "lead to the demobilization of the masses . . . by means of diverting workers from their real class interests."[23] Such criticism judged the Velasco government against a preconceived standard of popular mobilization, leaving little room for understanding the internal dynamics of the government's mobilization project or assessing its reception among different sectors of the population.

A more recent body of work takes a more nuanced approach. Historians have examined the complex relationship between local and national dimensions of the reform and situated it within the *longue durée* histories of particular regions. For example, Linda Seligmann shows how peasants invoked state narratives in their petitions to the Agrarian Tribunal (the court established to resolve disputes relating to the agrarian reform), directly engaging with the national government's rhetoric.[24] Jaymie Heilman argues that the uneven and in some cases disappointing application of the agrarian reform in the southern region of Ayacucho was part of a long tradition of state abandonment of rural communities and that this tradition was a critical factor in the growth and radicalization of the Shining Path terrorist organization, which waged war against the state throughout the 1980s and 1990s.[25] In a similar methodological vein—although reaching different conclusions—José Luis Rénique places the implementation of the agrarian reform in Puno within a larger history of agrarian conflict that was both particular to the region and a key aspect of Peruvian nation building, serving as the necessary "other" to the Lima-centric, "civilizing" political establishment.[26]

Such studies have considerably enhanced our understanding of state-society relations in the context of the agrarian reform, but there remain a number of questions regarding the political battles that opened up during the agrarian reform and their long-term impact on Peruvian politics. What role did the military government envisage for peasants within its plan of land redistribution? How was this received and contested at the local level? How did the intense state attention directed at rural areas alter the orientation of national political discourse? This book addresses these questions using a regional comparative approach.[27]

Starting from the position that local context and history were more than incidental to the lived experience of the agrarian reform, this book focuses on three regions in particular: Piura, Tacna, and Cusco. Across these three regions I compare local perceptions of the reform, government interventions that accompanied the reform, and the political debates that emerged on the ground. I look at the similarities and differences between the ways in which a variety of actors—political parties, SINAMOS, landowners, peasant organizations, government, and opposition mass media—intervened in the agrarian reform process in each region and what lies behind these similarities and differences. As well as enriching our understanding of the reform process in each of these regions, the book therefore tells a bigger story about the relationship between central government and the regions, how the idea of the region is consolidated and reshaped through state practice, and the challenges of establishing political hegemony in the context of great regional diversity.

Regional Comparison

Regional or subnational comparative research has boomed in the social sciences in recent years. Beyond the methodological advantages of studying a particular policy or state practice from different vantage points, subnational comparison can also make fruitful contributions to theory building. As noted by the political scientist Prerna Singh, subnational comparison can be used in a variety of ways to explain both regional and national policy outcomes. First, by comparing different regions one can assess whether the local outcomes owe more to the local context or the national policy. Second, subnational variations in the outcomes of national policies can help explain the overall national outcome (i.e., a national picture of moderate success might contain within it pockets of failure and great success rather than a consistent outcome across regions). Third, subnational comparison allows one to study subnational politics as an outcome of the interactions between various levels of politics, rather than as a contained unit. Fourth, subnational comparison can reveal new insights about the dynamics of a nationally observed process.[28]

Singh puts this last approach into practice in her study of social service provision and welfare outcomes in India. In answer to the question of why social development in some Indian states is so much higher than others, she argues that a strong collective identity provides an important impetus for state prioritization of social welfare. In states with a strong collective identity, such as Kerala, progressive policies are given high priority, whereas in states where subnational solidarity is weak, as in Uttar Pradesh, the sense of a common purpose is absent and public policies are significantly less development oriented.[29] Such comparisons in turn reveal the importance of subnational identities in the overall construction of India's national welfare state. In the case of the Peruvian agrarian reform, subnational comparison offers a means to understand both the uneven dynamics of its application and how regional identities shaped the ultimate outcomes of the Velasco government's national revolution.[30] This examination is particularly focused on whether the nationally produced slogans of the agrarian reform resonated with regional perceptions of the land problem and to what extent the modernizing vision projected by the Velasco government was challenged or reformulated within different local contexts. Ways in which localities and regions experienced the agrarian reform, which have been underappreciated, shaped how it is remembered and talked about in contemporary politics.

The regions of Piura, Tacna, and Cusco were selected on the basis of their contrasting histories and socioeconomic makeup. By comparing such different regions, I seek to analyze both the ways in which different regional populations responded to the agrarian reform and the continuities or differences in the interactions between local, regional, and national layers of government. A brief outline of each region will help clarify the point.

Piura, in the far north of Peru, is a coastal region that includes 20 percent coastal land and 2.8 percent highlands, with the remainder taken up by plains and desert.[31] Growth in the export trade of cotton and sugar in the mid-twentieth century led to the development of large agro-industrial complexes that used increasing levels of mechanization and were owned by economic associations rather than single families. Piura's valleys and plains were characterized by large cotton-producing estates belonging to powerful landowner associations, such as the Romero Onrubia group, which owned a total of 103,991 hectares (about 257,000 acres), while the highlands were occupied by smaller haciendas and peasant communities that produced livestock and farmed small plots of unirrigated land.[32]

Prior to the agrarian reform, the peasantry was weakly organized across Piura, in contrast to the large landowners, who operated powerful organizations, such as the Departmental Agricultural and Livestock League and the Association of Chira Agriculturalists. In 1966, President Belaúnde's center-right party, Acción Popular (Popular Action), founded the Federación Departamental de Campesinos de Piura (Departmental Federation of Piura Peasants [FEDECAP]) to represent peasant interests, but this was largely controlled by urban trade unionists who oriented their work toward indigenous communities rather than waged laborers.[33] The majority of peasants worked as temporary laborers on the large haciendas and were therefore not effectively represented by FEDECAP. During the Velasco era, Piura became an important political base for the left-wing parties Vanguardia Revolucionaria (Revolutionary Vanguard [VR]) and Movimiento de la Izquierda Revolucionaria-Cuarta Etapa (Movement of the Revolutionary Left-Fourth Stage [MIR-CA]), which mobilized peasants to demand a more radical agrarian reform. Piura's agriculture had been declining since the early 1960s due to global economic conditions and the threat of agrarian reform, which inhibited investment. The high degree of unemployment caused by this decline placed Piura's peasants in an economically and politically precarious situation. This made them both highly responsive to the agrarian reform and a target for left-wing activism, since they were considered to hold strong revolutionary potential.[34]

Cusco, in the southern highlands, has a subtropical highland climate that is generally dry and temperate, with two defined seasons: the dry season from April to October and the rainy season from November to March.[35] The varied landscape makes it possible to produce a wide range of agricultural products, from tea and coffee in the high forests to wheat and barley in the lower altitude valleys. In contrast to the agro-industrial plantations in Piura, Cusco farming methods were more traditional and less intensive, since the high altitudes and steep inclines did not permit the use of heavy machinery. In the late 1960s, agricultural land continued to be highly concentrated in the hands of a small number of hacendados and religious orders. The extent of capitalist penetration in the region should not be underestimated; peasant uprisings in the province of La Convención in the early 1960s were in large part a reaction to the tensions created by capitalist development in the highland jungle areas of Cusco. Nevertheless, the great haciendas of Cusco were more commonly seen by their owners as indicators of social status and regional power rather than centers of capitalist accumulation, as was the case in the agro-industrial complexes of Piura.[36]

Whereas peasant mobilization in Piura developed rapidly and largely in response to the economic decline of the mid-twentieth century and the new political context opened up by the agrarian reform, Cusco had an established history of peasant unions and popular mobilization against exploitative landowners. Although conditions varied across the region, labor scarcity in the remote highlands gave peasants a stronger bargaining position, particularly on the coffee-producing estates of La Convención and Lares.[37] Peasant activism ranged from strikes in protest against abusive landowners to hacienda occupations by campesinos who claimed historic ownership of the land. The activities of the campesino unions in the Cusco region reached a peak in the period from December 1963 until March 1964, when numerous haciendas were invaded simultaneously across the region.[38] Communist organizers played a significant role in these protests. The first communist cell had been established in the city of Cusco in 1929 and was affiliated directly to the Communist International.[39] In the 1940s, the Communist Party developed an important presence in the Cusco countryside via the Federación de Trabajadores del Cusco (Federation of Cusco Workers).[40] With the arrival of peasant activist Hugo Blanco in the valley of La Convención in 1958, the region gained a reputation as a communist stronghold.

Tacna, on the southern coast, presents a further contrast in geography, patterns of land tenure, and political tradition. It has a varied landscape, predominantly flat but with some mountainous areas to the west, with a mild desert climate and large amounts of sunshine year round.[41] Lack of irrigation and topographical limitations meant that in 1961, just 1.16 percent of the total surface area of Tacna was cultivated and by 1978 this had increased only to 1.49 percent.[42] At the time of the agrarian reform, Tacna had a large number of small landowners and few latifundios of the kind found in northern Peru. In 1961, some 73.76 percent of Tacna's cultivated land was held in plots of less than five hectares (classed as minifundios); 21.89 percent were extensions of between five and fifty hectares; and just 4.35 percent were more than fifty hectares.[43] Tacna's chief agricultural products were alfalfa and other food crops, rather than international exports such as coffee, sugar, or cotton. Alongside agricultural production, Tacna's economy centered on mining, industry, and fishing, while its proximity to the border with Chile made it an area of intense commercial activity.[44]

Politically, Tacna was not a stronghold for any of the major parties. In the 1963 election, the Alianza Popular Revolucionaria Americana (American Popular Revolutionary Alliance [APRA]), Peru's first mass political party, had gained just 14.02 percent of votes—the second lowest return in the country.[45] Unlike Piura and Cusco, which saw a growth of political activism during the agrarian reform, "party politics in Tacna were reduced to barely perceptible activities within the workers' trade unions, the local university and intellectual circles."[46] In Tacna the great political struggles of the twentieth century related to Peru's conflict with Chile, rather than localized land disputes and labor conditions. The fifty-year Chilean occupation of Tacna following the War of the Pacific (1879–1883) deeply affected the history and identity of the region, forging a political discourse that was both nationalistic and defiantly independent.[47] Unlike Cusco and Piura, which have been considered emblematic cases and received sustained attention in academic research, studies of the agrarian reform in Tacna are almost nonexistent. Yet Tacna's agriculture also formed part of the Velasco government's vision for a new Peru, and it was also subject to sustained media, education, and political campaigns throughout the reform era. This makes it an intriguing case to compare with Cusco and Piura, and one that helps highlight the agrarian reform's importance as an act of nation building.

Methodologically, the writing of comparative history poses a number of challenges. The first and most basic challenge concerns the unit of comparison. In a comparison of the experiences of agrarian reform in Peru's regions, the category of "region" is itself quite slippery and has been defined in multiple ways over the course of Peru's history. In fact, I soon found through examining government archives that the definition and management of regions through state practice is itself an interesting and important object of study and that the military government was particularly striking for its tendency to think in regional terms. As such, the three regions presented in this book should not be understood as fixed entities but rather as geographical locations in which multiple bureaucratic structures, cultural identities, and economic networks overlapped.

Second, comparative research must also negotiate the difficult balance between analytical depth and breadth. In this case, it was important to recognize the internal diversity of each region while synthesizing the material sufficiently to enable systematic comparison. For example, there was a marked contrast between Piura's indigenous highland communities, many of which had gained land titles long before the 1969 agrarian reform, and its coastal plantation workers, who were key protagonists in the region's agricultural production cooperatives. I have endeavored to remain alive to such variation while at the same time building a larger picture of the politics of agrarian reform at regional and national levels.

Finally, comparative history is extremely labor intensive, requiring in-depth archival work and field research in multiple locations. I found that archives available in one region often had no equivalent in another; interviews that were relatively easy to arrange in one place proved elusive elsewhere. It is partly for this reason that the book's final chapter, on the historical memory of the reform, departs from the regional comparative framework maintained in the rest of the book. The long-term ethnographic research that would be required to compare the formation and preservation of memory in Tacna, Cusco, and Piura in the decades since the agrarian reform was not possible within the scope of this project. Yet the question of the agrarian reform's place in historical memory was too important to leave out altogether. Instead, this chapter incorporates my regional fieldwork alongside secondary research on memory and contemporary politics in Peru.

Sources

Whereas many studies of land reform concentrate on specific land struggles and their articulation through the courts and state bureaucracy, I examine the agrarian reform's wider social impact in education, local politics, and mass communication. This approach involves the use of sources not normally analyzed in relation to land reform. By combining newspapers, political ephemera, visual media, government reports, and oral histories, I incorporate the perspectives of a wide range of interest groups involved in the reform. These varied perspectives provide a more comprehensive understanding of the tensions that emerged during the reform process than that provided by the historical record alone.

Archival material on the Velasco era is fragmented and widely dispersed. Following Velasco's removal from power in 1975, the incoming regime led by General Morales Bermúdez launched a steady campaign to destroy much of the documentation relating to state planning and popular mobilization, which was viewed as excessively radical.[48] A substantial amount of material relating to the agrarian reform remains in the General National Archive, but the majority of this is uncatalogued and therefore inaccessible to researchers. Historical documents have also been lost through inadvertent deterioration or poor archival infrastructure; at the regional government archive in Piura, I was informed that all correspondence over ten years old was routinely destroyed due to lack of storage space.

Visual and sound archives were even more difficult to trace. In the archive of Radio Nacional del Perú I found that although a number of radio recordings have been preserved, the technology needed to listen to them is rare and difficult to access, and in many cases the magnetic tape used for recordings is now too fragile to handle. Much of the information on radio in this book comes from written reports or interviews. In the case of television, newsreels were often reused or disposed of, and no television archive has been maintained. Peru has no national film archive; the country's existing film archives are largely the result of efforts by private individuals.[49] One of the advantages of the growth in internet access is that individuals have begun to upload their private collections to sites such as YouTube. However, these are often incomplete or provide little accompanying contextual information. The absence of a state-maintained archive is a telling indication of the agrarian reform's status within contemporary political discourse. As I discuss in chapter 5, successive governments have distanced themselves from the radical policies of the Velasco era and favored a neoliberal agenda that minimizes the possibilities for state-led reform.

The dispersed nature of the historical record raises important questions about its representativeness. In her article on the use of archives as sites of state ethnography, Ann Laura Stoler argues that rather than mining state archives for the content of government reports, researchers should engage with archives as sites of "knowledge production," where "facts" are created and classified in ways that reinforce state power.[50] In conducting the research for this book, I was in the reverse position. The government documents I encountered were not catalogued and stored in order to present a particular version of events. Rather, they often turned up unexpectedly in the national library and in the private collections of nongovernmental organizations. Given the absence of an organizing archival frame, how was I to determine whether the documents I encountered were representative, or what their importance was at the time? The solution I chose was to use a wide variety of source materials, including posters, pamphlets, film, newspapers, government reports, and oral history, to build up the most complete picture possible. Cross-referencing between these materials helped identify recurrent themes and tensions. It also proved an effective way of identifying the key images, symbols, and motifs used across different forms of government propaganda.

While it was often difficult to bring all these materials together to build a consistent historical argument, using such a variety of sources also helped to reconstruct a process that was rich in competing voices, ideas, and ways of remembering. For his book *Ugly Stories of the Peruvian Agrarian Reform*, Enrique Mayer interviewed a variety of people from different social backgrounds about their experiences of the agrarian reform. He observed that his interviewees "mixed personal memories, shared experiences, popular opinions produced at that time or collectively elaborated afterward, apt examples kept in mind as cautionary tales, unconfirmed gossip, and political opinions."[51] Attitudes toward the agrarian reform (both at the time and subsequently) were not motivated by personal experience alone; they reflected ideas expressed in the mass media, government institutions, education, and political activism. By combining sources from each of these social spheres, I was able to examine the different ways in which ideas circulated and reflect on how they were received at the time.

Regional and national newspapers provided important information on the public discourse that surrounded the agrarian reform. Each of the regions included in my research had one or two prominent regional newspapers. I was interested both in the specific events reported (expropriations, land adjudication ceremonies, public rallies and protests) and the political interpretations given through editorial style and opinion pieces. Local newspapers are particularly valuable in offering alternative perspectives on the agrarian reform, since they were not subject to government censorship and remained exempt from the 1974 press reform that expropriated all national daily newspapers.[52] My use of newspapers is qualitative rather than quantitative; I examine the meanings established through language and argumentation, rather than using statistical methods of linguistic analysis. While this approach holds the danger of subjective selection, I find it a more effective way of establishing broad patterns in news reporting. To surveying the day-to-day reports on the progress of the agrarian reform, I added and focused on key dates (such as the announcement of the agrarian reform) and their anniversaries across the 1968–1975 period.

Given the high rate of illiteracy in Peru at the time, the imagery included in both government and opposition publications often had to do a lot of the communication "work." While the scarcity of certain sources (particularly films and posters) precludes a systematic survey of government imagery, visual analysis adds an important dimension to my interpretation. For example, I found that campesinos wielding the Peruvian flag were a recurrent image in government pamphlets about the agrarian reform, expressing the government's desire to use the reform to "incorporate" the peasantry into the nation. Comparing the different ways in which campesinos, the government, and "the new Peru" are portrayed across government and opposition publications also highlights the points of friction within this state project. While the government used iconography to suggest continuity between its "revolution" and the indigenous political heroes of the past, this claim was heavily satirized in cartoons produced by left-wing political party VR.

A large number of anthropologists and sociologists were employed by the government to assess the progress of the reform.[53] Their reports are not dry statements of official policy but often surprisingly candid reflections written by people who felt personally committed to the reform process. In addition, I draw on central government reports (published and unpublished) and the internal correspondence of government officials working in the regions of Piura, Tacna, and Cusco. This provides multiple angles on state activity and highlights the different social and political problems that officials encountered in each of these regions.

Oral interviews with people involved in the agrarian reform considerably enrich this book. I conducted interviews with a total of 49 individuals, including former government employees, cooperative members, landowners, political activists (from VR and MIR-CA) and workers for nongovernmental organizations. Beginning with one or two contacts in each location, I used the "snowball" interviewing technique. That is, during each interview I asked the interviewee to identify four or five other people whom they thought could provide useful information for my research. Given the relatively short research period (nine months), who I was able to interview often depended on luck and individuals' willingness to participate, rather than the construction of a systematic sample. Taking these limitations into account, I have tried to represent a range of different voices within the book. While the citations used in the text are necessarily selective, the often long conversations I shared with different interviewees have informed my interpretation in important ways.

Oral history has certain limitations as historical evidence: it centers on particular individuals whose personal stories are not necessarily representative of wider historical trends. The fallibility of memory can alter the telling of events, while the personality or conduct of the interviewer can influence the interviewee's response in significant ways. Yet oral interviews have the advantage of gathering histories that rarely make it into written sources, such as the day-to-day experiences of cooperative members and government employees. In this project, interviews also helped fill gaps where other sources (government records, film, radio, posters) had been destroyed or perished. Perhaps most significantly, oral history provides a vital way to study memory and the complex relationship between the past and present.[54] It reveals, for example, how primary experiences of the agrarian reform can be displaced by the force of propaganda that circulated at the time or by later politically motivated revisions. Interviewing several individuals from a single group (e.g., former SINAMOS employees) also highlighted the role of collective memory in the formation and maintenance of group identities.

Chapter Outlines

In chapter 1, I examine the origins of the land problem in Peru and set out why the agrarian reform came to be viewed as the central question of national politics. For those already aware of the Peruvian case or the wider history of twentieth-century land reforms in Latin America, this chapter will cover much ground that is familiar and may be passed over. However, for readers with no prior knowledge of Peru's agrarian reform, I hope this chapter will provide a useful introduction and guidance on further reading. While often expressed as a question of land scarcity, Peru's land inequality had deep historical and political origins in the development of the hacienda system. The concentration of land ownership had been intensifying since the start of the twentieth century, with the insertion of Peru's agricultural industry into global capitalist markets, and was sustained by a political system that defended elite privilege and excluded the peasantry on grounds of race and class. Government attempts to introduce land reform in 1962 and 1964 were limited in scope and stymied by landowner opposition. I place the 1969 agrarian reform law in historical context and describe the opposition it encountered from both the Left and Right. The political tensions outlined in the chapter are crucial for understanding the politicized nature of the state interventions discussed in the subsequent three chapters.

In chapter 2, I look at the military government's perception of regional diversity and its efforts to communicate effectively with different regional populations. In particular, I examine the work of SINAMOS, a state organization established to promote the government's reforms. By linking the experiences of Piura, Tacna, and Cusco, I build a more complete picture of the state apparatus used to deliver the reform and show how government "promoters" tried to establish political hegemony in rural areas by responding to regional cultural diversity and translating the revolution into locally meaningful discourse.

In chapter 3, I address the Velasco government's use of education to create a new kind of citizen, one able to participate in "the new Peru." Alongside its 1972 education reform and national literacy program, the Velasco government made extensive provision for education and training within agricultural cooperatives. In comparing rural education programs in Piura, Tacna, and Cusco, I show how the cooperative ideology espoused by the military government clashed with regional traditions of mutual assistance and understandings of the collective. At the same time, the chapter delineates how, in all three regions, the emancipatory discourse promoted through government education programs helped propel a generation of peasant leaders into politically prominent roles and paved the way for the extension of suffrage to illiterates in 1979.

Alongside local politics and education, the Velasco government used the mass media extensively to promote its reform agenda. The conservative bias of the major newspapers and radio stations had been a significant source of opposition to comprehensive land reform throughout the 1950s and 60s. By contrast, the Velasco government saw the agrarian reform as a means to incorporate the country's long marginalized peasants into national political life and engaged in mass media campaigns that emphasized popular participation. In chapter 4 I show these campaigns were often innovative in their style and approach, capitalizing on emerging trends among Peru's intellectuals and artists.[55] But the most radical and controversial step taken by the Velasco government with regard to the mass media was the expropriation of the national newspapers in 1974. I look at what motivated this action, and the cultural experiments that occurred within state-controlled media. I demonstrate that, contrary to common assertions about the repressive nature of dictatorship, the agrarian reform created a precedent for social dialogue, evident in new uses of the mass media (radio fora, political documentaries, worker-controlled newspapers) and the proliferation of new publications produced by different social sectors. The style, content, and reception of government media campaigns varied substantially between regions, but their comparison reveals a consistent finding: unusually for a military dictatorship, the Velasco government oversaw an eruption of public debate that resulted in an irreversible widening of political participation in Peru.

The continued political significance of the agrarian reform is reflected in the ongoing battle to define its place in history. In chapter 5 I argue that the reform remains contentious both because of the conflicts it generated at the time and because of its symbolic importance in establishing a more inclusive political system. While conservatives criticize the reform as an economic disaster inflicted on the country by a resentful military dictator, others celebrate it as a turning point in struggles for greater equality. Using oral history interviews and analysis of the mass media, I reveal how these different versions are constructed and circulated. Drawing on Elizabeth Jelin's idea of historical memory as a political resource, I show how different groups in Peruvian society have tried to control popular perceptions of the reform. I also analyze people's efforts to order local histories of the agrarian reform around a variety of (often competing) local, regional, and national identities. I argue that while the neoliberal turn has tended to marginalize the history of the agrarian reform, it retains vital political currency among the population. Thus, the agrarian reform continues to anchor narratives of change and continuity and delimit the possibilities for significant social reform in Peru.

In the conclusion, I reflect on the importance of understanding land reforms—particularly those of the twentieth century—as an ideological struggle. Conservative critics of Peru's agrarian reform have been remarkably successful in shifting popular attention away from the politics of land redistribution to a much narrower set of economic issues, a strategy that has helped define the conventional view of the reform as an economically disastrous agricultural policy. Refocusing attention on the political dialogue that surrounded the reform illuminates the ways in which it contributed to Peru's formation as a modern state and the key role it played in the development of citizenship and social mobility. Moving beyond the Peruvian case, I argue that a return to the political debates that surrounded Latin America's multiple land reforms will deepen our understanding of the land question and its implications for the distribution of political power.

CHAPTER 1

The History of the Land Question in Peru

The land struggles that came to the fore of Latin American politics in the twentieth century can be traced back to the colonial era. In the years immediately after the 1532 invasion, the early Spanish settlers were granted an encomienda by the Spanish Crown, which gave them rights to the tribute and labor of the subjects of certain indigenous chiefs, or caciques.[1] However, as Robert Keith shows, the encomienda system collapsed about thirty years after the Spanish invasion due to massive decline in the indigenous population and a simultaneous increase in the settler population and its consumption needs. Keith's study of Peru's central coastal valleys finds that by the late sixteenth century, the conquest society that lived off tribute from indigenous producers had shifted to a colonial society that was directly involved in the production process.[2] The central productive unit in this new colonial society was the hacienda: an agricultural estate producing goods that could be traded on local and international markets. With the emergence of the hacienda, land ownership became much more significant and contested, since the land itself formed the basis of the settlers' wealth.[3]

Origins of Land Inequality

During the sixteenth and seventeenth centuries, the lands occupied by indigenous communities (known as *ayllus*[4] in the highlands) were increasingly absorbed by the haciendas. According to Keith, methods of acquiring land differed from region to region. They included marriage (e.g., to the daughters of local *curacas* [chiefs]), land auctions, and formal land grants from the viceregal government. It was thus not always a case of violent dispossession. Keith notes, for example, that the density of the Spanish population on the central coast increased the demand for land and hence the ability of Indian chiefs to negotiate its sale.[5] Yet the vacating of former communal lands also occurred through the disintegration and dislocation of indigenous communities due to disease, political breakdown, and the colonial reorganization of dispersed indigenous populations into *reducciones* (reductions or concentrated settlements) as part of the Toledo reforms that began in 1567.[6]

Using different forms of labor (slaves, salaried workers, and tribute labor), the haciendas were able to develop as profitable enterprises. Despite the increasing dominance of the haciendas, however, the communal tribute system practiced by indigenous communities retained a significant presence, not least because these communities constituted a valuable source of labor for the haciendas. The communities' self-sufficiency allowed the hacendados (landowners) to call on servile labor when required without assuming the costs of maintaining a permanent workforce. The mines also had a strong interest in preserving access to indigenous labor, and the Spanish treasury continued to use indigenous tribute as an important source of state revenue. The Spanish Crown therefore permitted the titling of communal lands both to protect its "Indian" subjects and to maintain indigenous communities as an economic resource for the Empire.[7]

The limited protections afforded to indigenous communities under colonial rule were steadily withdrawn following the declaration of Peruvian independence in 1821. Indigenous communities ceased to exist in legal terms and could no longer be recognized as landowners: only individual property titles were recognized. The creole elite who assumed political control of the republic argued that communal landholdings restricted the development of commercial agriculture and hence the economic development of the country as a whole.[8] Similar arguments were made across the emerging independent states of Latin America.[9] This type of capitalist agriculture became particularly dominant after 1840 (with the advent of the guano export industry and the capital it made available).[10]

With communal property officially invalidated, the expanding haciendas were free to accumulate former indigenous lands either through commercial transactions or forcible occupation.[11] The loss of communal lands pushed indigenous communities into inhospitable areas of the sierra (Andean mountain range) and less productive areas of the coast. At the same time, the continued requirement for indigenous communities to pay tribute to the provincial authorities caused them to seek employment on the haciendas as a way of obtaining the cash needed to pay the tribute.[12] Others lived on the haciendas as *yanaconas*—servants who were given a portion of land on which to practice subsistence farming in return for personal service to the landowner.[13] As demographic pressure and land shortage increased over the nineteenth century, various forms of semifeudal labor emerged, particularly in the highland regions where indigenous communities were concentrated.[14] The privatization of former communal lands also gave rise to a class of small landowners or *parceleros*, who survived primarily through subsistence farming.[15] These minifundios (small farms) struggled to compete with the haciendas, which were often able to control water access and the marketing of agricultural produce.

Within this broader trend, the production methods and labor structure of the haciendas varied considerably according to local social and economic conditions. In the northern coastal departments, large areas of flat, irrigated land and ready access to seaports facilitated the growth of plantations producing major export crops such as cotton and sugar. Initially these large haciendas or latifundios relied on black slaves for labor, but following manumission in 1854, they turned to Chinese unskilled laborers. By the end of the nineteenth century they had developed a large migrant workforce and recruited heavily among highland communities.[16] In the sierra, by contrast, capitalist development was concentrated in mining and major centers of livestock production, while other forms of agriculture continued to serve local and regional markets. Here the traditional relationship between haciendas and indigenous communities persisted: the land was not farmed directly by the hacendado but leased to peasants for small-scale agricultural production in return for personal service and rent paid in cash, produce, or labor.[17]

Peru's Amazonian regions provide a further contrast: the low proportion of land suitable for agricultural production and the low population density made it virtually impossible to transform these regions into areas of capitalist production using the hacienda model. Instead, these regions were at the center of the Peruvian rubber boom (1870–1915) and later became the focus of sporadic government attempts to colonize Amazonian forest lands using landless Andean peasants.[18] For this reason, the Amazonian regions were not included in the 1969 agrarian reform but were subject to separate legislation through the 1974 "law of native communities and agricultural promotion of the jungle regions."[19]

During the first half of the twentieth century, expansion of the coastal haciendas proceeded rapidly, as Peru's export crops became increasingly integrated into global markets. This capitalist expansion was accompanied by substantial foreign investment and the adoption of modern production methods. The consolidation of the sugar industry resulted in the dislocation of the traditional haciendas and the concentration of land ownership in latifundios at the expense of small landowners and indigenous communities. The inequality of the latifundio-minifundio agricultural structure grew ever more extreme. At the same time, however, the concentration of migrant laborers on the sugar and cotton plantations paved the way for trade union activism, in some cases achieving notable improvements in wages and working conditions.[20]

In the southern sierra, by contrast, the traditional haciendas continued to extend their territorial control, with some indigenous communities being displaced to the least productive areas and others becoming captive labor for the haciendas.[21] These regional differences would become extremely important when it came to implementing the 1969 agrarian reform: regional social and economic conditions determined what kind of agricultural enterprise was possible and shaped what people wanted from the reform. While campesinos in the sierra sought the return of their ancestral lands (which had often been lost relatively recently to hacienda control), agricultural laborers on the coast were more concerned with securing better remuneration and working conditions. Peasant movements, political parties, and successive governments were also responding to the so-called land question in their own ways.

Responses to the Land Question

Peasant Movements

In his study of Peruvian peasant movements across the nineteenth and twentieth centuries, Wilfredo Kapsoli Escudero highlights the range of protest strategies that were used to contest conditions of land shortage, servitude, and abuse at the hands of the hacendados. These included petitions, land occupations, strikes, violent attacks, and banditry.[22] Peasant protests, he argues, "are like the waves of the sea or the flow of the Andean rivers. They have their ups and downs, their growths and retreats."[23] Kapsoli nevertheless identifies 1930 as a key dividing line. Before 1930, peasant protests were contained with relative ease using repressive force, often resulting in violent massacres of the protesters.[24] In the latter period, however, both the scale and organizational capacity of peasant protests presented a greater challenge to the landowners.

Alberto Flores Galindo observes a similar process of expansion of peasant movements across the twentieth century, but he proposes a division into three distinct phases: uprisings and banditry (1910–1925), peasant land invasions and trade unionism (1945–1965), and the new peasant movements that emerged in the context of the agrarian reform (1969 onward).[25] Whereas the first period was characterized by short-lived, localized protests that did not gain the support of other social groups, the second period was marked by protests of a regional or national scale that were highly organized. During the latter period, peasant demands extended beyond land to a wider set of social issues, including education and better working conditions, issues which in turn enabled the protesters to build alliances with student and labor movements. Flores Galindo emphasizes the intensification of capitalist development in the countryside as a key factor underpinning this shift in peasant organizing: the growth of waged labor in place of (or in combination with) feudal systems opened the way for greater bargaining power, which was in turn strengthened by the emergence of peasant unions and peasant assemblies, such as the Confederación Campesina del Perú (Peruvian Peasant Confederation [CCP]), founded in 1947.[26]

Throughout the twentieth century, peasant protests retained important regional characteristics. In the central and southern highlands, the tactic of occupying hacienda land (*tomas de tierra*) became prevalent as a form of protest, whereas strikes and boycotts were more common in the plantation economy of the northern coast. As Peter Klaren has shown, it was on the coastal latifundios that APRA, Peru's first mass party, developed its base. Founded in 1924, APRA played an important role as the organizer of strikes, boycotts, and armed uprisings, despite frequently being forced into clandestinity by a series of authoritarian governments.[27] The proletariat of the coastal agro-industrial complexes provided a more fertile ground for mass party politics than the traditional haciendas of the central and southern highlands.

Capitalist development also created tensions in the southern *ceja de selva*—the eastern edge of the Andes, toward the Amazon basin. In particular, from 1958 to 1963 the province of La Convención in the department of Cusco was "the scene of the most important peasant movement of that period in Peru, and probably in the whole of South America."[28] Eric Hobsbawm explained this movement as a consequence of neofeudalism: as the international price of coffee grew and new transport connections facilitated access to global markets, the landowners sought to profit from these economic opportunities using land tenancies tied to traditional forms of feudal exploitation. In the short term this enabled the hacendados to reduce production costs to a minimum while expanding production to meet growing demand. However, while migrant laborers—lured by the possibility of acquiring land—accepted these onerous conditions in the short term, they soon turned to collective organization to challenge their situation. The tendency for landowners to terminate a tenancy once the land had been improved and cultivated by the settlers was a particular cause of peasant discontent.

Hobsbawm notes that Communist propaganda and organizers from Cusco were active in the region from the 1930s onward.[29] Among these organizers was Hugo Blanco, a central figure in the peasant protests that swept across the southern sierra in the early 1960s. In 1963, the city of Quillabamba (provincial capital of La Convención) was seized by peasants led by Trotskyist Blanco. The protesters proceeded to occupy the Hacienda Chaupimayo along with numerous other haciendas in the region, and occupation became a tactic that spread rapidly across the southern departments and continued until March 1964.[30] The protesters included indigenous communities, tenant farmers, and hacienda workers. They demanded the return of ancestral lands and the abolition of servile working conditions.[31] The scale and coordinated nature of these protests distinguished them from previous peasant movements and caused notable unease among the landowning elites. Warning that Peru was facing the prospect of a Cuban-style insurrection, one of Lima's principal daily newspapers, *La Prensa*, called for urgent agrarian reform as a way of preventing the growth of the movement. Land reform now seemed like a way of containing insurgency that was more viable than the violent repression used in the past.[32]

Political Parties

During the 1910s and 1920s, the activities of various *indigenista* organizations—which engaged in political campaigns on behalf of the indigenous population—began to raise public awareness of the abuses being committed by powerful landowners. Initially, the potential solutions discussed centered on the availability of legal redress and greater educational provision for indigenous communities. However, in 1928 intellectual José Carlos Mariátegui called for the so-called Indian problem to be reexamined as an issue of land distribution. In his popular and widely read *Siete ensayos de interpretación de la realidad peruana*, he commented: "When the agrarian problem is presented in these terms, it cannot be easily distorted. It appears in all its magnitude as a socioeconomic, and therefore a political, problem, to be dealt with by men who move in this sphere of acts and ideas. And it is useless to try to convert it, for example, into a technical-agricultural problem for agronomists."[33] Mariátegui founded what would later become the Partido Comunista del Perú (Communist Party of Peru [PCP]), and his ideas remained highly influential within left-wing politics for decades to come.

At the same time, agrarian reform was being used as a mobilizing slogan by the populist, anti-imperialist party APRA. The party saw land reform as a way to stop the extraction of wealth by foreign landowners and consolidate agriculture as a productive national industry. Yet rather than trying to eliminate foreign capital, APRA sought to control it.[34] This position appealed to the traditional hacendados who had been displaced by the massive growth of the sugar and cotton plantations, a large proportion of which were foreign-owned or allied to foreign investors. It also appealed to the laborers who worked for these large corporations and felt dissatisfied over pay and conditions. In addition, APRA's anti-imperialist discourse conjured up images of reclaiming Peruvian land for Peruvians in a way that appealed to the landless proletariat (although the party remained evasive about the prospects for redistribution).[35]

Forced into clandestinity as a result of government oppression during the 1930s and 1940s, APRA concentrated its efforts on developing a support base among the northern plantation workers. As APRA's role as broker between the workers and the large landowners grew stronger, the party became less inclined to challenge the property structure, preferring to use its lobbying power within the existing system.[36] Despite projecting itself as a "revolutionary" party, APRA was to become one of the main voices of opposition against major land reform during the Belaúnde government (1963–1968). In particular, it supported the view that only "inefficient" agricultural estates should be expropriated and that the industrialized coastal estates should be left untouched.

Alongside APRA, the other major political party to represent large landowners' interests was the Unión Nacional Odriísta (National Odriísta Union [UNO]). Led by former president Manuel Odría, the UNO was a key defender of the agricultural exporters and international mining companies that made up the Peruvian oligarchy. Despite having led severe repression of APRA while in office (1950–1956), during the Belaúnde government Odría agreed to a political coalition with APRA, known as APRA-UNO. This provided sustained opposition to the reforms of the Belaúnde government, particularly the 1963 agrarian reform.[37]

In addition to the lobbying power of major political parties, the interests of large landowners were represented through the Sociedad Nacional Agraria (National Agrarian Society) and the Asociación de Criadores de Lanares del Perú (Association of Livestock and Wool Producers). Latifundistas also enjoyed close relations with the major newspapers and a wide span of financial interests in other commercial sectors, which gave them considerable political influence through both formal and informal channels.[38] For example, the Gildemeister family was the largest producer of sugar and rice in the country, owning a total of 32,213 hectares of cultivated land and 105,131 of pastureland on the coast and approximately 420,000 hectares in the sierra. Outside the agricultural sector, the Gildemeisters had substantial shares in fish meal, oil, insurance, and the newspaper *La Prensa*.[39]

At the other end of the political spectrum, the growth of peasant protests during the 1950s and early 1960s convinced left-wing radicals that the countryside contained revolutionary potential, a position reinforced by the triumph of the Cuban Revolution in 1959.[40] In 1965 two radical left-wing parties launched a guerrilla insurgency in the central and southern highlands. The Movimiento de Izquierda Revolucionaria (MIR) (Revolutionary Left Movement) had formed as a breakaway movement from APRA around 1959, after the party's drift to the right.[41] The Ejército de Liberación Nacional (National Liberation Army) emerged at the same time among Peruvian Communist Party members who sought a radical alternative to the Soviet-allied party leadership. Despite sharing certain political objectives, the MIR and Ejército de Liberación Nacional worked independently of one another to promote revolution in the central and southern highlands. The guerrillas suffered from a number of weaknesses, not least their small number and their unfamiliarity with the local area (the majority of the guerrillas came from Lima or other coastal cities). By the end of December 1965 they had been defeated by the armed forces, with heavy loss of life.[42] Although the Peruvian armed forces were not seriously threatened by the insurgency, the experience strengthened their resolve to achieve economic development as a way of staving off revolution.[43]

Government Legislation

Parliamentary efforts to introduce land reform in Peru began in the 1950s as a response both to the internal political pressures outlined previously and to an international trend toward state-led agrarian reform. By the late 1950s significant land reforms had been carried out in China, the Eastern Bloc, and several Latin American countries.[44] While they occurred in different political circumstances, these land reforms were mutually influential and served as precedents for Peruvian legislation. Agrarian reform would later receive explicit backing from the US government, which saw it as a way to prevent the spread of Communist revolution. If land had been more equitably distributed, it was argued, Cubans would not have supported Fidel Castro's uprising. In 1961 President John Kennedy established the Alliance for Progress to stimulate economic cooperation between the United States and Latin America. Among the aims to which the Alliance members agreed was a commitment "to encourage, in accordance with the characteristics of each country, programs of comprehensive agrarian reform."[45]

The first major government initiative on land reform in Peru came in response to growing peasant protests. In 1956 President Manuel Prado created the Comisión para la Reforma Agraria y la Vivienda (Commission for Agrarian Reform and Housing [CRAV]) to investigate the causes of rural unrest. Although the commission identified as problematic the predominance of the latifundio-minifundio dynamic, its report placed greater emphasis on the need to colonize new areas for agriculture and improve productivity. It recommended only minor changes to exploitative land tenancy arrangements such as *yanaconaje* (indentured labor). In general, the traditional haciendas of the sierra were seen as warranting reform, while the large coastal estates were believed to be modern and efficient, despite the entrenched poverty maintained on these estates. As Matos Mar and Mejía note, the solutions proposed by the CRAV reflected its bias toward large-scale capitalist agriculture. This bias is unsurprising given that the CRAV's director was Pedro Beltrán, a well-known businessman and landowner who was a key member of the Sociedad Nacional Agraria and an editor of *La Prensa*.[46]

Although the CRAV's proposals were never passed into law, the need for agrarian reform continued to be hotly debated. It was a key issue in the 1962 general election, with all the major candidates proposing some form of agrarian reform. After an extremely close result and accusations of electoral fraud, the armed forces intervened with a coup d'état against President Prado. The military junta, led by Generals Ricardo Pérez Godoy and Nicolás Lindley López, announced that it would act as a caretaker government, with a general election to be held the following year. It also made agrarian reform in La Convención (southern highlands, a site of growing unrest) a priority and in November 1962 promulgated the "Law of Bases for the Agrarian Reform." This incorporated elements of the CRAV proposals and laid the groundwork for the implementation of limited agrarian reform in the valleys of La Convención and Lares in March 1963.[47]

Lindley's agrarian reform went some way toward addressing the demands of the peasant movements in La Convención, but it was clear that the need for reform extended far beyond this limited area. In campaigning for the 1963 general election, Acción Popular candidate Fernando Belaúnde Terry promised a major national agrarian reform and duly presented a bill to parliament a month after his election as president.[48] Yet despite the escalation of peasant-led land occupations throughout the southern sierra, the Congress continued to exhibit a remarkable degree of inertia on the question of land reform. Acción Popular did not have a parliamentary majority and, for reasons alluded to earlier, APRA formed an alliance with Odría's right-wing UNO to oppose key elements of the bill.

The government's frustration at this stonewalling was palpable in the words of Vice President Edgardo Seoane Corrales. In a pamphlet published to defend the government's reform proposals, he wrote: "Faced with the decision of the government, and the resolve already shown by the Peruvian people in the invasions of rustic and urban land that have occurred in the last decade, a minority of the country closes its eyes to our reality. Once again, history shows that the privileged classes of the economic order have never given in to the needs of the general welfare, justice and reason."[49]

The reform eventually passed by Congress in May 1964 (Law No. 15037) went further than previous proposals by making land redistribution a priority and creating provisions for land to be expropriated across all types of agricultural units (not just the traditional sector). It was also national in scope, in contrast to the limited reform introduced by General Lindley. However, the reform offered multiple concessions to large landowners, including the ability to parcel land privately (in effect allowing an estate to be divided among different members of the same family), a system of graduated affectation that restricted the total area of land that could be expropriated, and an exemption for agro-industrial complexes. Moreover, landowners were able to evade the reform if they could demonstrate the "efficiency" of their farm. The processes of expropriation and adjudication were extremely bureaucratic, providing ample opportunity for landowners to obstruct the law.[50] Matos Mar and Mejía calculate that by 1968 only 2 percent of the peasant population in need of land had benefited from the reform.[51]

The 1969 Agrarian Reform: Motivations

The desire to deliver meaningful agrarian reform was a key motivation for the 1968 coup led by General Juan Velasco Alvarado. According to Dirk Kruijt, the group of officials that surrounded President Velasco was "small and relatively closed."[52] It comprised three generals and 11 colonels. Like Velasco, the latter all came from "humble families that lived in small provincial cities or came from peasant communities."[53] They had all witnessed or experienced rural poverty and felt morally committed to addressing it.

Beyond the personal convictions of the coup leaders, the government's political agenda was inspired by a shift in the political orientation of the Peruvian armed forces that began in the 1950s. The Centro de Altos Estudios Militares (Centre of Advanced Military Studies [CAEM]), created in 1950, encouraged members of the armed forces to consider issues of national development and advocated their involvement in civilian life.[54] The CAEM reflected a tendency across much of Cold War Latin America to see the armed forces as key agents of modernization and counterinsurgency, with national military resources being directed toward preventing Communist insurgency through social programs and developing specialist military tactics to combat guerrilla groups. As Cynthia McClintock comments, "Anticommunism was a basic premise in military schools in most Latin American nations during the postwar period and Peru's military schools were no exception. An intense, visceral anticommunist stance characterized even many officers later to be classified as progressives."[55]

Within Peru's military intellectual circles, the center-left Partido Demócrata Cristiano (Christian Democrat Party) and the Movimiento Social Progresista (Progressive Socialist Movement [MSP]) were particularly influential. Alberto Ruiz Eldredge, a highly respected lawyer and member of the MSP (who later became a significant figure in the Velasco government), recalled that various members of the MSP were called upon to give talks at the CAEM, and many of the Velasco government's reforms reflected ideas first proposed by the MSP in the 1962 election.[56] Two MSP sympathizers, Benjamín Semanez Concha and Guillermo Figallo, played a critical role in the drafting of the reform law.

The agrarian reform law (D.L. 17716) was drafted by a special commission that included the minister of agriculture and five advisors. The commission members drew on the growing body of research on rural issues that had emerged since the late 1950s in the fields of anthropology, sociology, and economics as well as their previous experiences with land reform. Both Peruvian and foreign researchers had addressed such questions as the nature of power relations in rural communities, differences in systems of land tenure, the factors determining agricultural productivity, and the prospects for social change.[57] This research would continue to develop throughout the agrarian reform process, driven by a strong political engagement with the issues affecting the countryside and the unusually direct opportunity to contribute to government policy.[58]

According to Semanez Concha, the initial proposal drawn up by the agrarian reform commission "was largely a copy of . . . Law 15037, passed by Belaúnde, which left the latifundio and the sugar complexes untouched."[59]

After he and Figallo raised concerns that the law did not go far enough, a new commission was formed, this time overseen by the more progressive General Leonidas Rodríguez. Semanez Concha described the guiding principles of the law as follows: "We wanted to carry out a structural agrarian reform, not a conventional reform like that created by Law 15037 and like those which existed in other countries [but] an advanced law that proposed an agrarian reform that could be massive, rapid and drastic."[60] Unlike Bolivia, where plans for the country's 1953 agrarian reform were developed in consultation with the United States government and scaled back because of fears that the United States would withdraw support, the drafting of D.L. 17716 was carried out in closely guarded secrecy. The Velasco government remained defiant in the face of the US government's publicly voiced concerns on behalf of US firms, such as Grace & Co., one of Peru's major sugar producers.

The Terms of the Law

The 1969 agrarian reform law had much in common with land reform programs developed elsewhere in the world—its slogan of "land to the tiller" was shared by almost all land reform processes of the era, from India to Yugoslavia—yet its specific terms also defined the nature and pace of change that it stimulated in Peru. Unlike land reforms in Mexico and Bolivia, the Peruvian agrarian reform expropriated land according to the priorities identified by government officials, rather than responding to petitions for land. That meant it could be implemented more quickly than previous reforms had been and under conditions that were favorable to the peasantry.[61]

D.L. 17716 created a new, semi-autonomous unit within the Ministry of Agriculture to implement the reform: the Dirección General de Reforma Agraria y Asentamiento Rural (General Office of Agrarian Reform and Rural Settlement [DGRAAR]). Local administration was undertaken by the offices established in each agrarian reform zone.[62] Once an agrarian reform zone had been declared, all landowners within the zone were requested to present their land titles for review by the DGRAAR. Land that exceeded the maximum area that could be farmed directly by the landowner, known in Spanish as the "*inafectable*" area (variable according to geography and land type),[63] was expropriated according to a fairly rapid timetable. Although the expropriations were compulsory, landowners received payment for their land in the form of industrial bonds and/or cash, following a detailed assessment of the value of the land by government administrators.[64]

Once expropriation was complete, the DGRAAR began the process of adjudication. It was at this point that peasants could present their case for receiving the expropriated land, and this was often the most contentious part of the reform process.[65] Land claims were processed by newly established "land judges," who were in turn accountable to a national agrarian tribunal. This new land court system was largely independent of the civil courts—which had historically tended to favor the landowners over the peasantry—and permitted oral hearings, including the use of Quechua.[66] In receiving the land, the awardees agreed to pay for it over the course of 20 years, in what became known as the "agrarian debt."

The primary form of adjudication was to Cooperativas Agrarias de Producción (Agricultural Production Cooperatives [CAPs]) and Sociedades Agrícolas de Interés Social (Agricultural Societies of Social Interest [SAIS]). While CAPs were composed of permanent laborers (i.e., the former hacienda workers) who were jointly responsible for managing a single estate, SAIS were broader associations made up of permanent laborers from a number of neighboring estates and local communities. By extending SAIS membership to communities living in areas surrounding the expropriated estates, the government hoped to widen the impact of the reform and recompense indigenous communities in particular, which had suffered encroachment on their lands.[67] Cooperative membership was determined by local surveys that registered the potential beneficiaries in a given area, but the cooperatives were frequently unable to absorb all the eligible workers, giving rise to considerable tension between landless peasants and cooperative members.[68]

Although indigenous property rights were explicitly guaranteed by Article 2 of the agrarian reform law, this applied only to land granted to indigenous communities after 1920.[69] As a consequence, members of indigenous communities were often forced to seek access to land as members of cooperatives or as a group of peasants that agreed to form a cooperative in the future, rather than on the grounds of ancestral land claims.[70] Even those indigenous communities that did receive land through the reform were forcibly renamed *comunidades campesinas* (peasant communities). This was part of the Velasco government's effort to rid rural society of what it saw as the racist, discriminatory associations of the terms *indígena* or *indio*. Yet as Juan Martín Sánchez argues, this imposition of a homogenous campesino identity upon a population characterized by great ethnic and social diversity tended to produce its own patterns of exclusion and discrimination, an issue considered again in later chapters.[71]

Beside the cooperative or peasant community route, peasants could receive land on an individual basis in the form of a family agricultural unit.

However, the government preferred the associative model on the grounds that it produced economies of scale and a more rational use of recourses. This is reflected in the fact that 65.3 percent of the total land adjudicated by the reform went to cooperatives, rather than to communities or individual peasants.[72] In addition, Article 92 declared that the cooperatives should be given preference in the distribution of agricultural credit.[73] Moreover, through the Special Statute on Peasant Communities (passed in February 1970), the Velasco regime tried (largely unsuccessfully) to "reorganize" peasant communities to make them more like cooperatives.[74]

This preference for the cooperative model was not unique to the Peruvian agrarian reform, nor to development policies more generally in the post–World War II era. In a recent doctoral dissertation that traces the emergence and development of ideas about cooperative systems within Peruvian intellectual circles, Ying-Ying Chu notes how the European cooperative model exemplified by the Rochdale Society of Equitable Pioneers (established in England in 1844) was studied and reworked by social scientists and policymakers in the Third World.[75] Scholars in the emerging field of peasant studies were particularly interested in questions of agricultural productivity and the relationship between modes of production and political consciousness. Within Latin America, the examples of the *ejido* in 1930s Mexico, the agricultural cooperative in postrevolution Cuba, and the Chilean *asentamientos* or rural settlements during the Eduardo Frei Montalva (1964–1970) and Salvador Allende (1970–1973) governments illustrate both the diversity of possible cooperative models and the wide appeal of cooperative theory as an organizing principle. As Chu highlights, "The cooperative contained significant elements that many post–World War II Latin American policymakers and their councillors—no matter capitalist, socialist, or communist—wanted: economy of scale, productivity, popular mobilization, and integration."[76] As will be discussed in later chapters, the cooperatives performed a vital role in the Velasco government's vision of mass political participation, yet the precise nature and limits of this participation would become a recurring tension throughout the era.

Although drafted in a top-down fashion by a closed commission, the 1969 agrarian reform did undergo a variety of modifications in response to peasant protests. Its implementation was also shaped by the new government agencies that were charged with explaining the reform, generating support, and training the new cooperatives. The most significant of these agencies were CENCIRA and SINAMOS, both created in 1971. While the Velasco government rejected the idea of creating a political party to promote its reforms, agencies like CENCIRA and SINAMOS ended up working in increasingly partisan ways, as they struggled to combat political opposition from both the Left and Right.

Opposition to the Reform

In comparison with countries such as Chile and Colombia, where landlords created their own paramilitary organizations to oppose agrarian reform, conservative opposition in Peru was relatively muted. Cynthia McClintock attributes this to what she terms the "politics of stealth": the government acted in unpredictable ways that did not give landowners time to mount a response.[77] The overnight occupation of the northern agro-industrial complexes immediately after D.L. 17716 had been passed is an example of this strategy. McClintock also notes that the manner in which the reform was implemented divided the landowners by beginning with the largest estates and later proceeding to the smaller ones: "The medium-size landowners did not come to the defense of the larger ones because they had believed only the oligarchy would be affected. Later, by the time the medium-size landowners were affected, the largest ones had been compelled to leave their enterprises and had no incentive to work on behalf of other landowners."[78]

Nonetheless, the conservative elites continued to have strong political influence via Manuel Odría's UNO party and frequently used the mass media to criticize the government (as will be shown in chapter 4). North and Korovkin note that part of the strength of right-wing opposition lay in its subtlety: "Like all good propaganda it appealed to 'common sense' and thereby was accessible to a mass audience. The intelligence of this campaign and its impact on the middle class and on the officers in power should not be underestimated, for in the arena of political ideological debate the right dominated with its alternatively fear-provoking and reasonable discourse."[79] In addition, a large number of the agronomists and engineers on whom the agrarian reform administration called for their technical skills came from landowning backgrounds and sometimes used their position to undermine the reform from the inside.

A further source of conservative opposition was APRA. As has been noted, despite claiming to be a revolutionary mass party, APRA resisted any change that might damage the interests of the sugar and cotton barons on the northern coast with whom it had important alliances. The party was also eager to retain its leadership position within the agricultural trade unions and responded to the new cooperatives as an encroachment on its territory. The suspension of provincial and departmental government elections and the closure of the national congress throughout the Velasco and Morales Bermúdez governments limited the opportunities for APRA to publicly voice its opposition. However, the party exerted a powerful presence from within the state apparatus, where numerous party members and sympathizers were employed. The political tensions that emerged within the state bureaucracy during the implementation of the agrarian reform are a recurring theme of this book.

On the Left, the Velasco government received the backing of the PCP. Party leader Jorge del Prado adopted a position of "critical support" for the military government, arguing that its progressive elements were to be encouraged, despite its broadly "bourgeois" and "reformist" character.[80] However, a variety of smaller left-wing groups openly criticized the government. Following the Sino-Soviet split in 1964, a number of different factions had broken away from the PCP, each declaring themselves the true Peruvian Communist Party. The most significant of these factions were the Partido Comunista del Perú–Patria Roja (Communist Party of Peru–Red Homeland [PCP-PR]) and the Partido Comunista Peruano–Bandera Roja (Peruvian Communist Party—Red Flag [PCP-BR]).[81] Both parties adopted a Maoist political orientation and sought to establish a worker-peasant alliance, arguing in favor of revolution and against reform.[82]

In addition to the Maoist groups, the government faced opposition from the MIR (one of the two parties that launched an unsuccessful guerrilla war in 1965, discussed above) and VR, founded in 1965 by left-wing activists from diverse party political backgrounds as part of the "new left" that was developing across Latin America at the time. Both organizations had a small membership base and often functioned as loose associations rather than traditional political parties.[83]

The main political strength of radical leftist organizations came from the alliances they built with trade unions and peasant organizations. For example, VR established strong links with the CCP and used them to mobilize peasant opposition to the government.[84] In 1974 VR played a key role in the peasant protests and land occupations that took place in Andahuaylas (south-central highlands), causing a major political crisis and forcing the government to negotiate directly with the protesters. Similarly, PCP-BR took control of the main teachers' unions, which were a powerful voice of opposition during the Velasco regime.[85]

Left-wing opposition to the Velasco government stemmed from, on one hand, mistrust of the military's motivations and ideological disagreement with its reformist approach and, on the other, frustration with the speed at which the government's reforms were implemented. Ideological criticism of the agrarian reform focused on the policy of compensating landowners for their land, the creation of cooperatives (seen as supplanting existing forms of political association and promoting authoritarian control), and the marginalization of indigenous land claims in favor of the cooperative system. Groups such as PCP-BR and VR also accused the Velasco government of installing a procapitalist agrarian reform that was driven by the demands of "US imperialism."[86] It was also argued that by ameliorating Peru's immediate social problems, the government's reforms would merely delay the socialist revolution, which these parties saw as both inevitable and necessary.[87]

President Velasco described his attitude toward communism as one of tolerant disagreement, rather than direct opposition; he argued that the communist systems operating in China, the Soviet Union, and Cuba were inappropriate to the Peruvian context and instead proposed a "third way" that was neither communist nor capitalist. In his 1973 message to the nation, Velasco said: "We reject communism, not from a conservative position of the Right, but from a revolutionary position of the national, autonomous Left." He dismissed the "dogmatic Left" as a series of insignificant minority groups.[88]

Internally, however, the government remained extremely concerned about the communist threat. In 1975, the government agency SINAMOS produced a series of political guides for its staff. The introduction to one such guide, entitled *Maoist Groups*, stated: "We believe it is important for the militants of the Peruvian Revolutionary Process . . . to know the positions of these Maoist groups, to be able to compete politically and ideologically with them within the popular organizations, and in that way orientate their actions in accordance with the Ideological Bases of the Peruvian Revolution."[89] The fact that government staff were being described as "militants" gives some idea of the intense political climate that surrounded the agrarian reform. Government agencies and the radical Left saw "consciousness raising" through education and political organizing as central in bringing about their preferred model of social change in the countryside.

Conclusion

Beginning with the consolidation of the hacienda system during Spanish colonial rule, the central tension in Peru's land question arose between large haciendas and indigenous communities, with the former frequently encroaching on the land of the latter. Indigenous land claims were further weakened in the nineteenth century by the shift toward liberal economics and in the twentieth century by the expansion of latifundios serving global capitalist markets. Indigenous communities were frequently forced to relocate to more inhospitable lands, and the inequality of the latifundio-minifundio agricultural structure grew ever more extreme.

As I have shown, land reform was a priority for the Velasco government. Peasant protests, the threat of rural insurgency, and international precedents all contributed to a growing awareness of the need for reform. Against this backdrop, the 1969 agrarian reform announced the Velasco government's intention to effect fundamental changes to the social structure. Whereas the reforms of the Lindley and Belaúnde governments had been introduced to pacify peasant uprisings and left the coastal plantations untouched, Velasco's agrarian reform openly confronted the oligarchy and sought to remodel society according to a system of cooperative ownership.

Given the deep historical roots of land inequality, the success of the government's reform would depend on its ability to transform both property relations and social attitudes. The experience of the Belaúnde government—whose 1964 agrarian reform had been whittled away by the conservative opposition—suggested that this could not be achieved through parliamentary debates alone. It required a sustained program of education, political organizing, and mass communication that would help overcome both conservative resistance and opposition from the radical Left and have consequences for political participation and national identity.

CHAPTER 2

SINAMOS: Promoting the Revolution in the Regions

The Velasco government is frequently characterized as an example of "revolution by decree."[1] The absence of formal checks on the power of the executive allowed the regime to implement reforms that were more radical and wide-ranging than any introduced under democratic rule.[2] Yet as the previous chapter demonstrated, the agrarian reform was an extremely contentious policy that faced opposition from various quarters, especially the landowning elites. To promote agrarian reform at the regional level, the government worked through targeted propaganda and grassroots organizing, and SINAMOS engaged with local politics and translated its message into locally meaningful discourse. Through these activities, SINAMOS linked the local experiences of agrarian reform to a broader narrative of revolutionary change and destabilized existing power structures. As a result, politics was no longer treated as the preserve of the capital city or major urban centers. In fact, the intense political organizing that surrounded the implementation of agrarian reform brought mass politics into rural areas to an unprecedented extent.

As Susana Aldana Rivera observes, "The region is a fundamental element in the vision and imaginary of any Peruvian. However, the construction of the nation-state model led to the creation of a totally homogenizing official discourse. Lima is the capital of the nation and, therefore, its best—and almost single—representative; the Peruvian state is reflected in the capital and is a reflection of it."[3] This is particularly true of the historiography on the Velasco government. Perhaps influenced by the government's own intensely nationalist rhetoric, analysts of the regime have tended to confine themselves to its national political strategy and decisions taken in Lima.[4] In the multilayered account that follows, detailed local research in a comparative framework reveals the state apparatus used to promote agrarian reform.

Focusing on the fieldwork of government promoters in the regions of Cusco, Tacna, and Piura illuminates the defining influence of local context on the strategies used to establish political hegemony.

I begin by analyzing the Velasco regime's conceptualization of Peruvian national territory and its approach to mass communication in the context of great national diversity. While propaganda to promote the agrarian reform was initially produced in the capital and distributed nationally on a sporadic and limited basis, the government soon realized that it required a more sustained regional presence. Significantly, the process to create SINAMOS began shortly after the promulgation of the agrarian reform law, reflecting the urgent need to mobilize support for the reform on a national scale.[5] Interviews with former SINAMOS employees reveal what kind of organization SINAMOS was and who it employed.

Of course, government communications strategies responded to regional diversity in the language, imagery, and narratives they employed, yet the government promoters still encountered problems at the local level. Both the armed forces and the SINAMOS leadership saw Peruvian national territory as a composite of regions and attributed different characteristics to each one. However, while undoubtedly influenced by political boundaries and physical geography, regional cultures come about through dynamic flows of people, ideas, and trade, developing a spatial logic that does not necessarily correspond to those established in other spheres, particularly legal or governmental realms.[6] At times, the military government's stereotyped view of particular regions meant that it communicated poorly with the population groups that it most sorely sought to inform and persuade.

Perspectives on the Regions

The idea of the region is a social construct that has historically been defined in different ways and for different cultural and political purposes. Peru's current system of regional governments did not exist until 1990. Before that, there was a system of departments governed hierarchically from the center, with each department containing a number of provinces.[7] Yet regions have more often been understood in terms of social and cultural identities than politically defined territories, most commonly in the formulation of three distinct geographical areas: the coast, the sierra (Andean mountain range), and the *selva* (Amazonian jungle). While framed in terms of naturally occurring geographical features, such descriptions are shaped by particular cultural assumptions and reflect broader ideological positions.

As Evelyne Mesclier has shown, changing representations of Peru's regions have also served to legitimize particular government policies. She argues, for example, that the characterization of the southern highlands as an area of isolation, poverty, and "backwardness" was particularly pronounced during the 1990s, when the turn to neoliberalism made it convenient to see the social problems experienced in the sierra as somehow endemic and particular to that region.[8] The armed forces' perception of Peruvian national territory, as described below, influenced government policy, as did the innovative approach to regional politics adopted by SINAMOS.

The Armed Forces

The Peruvian armed forces' perspective on the regions exerted a powerful influence on the Velasco government, both within the president's circle of senior advisors and in the implementation of policies on the ground.[9] Contemporary military magazines such as *Actualidad Militar* and *La Revista Militar* provide a good indication of the mentality of military personnel at the time. Kruijt notes that by the 1960s, *La Revista Militar* had moved from its earlier focus on military topics and armaments to addressing issues of economy, development, cooperative principles, and social analysis.[10] This reflected a broader shift in the political orientation of the military and its growing interest in social and economic reform (discussed in chapter 1). As Koonings and Kruijt rightly recognize, "Political armies"—those that consider their involvement in or control of domestic politics a central part of their legitimate function—have been the norm rather than the exception in the majority of nation-states that have emerged and been consolidated in the nineteenth and twentieth centuries.[11] This military urge to direct the course of national development became particularly dominant in the mid-twentieth century, with examples ranging from Nasser's Egypt to Suharto's Indonesia.

In the case of Peru, this sense of national mission was a product of decades of struggle on the part of the armed forces to overcome the destructive issues of *caudillismo* (strongman rule) and personalism. As historian Daniel Masterson writes, "The soldiers who deposed President Fernando Belaúnde on 3 October 1968 were products of an institution that labored for decades to define its national mission, limit the intrusion of national politics in the military's internal affairs, rid itself of personalism, and most of all, justify its worth to the nation and themselves."[12] A recurring theme in *Actualidad Militar* was the depiction of the army as a civilizing power. A 1970 article celebrated the role of the army's civic action organization in "breaking the isolation of extensive regions through the establishment of communication networks . . . and, within these, roads that penetrate the deepest parts of the territory, such as the vast Amazonian region."[13] The article gave the example of the Bagua-Río Marañon highway, commenting: "Thanks to this highway, extensive lands of the highest agricultural productivity have been incorporated into the national economy, principally in the province of Jaén, department of Cajamarca, contiguous with the truly amazonian department of Loreto and very close to the frontier with Ecuador. In sum, it is a route of triple value: socio-economic, logistical and strategic."[14] As this remark illustrates, the military expressed the advantages of territorial integration in strategic terms that made little or no reference to the people inhabiting the land. The needs and interests of the local population were relegated to a second order of significance beneath the perceived national interest of territorial integration. This world view was to play a critical part in the dynamics of policy implementation during the agrarian reform. While on the one hand SINAMOS ideologues advocated local control and popular participation, government personnel proved willing to override local suggestions and ideas when it was politically expedient to do so.

If the Amazon region represented the "deepest" parts of the national territory in the eyes of the military, the southern sierra was frequently described as an area of cultural and economic backwardness. A 1968 article in *Actualidad Militar* titled "The Army Educates" featured a photograph of two campesinos perched at the edge of a long table. The caption reads: "In the South of Peru the Army teaches the campesino the first letters." The text of the article revealed that the army's educational activities had in fact taken place across the country, with schools established first in Chorrillos and Rimac (both districts of Lima) and later in Tumbes, Papayal, and Arequipa, as well as Callao, Trujillo, and Chiclayo.[15] By using a photograph of campesinos from the southern highlands as its representation of "the uneducated," the article reproduced a common cultural trope that separated the "backward" sierra from the supposedly modern and industrialized coastal regions. The predominantly indigenous population of the sierra was criticized for willfully maintaining its marginal position within the nation-state by "clinging" to its traditional communities, even when these were economically connected with "national society." Commenting on a province of the central highlands, *Actualidad Militar* complained: "The incomes . . . earned beyond the environment in which they live allow the people of Hualcán to maintain their traditional institutions and values and remain separate from national society."[16]

While the army perpetuated negative stereotypes about highland populations, it also had a long history of recruiting among Andean populations, and there was an acknowledged affinity between the military and the peasantry.[17] Even after the professionalization of the military in the late nineteenth century reduced the army's dependence on the economic resources of rural society, the military continued to provide education and a way into civilian culture for Andean populations. For example, the Comité Pro-Derecho Indígena Tahuantinsuyo (the first pan-national indigenous rights movement in South America) was partially composed of individuals who had graduated from a military education.[18] *Actualidad Militar* described the military's educative role as not only a heroic mission—military educators being sent to the provinces to raise literacy levels—but also a collective endeavor involving both army recruits and civilians. In 1968 some 6,200 soldiers were learning to read and write in primary schools within the barracks, and the magazine acknowledged that "the barracks have been for many people their only school."[19] Thus, while the army defined itself as a centralized, professional institution that was separate from "isolated" rural populations, it was to a large extent composed of rural recruits and influenced by their provincial backgrounds and experiences.

General Juan Velasco Alvarado's personal trajectory is a case in point. Born in 1910 in Castilla, Piura, Velasco was one of 11 children. His father worked as a medical assistant, and he described his early childhood as a life of "dignified poverty, working as a shoeshine boy in Piura."[20] As president, Velasco frequently referred to his humble origins to distinguish himself from the so-called oligarchy, whom he labeled enemies of the Peruvian nation and the revolution. On a presidential visit to Piura in October 1969, much was made of the fact that Velasco was returning to visit his place of birth. Local newspaper *El Tiempo* reported:

> The President, who returns to Piura after five years [away], was affectionate with the press, telling them that the "journey has been excellent". Referring to education, he stated that "the *Piurano* has always been well educated. Poor and rich, we have had good direction from the cradle, because the *Piurano* parent knows how to direct his children. We *Piuranos* came out well orientated and the *Piurano* has always been characterized by being hardworking." Later he said that "the *Piurano* with money goes all over the world, to travel. But he always comes back" (we journalists alluded to his own return to Piura and he smiled).[21]

Later, as he toured the neighborhood in which he grew up, Velasco reportedly "showed himself to be moved, mopping his brow and passing a handkerchief over his moistened eyes."[22]

We might well interpret this episode as a carefully crafted piece of populist politics. But it also demonstrates Velasco's keen awareness of the importance of regional identities within Peru's political arena. Many of the intellectuals who collaborated with the Velasco government also had a strong understanding of different regional cultures. Francisco Guerra, who was the director of SINAMOS's regional offices, grew up in Cajamarca (northern highlands) and moved to Lima to attend university. His career path was typical of many of the civilians who participated in the Velasco government. "Lima is a melting pot," he said in an interview. "Velasco was *piurano*. Leonidas Rodríguez, the chief of SINAMOS, was *cusqueño*. Carlos Delgado, who was the important political advisor and also the most important SINAMOS politician, was *chiclayano*. And I could continue."[23] This firsthand knowledge of Peru's regions was a guiding influence within the Velasco government and was particularly important in the work of SINAMOS.

SINAMOS

Initially, posters and pamphlets to promote the agrarian reform law were produced by a small team of artists and intellectuals based in the capital and distributed across the country as required, for example, during official visits or local land expropriation processes.[24] Propaganda interventions in the regions were sporadic and limited.[25] Over time it became apparent that a more sustained regional presence would be required to maintain popular enthusiasm for the government's reforms. Established in June 1971, SINAMOS was a government agency that was designed—in the elevated language of the time—to "achieve the conscious and active participation of the national population in the tasks that economic and social development demand."[26] The key objectives of the organization, as set out in Article 2 of D.L. 18896, were training the general population, developing social interest bodies, and communication, "particularly the dialogue between the government and the population."[27]

The activities of SINAMOS were organized into different "operative areas": youth organizations, workers' organizations, rural organizations, organizations in *pueblos jóvenes* (shanty towns), social interest economic organizations (i.e., cooperatives), and cultural and professional organizations.[28] The so-called system was organized into eleven regions, one of which was assigned to the *pueblos jóvenes* across the country (i.e., not confined to a particular geographical area). Each of the remaining ten regions comprised two or more departments (see fig. 2.1). Within each SINAMOS region there were several zonal offices, each of which took responsibility

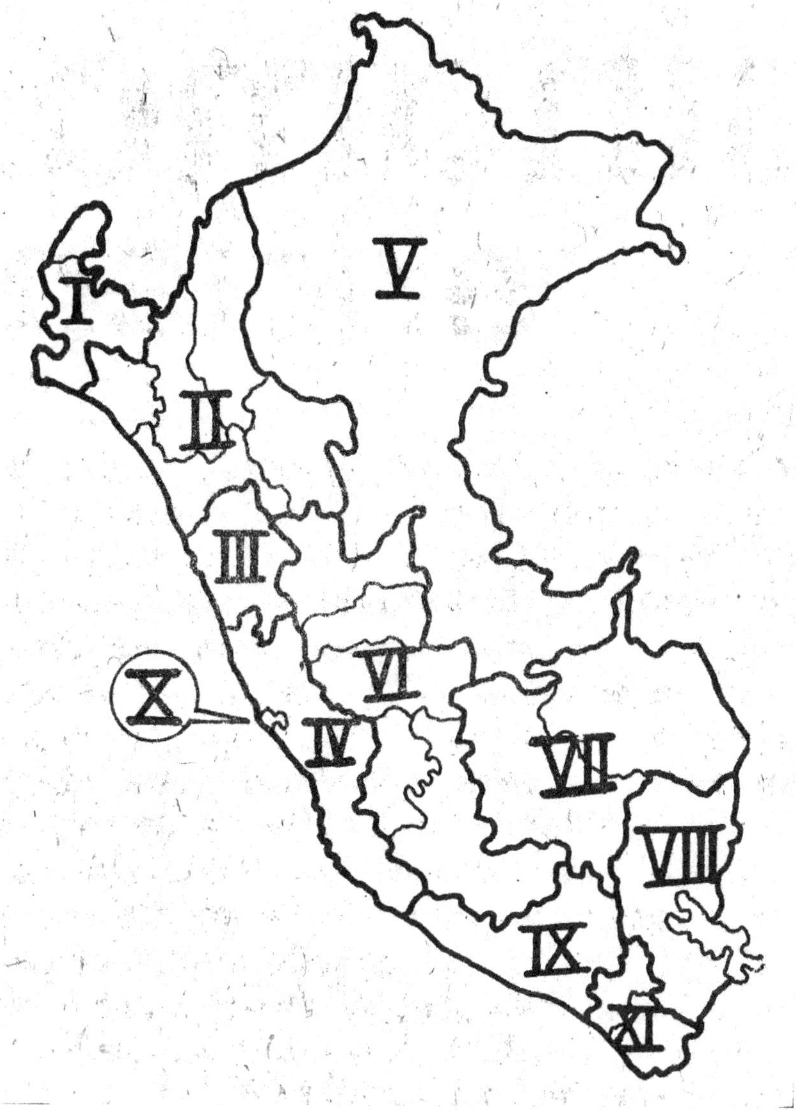

Figure 2.1. Map of regions as designated by the Sistema Nacional de Apoyo a la Movilización Social (SINAMOS). *SINAMOS informa* 1, no. 2 (1972): 5.

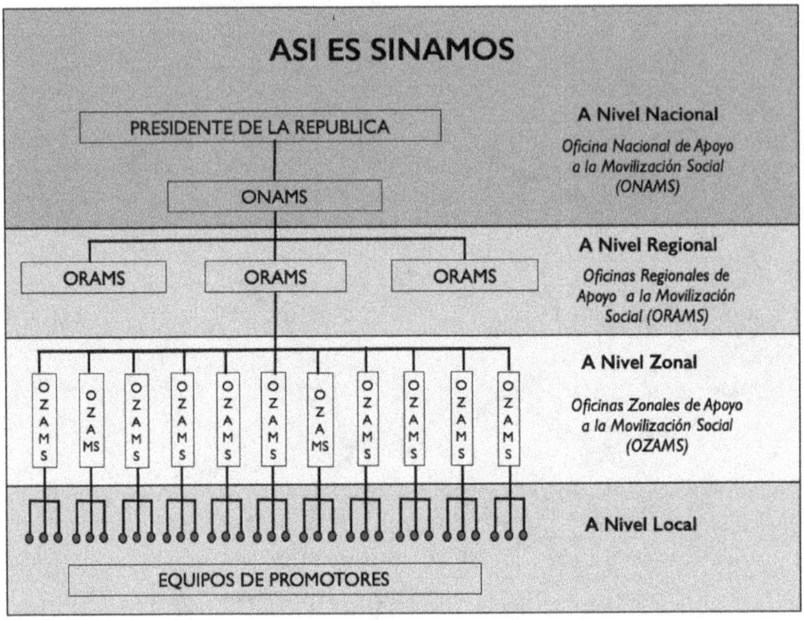

Figure 2.2. Diagram of SINAMOS organizational structure. Adapted from SINAMOS pamphlet *¿Por qué se ataca al SINAMOS?* (1974).

for the activities carried out by local promoters in one or more provinces. The overall organizational structure of SINAMOS therefore comprised four tiers: the local level (teams of promoters), zonal offices (OZAMS), regional offices (ORAMS), and the national office (ONAMS), each reflecting its level within the social mobilization movement in its name. This structure was designed—in theory—to facilitate the upward communication of ideas and opinions from the grassroots to the national government (see fig. 2.2).

The system of regions introduced by SINAMOS created a political geography parallel to the existing departmental and provincial boundaries.[29] Its regional divisions were also distinct from Peru's five military regions and its twelve agrarian reform zones, creating a complex set of institutional relations. The logic behind this was to introduce a kind of centralization in miniature, which would simultaneously create administrative efficiency and free up more resources to be used at the local level: "Regionalization should favor the concentration of administrative authorities and the reduction in the number of offices that function at departmental level, additionally allowing the extension of and vigorous support for the zonal level offices, with which the proposal for effective decentralization is achieved."[30] Thus, while the geographical boundaries of SINAMOS regions were defined somewhat arbitrarily, the mode of operation within each region was designed to ensure greater local access to state assistance. The system of local promoters ensured a closer and more collaborative relationship between state representatives and local populations than had previously been the case, particularly in rural areas.[31]

While the DGRAAR was formally responsible for the application of the agrarian reform, SINAMOS promoters informed peasants about the administrative processes, trained the new cooperatives, and established agrarian leagues and federations to mobilize peasants in support of the reform. As the members of staff in most regular contact with local populations, SINAMOS promoters were also charged with defending the government's policies and stimulating a new kind of political participation, captured in the following excerpt from a SINAMOS pamphlet:

> Participation should start with those closest to us, our neighborhood, for example. There, there are many things to do, many problems that are waiting to be resolved by us, without expecting that the solution will come "from above", from the government or whichever other institution. From the neighborhood, or place of work, or our children's school, [participation] will pass to other bigger levels: the city, the province, the region. In this way, in an ascending manner and in accordance with our practice of organized participation, we arrive at [the ability to] present and resolve the problems, be they economic, political, social or cultural, that affect the destiny of our country as a whole.[32]

Although in practice more hierarchical chains of command tended to dominate, the government's discourse on popular participation and more horizontal modes of organization attracted many people who were already employed at the community level, such as teachers, to work for SINAMOS. The former coordinator of the local SINAMOS office in Ayabaca (department of Piura) told me he was persuaded to join the organization on the basis that it would be a continuation of the work he had been doing within the local Communal Education Nucleus, an initiative to promote local involvement in the planning and management of education services. He commented: "They didn't oblige me to join, rather I myself joined, consciously and voluntarily. I said, 'It's good, we are going to continue planning.'"[33]

In addition, the organization recruited young graduates in the fields of psychology, sociology, anthropology, and journalism, through a rigorous selection process. According to a former SINAMOS employee who worked in the communications department of the Piura regional office, this consisted of various stages.[34] Following a written application, she was given a simulation exercise: to devise a plan for promoting a new law among Piura's rural population and present it to a selection panel. Having passed this stage, she was interviewed by a military official, who asked questions about her personality and her interest in social issues. Finally, she was interviewed by the director and subdirector of the regional office: "So everyone, according to the role they were applying for, went through that process. No one was recommended just like that. At least in my time. All of us who entered—there were a lot of us—we went through that process of selection and we passed."[35] An important element of the selection process was to establish whether the candidates had *mística*—a term that in this context meant a personal commitment to tackling Peru's social problems. This did not necessarily imply strict adherence to the government's ideas and approach; many of those recruited to the organization had previously participated in antigovernment protests, for example, in opposition to Velasco's proposed university reforms.

Given that SINAMOS sought a set of skills and experiences not usually found among military personnel (activism, public engagement, knowledge of social science models), its recruitment process was driven by a strong degree of pragmatism and admitted people with a variety of political affiliations. At times this openness created problems for the government as political parties such as VR—which saw SINAMOS as an instrument of dictatorship—deliberately infiltrated the organization.[36] Members and former members of the center-right party APRA also took up roles within SINAMOS. It seems that the issue of political infiltration was tackled through internal propaganda rather than any disciplinary action. In Tacna, for example, the regional SINAMOS office circulated a pamphlet in July 1975 entitled "Alert! APRA is infiltrating! What do you think?" with instructions for all the zonal offices to include a copy in their staff library.[37] Although the government rejected claims that SINAMOS was acting as the party of government, its political role became increasingly prominent.

However, the politically engaged new recruits represented a relatively small proportion of SINAMOS staff. The organization was formed from eight existing state institutions and retained large numbers of civil servants from the previous regime. This was a pragmatic move to avoid unpopular redundancies, but it meant that many staff lacked motivation to implement the government's reforms, or actively sabotaged them. A former employee of the SINAMOS regional office in Piura commented: "Within SINAMOS there were completely discordant voices, without feeling, bureaucratic. I would say that they had their backs to the reality, chained to their desks . . . . Perhaps they were not confrontational, but they delayed things. I would say that they delayed on purpose resolutions or projects that could have come out in one or two days."[38]

SINAMOS also struggled to overcome tensions between its military and civilian personnel. All but one of the SINAMOS regional office directors were military figures, meaning that military ideas about political organization often came into conflict with the more activist tendencies of civilian recruits. Carlos Franco, a key civilian member of the SINAMOS leadership, commented some years later in an interview with María del Pilar Tello: "Although the position of the military officials varied from one to the other, there were people who did not hide their doubts regarding the loyal or infiltrated nature of our collaboration. For others our style did not give them security, to the extent that we insisted that promoting [a] popular organization involved long periods, achievements by persuasion, respect for the differences and conflicts that there might be between members of the revolutionary team and partial or sectoral interests."[39] Military officials often favored an immediate, hierarchical mode of organization and feared that a more flexible approach would open the door to political infiltration. Added to this was the intense factionalism within the Velasco government: while the progressive group of generals supported SINAMOS efforts to promote popular participation, the centrist and right-wing members of the government were highly skeptical if not hostile.[40]

Regional Politics

In communicating the government's reform agenda to different regional populations, SINAMOS promoters and other government officials encountered resistance from both left- and right-wing opponents. They were also forced to question the cultural assumptions that informed the regime's vision of Peru's regions. At times, the military government's stereotyped view of particular regions meant that it communicated poorly with the population groups that it sought to inform and persuade. For example, the government's concept of northern Peru as the site of large agro-industrial complexes and the "engine of modernity" did not take account of the great internal diversity of a region such as Piura, the continued importance of communal identities (an idea the government associated almost exclusively with the southern highlands), nor the impact of migration flows between highland and coastal areas.

Piura

When examining the politics of the agrarian reform in Piura, an important distinction should be made between Piura's coastal valleys and its highlands, or sierra. In the coastal valleys, heavy investment in irrigation and industrialization during the first half of the twentieth century led to the development of large agro-industrial complexes producing fruit, cotton, and rice for the national and international markets. In the sierra, unirrigated agricultural production for local consumption was the norm, and land was held by a combination of haciendas, minifundios, and indigenous communities. In October 1969 the government declared that Piura would form part of Zona Agraria I (Agrarian reform zone I), comprising the departments of Tumbes and Piura and making it one of the first regions to be declared a zone of agrarian reform. However, priority was given to expropriating land in the coastal valleys—viewed as more modern and with greater potential for export-oriented agriculture—with the authorities turning their attention to the sierra (the provinces of Ayabaca, Huancabamba, and part of Morropón) only from 1973 onward.[41]

In Piura's coastal valleys, the agrarian reform was applied more quickly and decisively than in most other areas of the country. Between 1970 and 1973 almost all the major haciendas were transferred to the peasantry as CAPs or, in the case of the peasant communities of Catacaos and Sechura in Bajo Piura, as communal production units (UCPs).[42] Government promotors based in the region emphasized that the revolution was bringing liberation from latifundista control, with a variety of social benefits for hacienda workers. For example, a commemorative booklet entitled *Catacaos: 24 de junio de 1973 día histórico para el campesino piurano* was produced to mark the transfer of lands in several parts of Piura. The booklet included images of workers riding the finely bred horses that had previously belonged to the hacendado, asserting their control over the property of the latifundio.[43] Prior to the creation of SINAMOS, a propaganda film produced by the Dirección de Promoción y Difusión de Reforma Agraria (Office of Promotion and Diffusion of Agrarian Reform [DPDRA]), using footage from the northern agro-industrial complexes, featured interview extracts with the workers, who told how they were treated "like animals" and were "afraid, even of the guard." Images of animals kept in confined quarters were contrasted with the post-reform situation of animals in large pens and the workers participating in leisure activities, such as dancing the marinera.[44] The central theme of this propaganda was the idea of liberation from the oppression of capitalist landowners. Piura's campesinos were expected to embrace the cooperative model in much the same way as workers on the sugar and cotton plantations of neighboring departments La Libertad and Lambayeque had done.

To a certain extent this political rhetoric resonated with campesinos in coastal Piura. On the president's first official visit to the city of Piura in October 1969, local campesinos attended, bearing placards with slogans such as "Velasco: the master continues eating from our poverty."[45] However, the cooperative model envisaged by the government did not take account of the importance of existing social, economic, and political traditions of peasant communities (formerly known as indigenous communities). Despite the fact that members of these communities generally earned their wages from labor or subsistence agriculture on small, individually owned plots, they retained a strong sense of collective identity and wanted the adjudication of land to reflect this, rather than incorporating peasant communities into larger cooperative organizations. In addition, many believed that the cooperatives lacked the infrastructure to achieve true economic autonomy, as in the case of cotton cooperatives that did not receive the cotton processing plant as part of the adjudication.[46] Others complained that the restrictive nature of cooperative membership would leave many without work, exacerbating the region's long-standing problem of underemployment.[47]

In addition to disseminating propaganda about the reform and providing administrative support for the expropriation and adjudication of land, government promoters were charged with establishing peasant organizations. D.L. 19400, passed in May 1972, made provision for the abolition of the National Agrarian Society (seen as a bastion of the landowning oligarchy) and its replacement by the Confederación Nacional Agraria (CNA) and its affiliate organizations: agrarian federations at the departmental level and agrarian leagues at the provincial level. These organizations created immediate rivalry with the existing, independent peasant organizations. In the valleys of Piura and Chira, members of FEDECAP were fiercely critical of SINAMOS for what they saw as an antiunionist attempt to organize the peasants from above.[48] Whereas FEDECAP initially maintained a progovernment position, it adopted a more critical line after the passage of D.L. 19400 and the growth of SINAMOS activities in the area. Following its June 1972 Congress, FEDECAP changed its slogan from "Land for those who work it" to "United we will overcome." It began to develop strong links with VR and the CCP.[49]

Having been formed in the mid-1960s as a breakaway group from the PCP, VR was part of the Peruvian New Left, which took inspiration from the Cuban Revolution and rejected the PCP's pro-Soviet line. While initially supportive of the agrarian reform, the party was increasingly critical of the Velasco government. Armando Zapata was the leader of the VR regional committee for the north of the country at the time. He explained in an interview that the party worked mainly with peasant communities and landless peasants, establishing clandestine study circles and encouraging confrontations between these campesinos and what the party termed the "new agrarian bourgeoisie" of agrarian reform beneficiaries.[50] Like the SINAMOS promoters, VR organizers delivered talks, disseminated publications and leaflets among the study circles, and set different topics of discussion each week.

MIR—CA engaged in a similar style of activism, giving rise to strong competition between the parties that ultimately played out as factionalism within FEDECAP. While MIR had its political base in the Community of Catacaos in Bajo Piura, VR developed support in the Community of Querecotillo and throughout the Chira Valley. The division between these organizations became so intense that in 1974 FEDECAP divided in two, with a Querecotillo faction and a Catacaos faction. With hindsight, Zapata sees these ideological struggles as misguided: "In reality they made us lose the direction of what we wanted. Because in the end, seen from a distance, both groups wanted the same. What happened is that they were fighting for hegemony, no? Who was in front of the other, no? And that was the whole problem."[51]

Partly as a result of the activities of VR and MIR militants, the agrarian reform produced a dramatic rise in peasant activism in Piura's coastal valleys. In many cases this went far beyond the actions prescribed by D.L. 17716. For example, in 1971 a group of peasants launched a successful takeover of the Departmental Agricultural and Livestock League of Piura, which had previously been a bastion of the large landowners. There was also a series of peasant-led *tomas de tierras* (land occupations), designed to force a more rapid implementation of the agrarian reform. Over the course of 1972 and 1973, there were peasant occupations on a total of 31 haciendas.[52] These protests took the government by surprise and often forced it to ratify actions already taken on the ground. For example, on 21 February 1972, two thousand members of the Comunidad Campesina de Catacaos entered the property of the Compañía Irrigadora S.A. to reclaim their communal lands, occupying one thousand hectares in total. With more than twenty thousand inscribed members, the Comunidad Campesina de Catacaos was one of the largest peasant communities in the country. As Alejandro Diez notes, the community was ultimately successful in pushing the government to accept its proposal for UCPs, a variation on the standard cooperative model.[53]

The first UCP was recognized in 1973 and a further 60 were recognized in 1977, 104 in 1980, and 159 in 1991. This form of adjudication increased the number of beneficiaries and gave the community much greater political control than any of the proposals initially put forward by the Ministry of Agriculture or SINAMOS.[54] The Comunidad Campesina de Catacaos's success in forcing a modified application of the agrarian reform is an example of a wider trend. Colin Harding, writing in 1974, observed that "in most cases of land occupations—over 80 in Piura by mid-1973—the reform authorities have been forced to accept a fait accompli, expropriate the land very quickly and hand it over to a cooperative of the permanent and temporary laborers, despite the fact that invasions are expressly defined as an act of sabotage against the agrarian reform."[55] He concluded that the agrarian reform had been "pushed to the 'left' . . . by pressures from rural groups excluded from it."[56]

The intensity of the political struggles that occurred at the local level is revealed in cases such as the Comunidad Campesina de Querecotillo (Sullana province), where community members rejected the government's plan to establish an *empresa comunal* (a form of cooperative). Their reasons were much the same as those given by the community of Catacaos: it would benefit some *comuneros* (community members) more than others and would marginalize the community's existing administrative and political center. In a flyer produced by FEDECAP and backed by VR, the so-called blue list faction within the community denounced what it described as the treacherous actions of community members Jorge Cruz and Wenceslao Castillo, whom it claimed had sought support for their "green" faction from the director of the first military region and SINAMOS in return for backing the creation of a communal company in Querecotillo:

> This, the *comuneros* of Querecotillo will not allow, we are prepared to defend our community with our lives. This is the greatest betrayal that the traitors Wenceslao Castillo and Jorge Cruz do to their community, for that reason, the blue list that is headed by the comrade Víctor Alama calls on the individual property owners [*conductores individuales*] so that they do not fall into the trap that is being prepared by Wenceslao Castillo, with his little comrade and SINAMOS. . . . Together we will once again make them eat the dust of their defeat![57]

On the one hand, the case of Querecotillo exemplifies the local resistance that emerged in response to the government's cooperative model, which was often perceived as a threat to preexisting communal social structures. On the other, the previously cited flyer shows how decisions over land adjudication and cooperative formation came to be used as a political football by the emerging New Left, with factions within the community being identified as either "bourgeois" and progovernment or "classist" and revolutionary.

In the highlands of Piura, in contrast to the coast, peasant political organization was almost nonexistent at the start of the agrarian reform. SINAMOS promoters could operate with relative freedom, and their work centered on two key objectives: organizing the peasants who were potential beneficiaries of the agrarian reform (in many cases former hacienda workers who had already gained land through the private parceling off of hacienda land in the 1950s and early 1960s) and avoiding the decapitalization of the haciendas in areas where the agrarian reform had not yet been implemented.[58] As was noted earlier, the application of the agrarian reform in Piura began in the coastal valleys and only later—around 1973—reached the sierra. Nelson Peñaherrera, provincial coordinator for the SINAMOS zonal office in Ayabaca (Piura), recalled:

> [S]ince the agrarian reform began on the coast, therefore the hacendados of the sierra saw that the agrarian reform was expropriating everything from them. . . . So they at the level of the sierra begin to remove the livestock. They begin to remove, begin to sell. From the houses they begin to take off the roofs and try to reclaim the roof. . . . Practically if there was pasture they start to destroy all the pasture. . . . So that is where we formed the committees of support for the agrarian reform . . . to not let the hacendado, with his people, start to destroy everything that was to stay. So that they [the campesinos] would at least find something.[59]

Although a process of land parcelization that antedated the agrarian reform meant that the amount of land expropriated was small and few peasant communities were direct beneficiaries of the reform,[60] SINAMOS nevertheless developed a strong presence in the area due to its efforts to mobilize peasants. Former SINAMOS promoter Hugo Herrera described how he sought out individuals within the peasant communities to take on the role of Secretario de Difusión (dissemination secretary) to communicate with the community about political changes that were taking place in the region:

> [W]e looked among the youngest people, those who were most interested, those who asked [the] most questions in the meetings, no? And we began suggesting: "Do you want to help so that people find out about what is going on?" "Yes, ok," they said. And we consulted with the presidents of the peasant communities and they said, "Yes, yes, no problem." . . . The community sup-

ported them so that it wasn't presented as just "SINAMOS has put me here" but that the community had chosen them.[61]

These young people were charged with finding out what the different community leaders were doing and informing their own community via notices put up on the walls of the community center or in the village square. According to Herrera, this experience had a significant impact on the young people themselves, enabling them to learn about what was happening beyond their own communities. In later years, many of them went on to study at the universities in Piura.

The selection of dissemination secretaries is a good example of a strategy SINAMOS used throughout the country. In seeking to challenge the status quo, SINAMOS promoters engaged in the formation of what Antonio Gramsci described as "organic intellectuals." Defining intellectuals by their social function, Gramsci suggested that anyone had the potential to be an "organic intellectual." All it required was for these individuals to become involved in directing the ideas and aspirations of their class.[62] In that respect, SINAMOS not only communicated a set of ideas (the principles behind the agrarian reform) but tried to generate a group of organic intellectuals (cooperative leaders, agrarian league members) who would assume political leadership in the wake of the hacienda system.

It was partly through the work of these organic intellectuals that awareness of SINAMOS and the agrarian reform spread across the Piura region. Edita Herrera, who worked on communications for SINAMOS in the Piura regional office, recalled how, after visiting a remote village close to Ayabaca, a woman from the village came to Piura to seek her out: "After a few months she appeared in the Piura regional office, asking for Señorita SINAMOS. That is, the woman had no idea what an institution or an organization was. For her, I was Señorita SINAMOS, and she wanted to talk to 'Papa SINAMOS' so that he would receive her. Why? Because the mentality of the campesinos was that the master was the father, the *taita*."[63]

It would be easy to interpret such anecdotes as evidence of political naivete among Piura's peasantry. In Peru in particular, there is a strong tendency to characterize campesinos as politically innocent and disengaged from state institutions.[64] In fact, the woman in the story demonstrated a clear understanding of the political dynamics in operation by seeking out the person who could make state-backed decisions about her personal situation. The fact that this perception was formulated in terms of a family rather than a state-institution structure does not diminish the political understanding demonstrated by her actions. Moreover, the anecdote shows how quickly SINAMOS gained recognition as a major power broker in the Piura region, even in remote areas. While the military government's neat vision of a statewide structure of political organization did not match with how SINAMOS was perceived on the ground, the organization successfully penetrated existing political structures in the region.

Nelson Peñaherrera, the provincial coordinator previously cited, described how civil servants and other local authorities feared having any negative reports made about their work to the SINAMOS authorities, believing they would lose their jobs. Peñaherrera was required to send a political report on the province every three months:

> The political report was a report above all about the reality of the zone, the behavior of the institutions. For that reason, since we had to inform about more or less how this or that institution was performing, what were its merits and shortcomings, therefore the majority of people who worked in those institutions viewed us with certain distance, no? "With you, I'm watching you. But I'm not coming closer, because you are a risk for what I am doing." So that's why they said that we were the government's gossips [*chismosos*].[65]

Elmer Arce Espinoza attributed these tensions to the different organizational cultures of the Ministry of Agriculture and SINAMOS:

> [W]hile the Ministry of Agriculture responds to the criterion of executing actions from a "technical" point of view and its decisions are made within a suffocating centralization, . . . the SINAMOS apparatus responds to a political approach and, contrary to Agriculture, to a high degree of decentralization which leads the highest level functionaries at the regional level to take decisions that correspond to their "particular way of seeing things," many times diametrically different from the position that . . . the normative offices at the national level propose for these problems."[66]

In addition to filing regular political reports, the SINAMOS zonal office in Ayabaca kept a complaints book in which local people registered a range of issues, from impropriety on the part of police officers to corruption by land judges. Peñaherrera recalled, "I don't know whether in the other provinces, but here in Ayabaca we had a complaints book in which every day at least five complaints were received from people who felt that their rights had been affected by the institutions."[67] This kind of local engagement was not necessarily sanctioned by higher ranking officials within the military government. A SINAMOS promoter stationed in Ayabaca described how, when reviewing a bulletin produced by SINAMOS staff in collaboration with local people, the regional director told the promoters to scrap a section on local people's knowledge of their own history and replace it with more information on the government's agricultural policies.[68] While the promoters saw the bulletin as a way of connecting with the local population and inspiring collective action, the director treated it as a government mouthpiece. Moreover, in contrast to the local insight gained by the zonal promoters and coordinators, the SINAMOS regional plan produced in 1975 paints a stereotypical picture of campesinos in the Piura-Tumbes region. Their "sociological state" is described in the following terms:

a. Relative introversion
b. Difficult to communicate with
c. Tendency to be conservative
d. Distrustful
e. Conformist with their current economic, social, political and religious situation
f. Predisposed to suggestion on the part of leaders, sorcerers and healers, as to all kinds of superstitions.[69]

For Hugo Herrera, the disconnection between central or regional government objectives and his involvement in provincial-level activities became particularly marked after 1973 when Velasco suffered a pulmonary embolism that resulted in the loss of one of his legs. As Velasco's health declined, so did the so-called revolutionary process, culminating in the internal coup led by General Morales Bermúdez. In retrospect, Herrera feels that it would have been better to be open with people that the revolution had ended rather than continue to raise expectations: "We abandoned them. So that produced a doubly negative impact on them. . . . We continued talking to them about revolution because the leadership kept talking of revolution. But it had been making a revolution, and now it wasn't. That's what SINAMOS did."[70] Rather than the top-down, militaristic style of government that is often conjured up in reference to the Velasco government, the personal testimony of SINAMOS promoters in Piura suggests that there was considerable political engagement at the local level, even if it proved to be short-lived.

Cusco

Given Cusco's large indigenous population, an important part of SINAMOS's work in the region centered on guiding indigenous communities through the formal process of official recognition as a *comunidad campesina* (peasant community). Between 1968 and 1972 just three communities received official recognition in Cusco. Following the arrival of SINAMOS, this figure grew year on year: six were recognized in 1973, seven in 1974, thirty-one in 1975, peaking at thirty-three in 1976, the year after Velasco was removed from power.[71] The agency also had considerable success in establishing the new base organizations that were expected to mobilize in support of the agrarian reform process. According to official statistics, SINAMOS oversaw the creation of six provincial agrarian leagues and the region-wide Federación Agraria Revolucionaria Túpac Amaru del Cusco (Revolutionary Agrarian Federation Túpac Amaru of Cusco [FARTAC]). These organizations grouped together a total of 33,825 heads of household, equivalent to 90.29 percent of the department's peasant population.[72]

In presenting its agrarian reform to Cusco audiences, the Velasco government emphasized the idea that it offered an opportunity to reclaim ancestral lands that had been encroached upon by the haciendas. A propaganda film produced by the DPDRA combined highland rural scenes with the following voice-over:

> Four hundred years ago the Spanish invaded Peru. In the first hundred years of the conquest, eight million indigenous people and the system of the Inca leader were almost completely destroyed. Agriculture also suffered the consequences of the invasion. . . . Inca agricultural technology was destroyed. The indigenous were stripped of their lands and used as slaves. . . . The land now belongs to the tiller, but that is not sufficient. So that the change is true and complete, the campesino has to participate. The campesino has to organize and present his ideas. The campesino has to act.[73]

Although this message formed part of the government's overarching revolutionary narrative for the nation, the film's imagery and use of *sikuri* [panpipe music] clearly situated it in a highland context. Whereas propaganda on the northern coast emphasized the provision of new health and education services that would accompany the establishment of agricultural cooperatives, in the southern highlands greater stress was placed on the agrarian reform as a historic moment, in which the peasantry was called upon to make the reform a reality.

Constrained by the inertia of the regional bureaucracy and the influence exerted by large landowners, the reform in Cusco occurred at a slow pace and was often propelled into action only by the grassroots organizing of the campesinos. For example, despite being a prime target for expropriation according to the agrarian reform law, the Hacienda Huarán, situated near Urubamba in the Sacred Valley of the Incas, had, by 1971, escaped having any action taken against it.[74] The hacienda was owned by Oscar Fernandez Oblitas, a prominent landowner and former prefect of Cusco. He used his influence within the Ministry of Agriculture to secure an area of 48 hectares, which included the irrigated (and therefore most productive) areas of the estate. Oblitas wanted to make this land impervious to the claims of the campesinos.[75]

The *feudatarios* (sharecroppers) of the hacienda and the neighboring peasant communities of Arín and Sillacancha continued to petition the DGRAAR for the full expropriation of the hacienda. It was finally adjudicated to them as a cooperative in 1973, but only after they took collective action and occupied the hacienda by force.[76] The case of Huarán became well known throughout Peru after it was the subject of a feature film directed by Federico García Hurtado.[77]

The long history of land struggles in Cusco (discussed in the previous chapter) meant that the SINAMOS regional office could draw on a wealth of local experience of popular mobilization. The regional director of SINAMOS in Cusco, General Uzátegui, was an astute political operator who successfully co-opted well-known local political figures to work for the organization.[78] One such figure was Vladimiro Valer Delgado, a student leader and member of the workers' federation in Cusco who was recruited to help establish a SINAMOS presence on the Hacienda Huarán. Uzátegui told Valer that his criminal record for political activities would not bar him from joining the organization, commenting, "You've been in prison here and here, you've been in Sepa, no? . . . That's not important, for you it's a prize, a merit."[79] Valer was particularly familiar with Huarán, having helped to organize a trade union among the hacienda workers. The day after he joined SINAMOS, he was taken straight to Huarán to begin preparing the hacienda workers for the expropriation and adjudication processes.

As well as giving SINAMOS a strategic advantage, collaboration with local campesino leaders affected popular perceptions of the agrarian reform. While conducting interviews in Cusco, I found that interviewees frequently prefaced their accounts of the 1969 agrarian reform by talking about the struggles for peasant unionization and land occupations that began in the 1950s. In the province of Quillabamba I interviewed Hilario Pérez, former president of the Central de Cooperativas Té Huyro (Central Union of Huyro Tea Cooperatives). Pérez played a key part in forming peasant unions in the region during the 1960s and was a founding member of the Central de Cooperativas Agrarias Cafetaleras (Central Union of Coffee Cooperatives), established in 1967. He described that era as one of constant meetings, including meetings with the guerrilla fighters who were active in the region: "There were always meetings, there were sympathizers, there were people that connected us with them. So that helped us a lot, indirectly." Peasant activism was further fueled by the influx of magazines, published in Spanish, that detailed political events in Cuba and China at the time. "We read a lot," he commented, "So that's what we based our struggle on."[80] For Pérez, the agrarian reform represented a deepening of the politics of land redistribution that he had already been engaged in for some time. Similarly, the fact that individuals who had participated in Hugo Blanco's peasant political campaigns in the early 1960s went on to work for SINAMOS meant that, for many *cusqueños*, the agrarian reform formed part of a larger narrative of peasant struggle rather than arriving out of the blue, which is how it was commonly understood in the northern departments.

As well as engaging local campesino organizers to promote the agrarian reform on its behalf, the SINAMOS regional office in Cusco selected communication methods that incorporated Quechua and highland cultural traditions. According to the 1972 census, some 88.9 percent of the Cusco population was bilingual or monolingual Quechua speakers.[81] The regional office therefore produced radio programs and short films in Quechua, and government promoters were drawn from local populations to ensure they were fluent in the local dialect of Quechua. Quechua was also used in the slogans printed on flyers and posters. For example, the word "*Causachum*," meaning "rise up," was used frequently in connection with the government's actions, as in the slogan: "*Causachum Inkari! Causachum Revolución! Causachum Perú!*"[82] Against a historical background in which the Quechua language had been treated with contempt by state authorities and seen as a mark of backwardness within the education system, the government's deliberate use of Quechua held great symbolic and political significance.[83] During official ceremonies to mark the transfer of lands from government control to campesino groups and cooperatives, government officials spoke primarily in Quechua. The ceremonies also featured traditional instruments such as the *qina* (an edge-blown vertical flute) and the *pututu* (conch shell).

A common method used by SINAMOS to convey the principles of the agrarian reform was the traveling puppet show. This art form had the advantage of being highly mobile, accessible to an illiterate population, and adaptable to the local context. The teams of puppeteers employed by SINAMOS in Cusco went to surprising lengths to reflect local traditions in their shows. For each community they visited, the puppeteers altered the puppets' costumes to replicate the traditional clothing of the *comuneros*.[84] A short documentary film from the time, directed by Alberto Giudici, includes footage of one of these puppet shows being performed in the sierra (the precise location is unclear). In the show a campesino boy enters into a violent altercation with the landowner after discovering that the land of the hacienda was originally stolen from his ancestors. When he seeks redress from the priest, judge, and policeman, the boy suffers only more violence and condemnation. A striking aspect of the show is the depiction of the local priest as corrupt and deferential toward the landowner, refusing to help the boy and instead condemning him for hitting "a gentleman who has a lot of money." It is the *jefe anciano* (chief elder) who finally comes to the boy's aid, telling him: "Since I was young I grew up with the *gamonales*, and I have learned that there is no justice. Son, don't go to the judge. Don't go to anyone. We are going to complain to the assembly of the agrarian league. And afterwards we can sow [the land] happily."[85] The fact that the agrarian league is introduced through the figure of the community elder indicates SINAMOS's concern about presenting the reform as a natural progression from existing community struggles. Moreover, the show is conducted entirely in Quechua. As the camera pans around to the audience, it is clear from its laughter and close attention to the story that the performance is striking a chord.[86]

SINAMOS's use of Quechua, local costumes, and recognizable Cusco characters created a seemingly strong connection between Cusco's peasantry and the agrarian reform. It also promoted the idea that Velasco's revolution as a whole valued Peruvian indigenous identity. This idea was reinforced by repeated use of iconography linked to Túpac Amaru, the eighteenth-century leader of an indigenous rebellion against Spanish colonial rule, who was ultimately captured and hung, drawn, and quartered, in Cusco's central square in 1781.[87] Although heavily suppressed under colonialism and marginalized within nineteenth-century Peruvian nationalism, the memory of Túpac Amaru gained increasing importance from the 1920s onward as a symbol of the country's indigenous past and trajectory toward independence. The celebration of Túpac Amaru reached its apogee during the Velasco government when the Peruvian revolution was presented as a continuation of the rebel's efforts to fight imperial control and economic exploitation.[88]

Túpac Amaru was referenced repeatedly in government speeches (most famously in Velasco's announcement of the agrarian reform) and invoked in the naming of streets, institutions, and cooperatives. His image was reproduced across government publications and on placards and banners displayed at public rallies. An interview conducted by Thomas Turino with two musicians of rural-mestizo background in Cusco in 1988 suggests that the government's Túpac Amarist narrative was broadly accepted:

TT: And why was highland music of concern to Velasco?

EV: Because his political position was Túpac Amarist. And Túpac Amaru was the first precursor of independence, the first mestizo who went out in defense of the Indian, the campesino. Hence, because he [Velasco] identified with the campesinos, it was necessary for him to give value, not only to the campesino himself, but also to his culture.[89]

The government's self-identification with the history and legacy of Túpac Amaru proved effective as a strategy for generating peasant support and had particular resonance in Cusco, Túpac Amaru's birthplace.

As Raúl Asensio has shown, the Velasco government's adoption of Túpac Amaru as the principal emblem of its revolution coincided with Cusco's long-standing tradition of *tupac amarismo*, the veneration of Túpac Amaru as a leader and revolutionary example. What he describes as the Túpac Amaru cult—expressed through commemorative statues, artistic representations, and annual festivals—had been promoted by the region's public intellectuals since the early 1950s: "On the eve of the [1968] coup d'état, it was now a firmly established current in Cusco. From their modest rural beginnings, the *tupacamaristas* had extended to the urban zones, almost to the point that it became a transcendent ideology, shared by the majority of the population of the *cusqueño* cultural elites."[90] The rural origins of the cult were particularly significant for those seeking to promote the agrarian reform in the countryside. Most notably in the high provinces of Cusco, SINAMOS promoters could count on widespread identification with Túpac Amaru and a favorable reception of Velasco's "Tupac Amarist" discourse.

As well as devising communication strategies that would appeal to rural Cusco audiences, SINAMOS promoters had to navigate local power structures. A 1974 report by the regional SINAMOS office identified the "power groups" it believed were obstructing SINAMOS's work in the province of Urubamba. These included the judiciary, landowners, tradesmen, and the police (*Guardia Civil*), which "in these historic moments . . . do not comply with the proposals and conquests of the revolution. . . . [O]ften they act in collusion with the landowners."[91] The report provided details on the activities of APRA in the province, noting that the party had been one of the best organized political parties in the provincial capital of Urubamba prior to the 1968 coup: "For their [political] dissemination and communication, they had their office in the Plaza de Armas equipped with transmission equipment; to attract the youth into their ranks they carried out social, cultural, sport and folklore activities and later began the indoctrination, through sessions and plenaries, with students of different ages and social status."[92] According to this promoter, teachers affiliated with APRA continued to exert political influence over their students and incited them to participate in teachers' protests against the government. The report also criticized priests for evading the agrarian reform by selling lands belonging to the Catholic Church and using their position of authority to oppose the government: "during the mass they preach against the current government and the leaders, telling the parishioners that the current process is communist and promotes atheism."[93]

The PCP also had an important presence in the Cusco region, exercised through the Federación Departamental Campesina del Cusco (Departmental Peasant Federation of Cusco [FDCC]). Although the agrarian reform authorities initially had a positive working relationship with the FDCC, the federation soon divided between members who wanted to give unconditional support to the agrarian reform and others who sought complete independence and a more radical land redistribution. In June 1970 Hugo Blanco issued a letter calling for the participation of "classist elements" in the leadership of the cooperatives and supporting the proposal for nonpayment of the agrarian debt and total expropriation of the land. In 1972 and 1973 the FDCC organized a number of protests, including meetings in Yauri, Calca, Cusco, La Convención, Lares, and Quellouno, to reject D.L. 19400.[94] This shift toward a more combative position following the passage of D.L. 19400 tallies with political developments in Piura at the same time. Yet whereas Piura's FEDECAP experienced a moment of political ascendency during the agrarian reform, Cusco's FDCC had been weakened substantially through government repression in the aftermath of the 1963 land occupations and internal divisions brought by the failure of the 1965 guerrilla uprisings in the region.[95] Moreover, the SINAMOS regional office's policy of recruiting promoters and coordinators from among existing peasant movements enabled it to neutralize much of the opposition mobilized by the FDCC. According to one observer, this strategy gave its work "particular characteristics in relation to other areas of the country, permitting greater penetration in various peasant areas of the region."[96]

Beyond party political opposition, SINAMOS promoters faced open confrontation from landowners when they tried to form cooperatives in rural Cusco. In contrast to the large sugar and cotton plantations in Piura, where a CAP could be formed from a single agro-industrial complex, the predominant form of cooperative in the sierra was the SAIS, a looser form of association that brought together dispersed groups of peasants into a single organization. In the case of Oropesa, a highland district of the province of Quispicanchi, establishing the SAIS required promoters to reach campesinos across a wide geographical area and in places where the hacendados still exerted considerable social and political control. A report filed by the chief promoter at the Cusco zonal office in January 1974 complained that Alcides Velasco, the son-in-law of a local landowner, had disrupted a meeting organized to inform the small landholders of Chingo Chico about the SAIS. As the organizers waited for participants to arrive, Alcides Velasco "presented himself suddenly in a thuggish and presumptuous manner without any consideration, given that women and children were present, and without any cause hurled vulgar abuse against the Ministry of Agriculture representatives, SINAMOS, and the beneficiaries that had gathered."[97] The account includes verbatim quotes of what Alcides Velasco is reported to have said: "Don't think that I'm an ignorant *indio* like you that you can trick me," for example, and "I'm going immediately to see General Guzmán Fajardo, so that they [*sic*] get rid of you and your little bosses."[98] The language used here is significant, for it shows the persistence of racist attitudes among the landowners and the belief that even under the new regime, a word with the right person would see the removal of the "little bosses" of SINAMOS.

The fact that the promoters, Luis Urquizo and Guillermo Guzmán, remained in their jobs and were able to file a report critical of the episode suggests that this particular landlord's influence was not as great as believed. Nevertheless, a later report on the same SAIS commented that the lengthy adjudication process had allowed landowners to obstruct the formation of the SAIS by occupying the casa haciendas—required for training and organization purposes—and stripping their estates of assets. In addition, a number of landowners made requests under special provision, as described, to retain a portion of their property as "*inafectable*" [land exempt from expropriation], which had a negative impact on local support for the SAIS: "[S]uch is the case of Estanislao Gonzales of the property Huambutío L-2 to whom an *inafectable* area was granted and as a consequence of this fact the tenants of the property identify more with this gentleman, defending him and not wanting to know anything about the Company [i.e., the SAIS]."[99]

Developing and maintaining local campesino support for the cooperatives and associations established by the government required a continuous presence in the area. It was common practice for SINAMOS promoters to live in one of Cusco's remote villages and base themselves among the population. Establishing such a presence was not easy, however, and several interviews revealed that certain sectors of the department of Cusco remained untouched by SINAMOS because the landowners' power was too great. In the case of Maras, situated forty kilometers (about twenty-five miles) north of Cusco, the newly arrived SINAMOS promoter was forcibly evicted by "notable residents" of the village:

> There was a governor, a judge, the mayor, the priest. . . . They gathered here on the corner, the notable residents, and they said: "What? Promoter for what? And Peasant Community—what for? We don't want [that]. This little captain—no." So they talked among themselves: "Right, we'll give this young man forty-eight hours to vacate his room. If he doesn't, something will happen to him." By the following day he wasn't there; he had left that night.[100]

As this example illustrates, the passage of the agrarian reform law did not guarantee its implementation. While SINAMOS played an important role in emblematic cases such as Huarán, government promoters were unable to penetrate other parts of the region. In January 1973 local newspaper *El Sol de Cusco* reported on the dissatisfaction among peasants in Vilcabamba (La Convención province), who claimed that despite having been certified as beneficiaries by the subdirector of Agrarian Reform and Rural Settlement, their right to receive land as former hacienda workers had been undermined by two hacendados, who had made a deal with the Comunidad de Incahuasi, "leaving practically defenseless 150 feudatory families before the Land Judge." In a statement addressed to the agrarian reform authorities, they called for this transaction to be annulled and for the agrarian reform authorities to provide protection "against the threat of being evicted and having our rights denied."[101]

The impression gained from local newspaper coverage and the reports filed by promoters in Cusco is that both SINAMOS and the agrarian reform received substantial support and recognition among the region's peasants, who participated in cooperatives, agrarian leagues, and public rallies in support of the revolution. The effective co-opting of local campesino leaders gave the organization credibility, and the skillful use of propaganda helped project a triumphant image that raised expectations in rural areas. Yet while the provincial and district elites could do little in the way of overt opposition to stop the agrarian reform, they retained substantial power within village politics, in cooperative structures, and through personal connections in the government bureaucracy.

Tacna

In Tacna, both the nature of the reform's implementation and its results were less dramatic than in Piura or Cusco. What is significant is that Tacna was not declared a zone of agrarian reform until 26 February 1975. Until this point, Ministry of Agriculture officials could not compel landowners to present their land titles for official assessment and potential expropriation, and SINAMOS's actions centered on forming cooperatives and advising campesino communities, rather than pushing for expropriation and adjudication. The predominance of minifundism—over 70 percent of Tacna's cultivated land was held in plots of less than five hectares in 1961[102]—also meant that the terms of the agrarian reform law tended to be used for the resolution of disputes between relatively small landowners rather than for reclaiming communal territories or overthrowing abusive landlords.

Indirect exploitation of the land (i.e., leasing it to nonfamily members) by agrarian reform beneficiaries was expressly forbidden by D.L. 17716. Proving that a particular reform beneficiary or landowner was engaging in indirect exploitation (even if on a relatively small scale) could therefore result in the reallocation of land. During archival research in Tacna, I encountered several such cases, including disputes between family members.[103] For example, Armandina Liendo's request in 1972 for the Chañal estate in Tacna province to be adjudicated in her favor was initially approved on the grounds it would avoid the further subdivision of the property, which consisted of only three hectares. However, the claimant's uncle protested that the property had been subdivided some twenty years previously and was already being cultivated as three separate plots. The subdirector of agrarian reform ultimately brokered an agreement between the parties that Armandina would purchase the contested plot in two years' time.[104] As this case illustrates, the agrarian reform in Tacna resulted in small-scale transfers of ownership, and its effects were relatively limited when compared with those in Cusco and Piura.

Local newspaper coverage also indicates that the agrarian reform was not accorded the same political importance in Tacna as in Cusco and Piura. When President Velasco made an official visit to the region in October 1971, an editorial published in *La Voz de Tacna* claimed that in contrast to other regions, which had long been subjected to colonial exploitation, Tacna had maintained the agrarian structure brought by the Incas: "For that reason we have not experienced the excesses of *gamonalismo* nor have we been subjected to the domination of the latifundios. And because neither exploitation nor abuse by the powerful were known in Tacna, that is why [the people] learned to love and defend liberty with passion and rebelliousness."[105] The picture painted here is of a people who need neither liberation from the yoke of the landowners nor government intervention to change oppressive power structures. The editorial went on to express its faith that Velasco would deliver on the infrastructure projects it saw as most vital for the region: the building of an asphalt road to Bolivia, the diversion of water from Maure to the Tacna valley, and construction of a port in the Bay of Sama. Although broadly welcomed by the Tacna press, the agrarian reform was not regarded as a key priority for the region.[106]

Reaction to the agrarian reform among Tacna's campesinos was similarly muted. In 1975 the government-sponsored Federación Agraria Revolucionaria de Tacna y Moquegua (FARTAMO) observed:

> In the region of Tacna and Moquegua obvious structural changes have not been noted with the application of the agrarian reform, given that there were no large haciendas, except in the case of Totora and the Colonization of La Yarada, the majority of the properties are medium and small. In terms of the management of land tenancy, on many of [the properties] indirect management is observed. For that reason we can say that the agrarian reform is benefitting the peasantry of the region very little.[107]

Whereas government communication efforts in Piura and Cusco engaged with regional histories of social injustice and portrayed the agrarian reform as a continuation of local struggles, SINAMOS promoters working in Tacna complained of indifference among the population. In January 1974, staff completed a questionnaire that asked them to list, in order of importance, the main problems they met with in carrying out their daily work. A number of promoters referred to the apathy and/or resistance they encountered among the target population. One response stated that "rejection from the base population [and] lack of awareness about the current process among the population" were the key problems, while another listed "the population's rejection of the system [i.e., SINAMOS], excessive individualism, [and] influence of some power groups" as the main difficulties.[108]

Tacna's history as an occupied territory was an important factor in shaping the population's response to SINAMOS. Being on the border with Chile, Tacna had been subjected to Chilean occupation for fifty years following Peru's defeat in the War of the Pacific (1879–1884). When SINAMOS was first established in 1971, the SINAMOS office in Tacna was a zonal office, under the supervision of the regional office in Arequipa. When it was announced in June 1972 that Tacna was to be granted its own regional office, the news was greeted with rapturous support in the local press. In melodramatic prose, *La Voz de Tacna* proclaimed that the news had resounded "like redemption bells in the Tacna sky": "Juan Velasco Alvarado, the chief of the military government that governs the country with the stroke of a pen, has cut the guardianship that Arequipa had been exercising with respect to SINAMOS. And it could not be any other way[;] Tacna experienced for more than half a century the martyrdom of foreign guardianship. And it was not correct or right that once again its development and all its activities be subjected to a new guardianship."[109]

Fredy Gambetta, who worked for the "pueblos jóvenes" section of SINA-

MOS in Tacna, recalled that "the day of the creation of the Region XI office, caravans took to the streets to thank the government for 'granting us independence' from the arequipeños."[110] The tenor of this reaction indicates that among *tacneños*, greater attention was given to the arrival of state institutions per se than to the revolutionary messages they carried.

By 1973 five CAPs and five agricultural service cooperatives had been established in the departments of Tacna and Moquegua (Agrarian Reform Zone VII), as well as the SAIS Totora (Agrarian Social Interest Society), which grouped together 200 families and two comunidades campesinas, which were in turn members of service cooperatives. With relatively few targets for expropriation that could be converted into large-scale cooperatives, the attention of SINAMOS promoters shifted to consolidating those cooperatives that had been established—some of which antedated the agrarian reform law—through training and advice. A 1973 SINAMOS report on Tacna's agricultural cooperatives found that the majority did not comply with such basic requirements as the keeping of accounts and maintaining regular meetings of the vigilance, administrative, and general councils. According to the report, this reflected members' limited understanding of the principles and functions of a cooperative and the dispersed nature of the membership: "Because the members are from different places and origins, generally [indigenous] communities, the scope of the cooperatives did not tend toward integral development, and consequently [they] have not achieved a structure that assures their stability as a company."[111] Rather than CAPs and SAIS, there was popular support for the formation of Asociaciones Agrarias de Conductores Directos (Agricultural Associations of Owner Occupiers).[112]

There was also a considerable amount of public distrust toward SINAMOS. In an internal meeting, a group of SINAMOS employees reported that among their own friends and people on the street, they had heard SINAMOS described as "gestapos, politicians, that we are the political group of the day, that there is no freedom of the press, that when we go to work in another company as employees of SINAMOS we are not going to have access."[113] Others revealed that "in the neighbor Republic of Chile (in Arica)[,] they had heard it said that the workers of SINAMOS were something like a government secret police."[114] Made in June 1974, as General Pinochet was consolidating his power in Chile, this comment is a clear example of how Tacna's proximity to Chile could shape local responses to SINAMOS and fuel suspicion toward its activism in the local area.

However, there are signs that opportunities for greater political engagement between SINAMOS promoters and local populations were missed in

Tacna as a result of the government's misplaced assumptions. For example, the notion that Tacna was a fundamentally mestizo region meant that there was little provision for communication using indigenous languages and the importance of Quechua in particular was underestimated. Evaluating a training course for peasant community leaders, a report by the zonal SINAMOS office in Moquegua stated: "While it is true that those attending the course speak Spanish[,] a better understanding and integration between the Comunidades Campesinas and presenters would have been achieved using the language of the zone (Quechua)."[115] The failure of government promoters to engage with Tacna's regional cultures ultimately shaped how the agrarian reform has been remembered in the region. Whereas in Cusco and Piura the agrarian reform is remembered as a period of great political tumult, in Tacna it has left a relatively small impression on the region's history.

Alongside its promotion of cooperatives, the Tacna-Moquegua SINAMOS office worked with indigenous communities to support their recognition and institutionalization as comunidades campesinas. In this area too it seems that promoters were not successful in generating enthusiasm for the government's model. In one particularly interesting case, a peasant community that had been established in 1948 sought dissolution in 1971. Despite receiving substantial encouragement from government promotors to reorganize and gain access to the benefits available to peasant communities under the agrarian reform law, members of the Comunidad Campesina Quilahuani (Tarata province) reportedly told community leader Felipe Ramos that they wanted "to know nothing about the community and for me to never again speak to them about it."[116] The reasons given for the dissolution request were that the *comuneros* had not benefited from community status, they wanted their properties to be privately owned and registered as such, and the community had not had "institutional life" since 1955, when Quilahuani became a provincial district.[117] And yet in relaying the community's demands to the department of peasant communities within Agrarian Zone VII, Ramos writes of the strong desire among community members to have their minutes book returned to them immediately: "[T]he inhabitants of both sexes in no way want to let this little book go anywhere, there is a tremendous protest, they have told me that I am a simple manager [*encargado*] and as such I should not get involved in anything, we are civilized people, district capital, small landowners of private lands [*sic*] we live peacefully, they told me."[118]

This letter simultaneously reveals a strong sense of collective, community identity and a complete rejection of official community status and all that it entailed. It is also indicative of the way in which government officials developed relationships with particular individuals in order to exert influence within the peasant communities. Adopting a somewhat familiar tone, Ramos writes: "As you recommended to me so much, that by all means possible I try to convince the inhabitants of Quilahuani to reorganize the Community, I have done everything possible, so much so that I have delayed sending you the certified certificate of dissolution, because some [of the community] gave [me] hope."[119] This comment suggests both a long-standing relationship between Ramos and the government official and a deep personal commitment on the part of the community leader to achieve what had been asked of him.

In a similar case, the government's program of community reorganization became a bone of contention within the Comunidad Campesina Huanuara (Candarave province). In December 1974 a memorandum signed by 145 members of the community was sent to the SINAMOS regional office declaring their complete disagreement with the recent organization of the community. The SINAMOS promoter cited the influence of the local priest in generating this memorandum, as well as the actions of "the campesino Lorenzo Vargas," who was not in agreement with the organization "and even less with the structural problems and the objectives of SINAMOS, because, he clearly stated, 'SINAMOS is a political institution, that comes to perturb the tranquility of the inhabitants of different villages and at no moment would I accept the help of SINAMOS.' "[120] On the other hand, a group within the community openly welcomed the arrival of SINAMOS and wrote to the regional office to request a training course specifically for their community. Their letter began by referring to "the problem of pervasive divisiveness: some of us are true *Comuneros* identified with the postulates of the Revolutionary Government of the Armed Forces and others, the great majority, [are those] who believe they are Direct Conductors [of the land]."[121]

The interpretation that SINAMOS and its allies gave to such difficulties centered on the question of mentality and political orientation. In requesting a training course for their community, the president and secretary of the Comunidad Campesina Huanuara asserted that this was the only way out of the tensions affecting their community. Primary objectives of the course included elevating the "ideological level of the members of the community, based on the analysis of the national and global problematic," and incentivizing and strengthening "the analytical and creative capacity of the *comuneros*, intervening in the development of criticism and self-criticism that make solidarity action possible."[122] Similarly, in his report on peasant communities' noncompliance with internal electoral procedures, a local Ministry of Agriculture official observed, "[W]hen their election results have been returned to them to be corrected or new elections called, [they] have opted to pronounce for the dissolution or extinction of the Community[;] it is clear that they act that way because of the noninterpretation of the law to which the undersigned is dedicated, but that requires time, to adapt the *comunero* to the change of mentality."[123]

The need for a change in mentality among SINAMOS staff was also viewed as one of the principal problems limiting the organization's impact in the Tacna-Moquegua region. The senior management organized study circles in which staff worked through a series of "reflective guides" and recorded their answers to the questions posed in the guide. The minutes of these study circles reveal a high degree of indoctrination, with staff expected to repeat and celebrate the government's "revolutionary" mantras on political participation and the threat posed by "counter-revolutionary" forces. In 1973 there was also an intensive regional training course spanning more than twelve days, which was organized with the assistance of the SINAMOS national office and included the participation of Héctor Bejar, a former guerrilla and key leader within SINAMOS. The aim of the course was to "influence the ideopolitical training of the promoter. . . . This political training refers to knowing how to understand what the fundamental objectives of our noncapitalist, noncommunist Process are, and what its political differences are with other doctrines and forms of work." Despite these efforts, an internal evaluation report dated January 1975 observed: "In the course of the past two years there has been a lack of identification with the process and the interests of the population and indifference toward the political work on the part of some [civil] servants."[124] Whereas in Cusco SINAMOS had been able to recruit politically conscious promoters from the ranks of the region's peasant unions, in Tacna a large proportion of SINAMOS staff came from the technical professions, resulting in a more technocratic style of operation and little sense of camaraderie or political mission.

Ultimately, the largest obstacle faced by SINAMOS in Tacna was the entrenched conservative opposition. An evaluation produced by the regional office in January 1976 noted that organizations such as the government-sponsored agrarian leagues were being displaced by the provincial council (whose membership was established before the 1968 coup and had not been altered by the military government), which promoted individuals who "spoke in the name of base organizations but who are known political activists of the parties who oppose the Process (APRA-UNO)."[125] It is significant that it was in Tacna that General Morales Bermúdez launched his coup against President Velasco in August 1975, an event that became known as "el Tacnazo." Unlike Cusco, where peasants and workers would reliably join public rallies in support of the Velasco government when asked, in Tacna, as Morales Bermúdez correctly anticipated, residents showed little reaction to such requests.

In summary, in Tacna SINAMOS promoted the agrarian reform as part of a nationalist revolution that would transform all aspects of Peruvian society and emphasized Tacna's importance as a regional leader in the reform process. Local actions centered on the reduction of minifundism, the formation and maintenance of cooperatives and peasant companies, and resistance to the counterrevolutionary opposition of conservative political parties. However, given Tacna's political history and the predominance of small-scale agriculture, there was limited popular enthusiasm for the agrarian reform. A 1975 report by FARTAMO representatives in Tacna cited rural-to-urban migration, poor irrigation, limited use of technology, and unfavorable trading terms as the region's principal agricultural problems.[126] FARTAMO also pointed to an absence of coordination among the organizations that were designed to represent campesino interests, echoing similar statements made by SINAMOS promoters on the difficulties they faced in establishing and maintaining relationships among the rural population.

Conclusion

Government efforts to promote the agrarian reform at the regional level generated a series of tensions between existing bureaucrats and new recruits and among local elites, political activists, and SINAMOS promoters. In an interview shortly after Peru's return to democracy, former SINAMOS official Carlos Franco commented: "Most people believed that SINAMOS was a very powerful institution, with great economic resources and . . . an extraordinary level of political confidence from the president. . . . That was the public image."[127] In reality, SINAMOS's power had to be carefully constructed through persuading stakeholders, building alliances, and adapting to the local political context.

Efforts to promote the agrarian reform varied considerably between the regions of Piura, Cusco, and Tacna. The local context dictated the story that SINAMOS representatives chose to tell, from a popular celebration of economic progress and liberation from latifundio control in Piura to the vindication of indigenous land rights in highland Cusco and "revolutionary nationalism" in Tacna. Variations in literacy levels often determined the kinds of propaganda that could be deployed. Promoters also used local historical and cultural resources to link the agrarian reform to the broader historical trajectory of each region, with varying degrees of success. While SINAMOS developed a reputation for its "octopus grip" on power in rural Piura, its representatives were forced out of villages in Cusco and met with indifference in Tacna. Differences in the local activity and reception of government promoters helped determine the pace of change in each region and shaped how the agrarian reform is remembered today (a theme revisited in chapter 5).

Yet alongside these differences, this comparative study of SINAMOS's interventions in local politics reveals a number of significant continuities. First, it is clear that regardless of their success rate, SINAMOS promoters in each region tried to effect political change by cultivating what Antonio Gramsci described as "organic intellectuals." The young people whom SINAMOS recruited as dissemination secretaries in highland Piura, the individuals charged with reorganizing peasant communities in Tacna, and the peasant organizers who took up leadership roles in Cusco's agrarian leagues and cooperatives are all examples of this strategy.

Second, in all three regions SINAMOS promoters clashed with other government departments and agencies, particularly the Ministry of Agriculture. Whereas the Ministry of Agriculture was an established part of the state bureaucracy that long preceded the Velasco government, SINAMOS was a national agency, forged in the feverish climate of revolution, that explicitly sought to break with established norms. SINAMOS was larger and more heavily funded than any previous state institution, but its magnitude also gave rise to significant resentment and rivalry from other government departments.

Finally, while the impact of SINAMOS promoters varied both within and between the regions studied here, the very fact that they engaged in local struggles with political party activists and landowners changed the dynamics of rural politics across the country. Prior to 1968, the major government ministries had been centered in Lima, and peasants would often be forced to travel to the capital to state their case. As a consequence of the agrarian reform and the political mobilization prompted by it, Peruvian regions developed new significance as distinctive entities within Peruvian politics, and political actors in the regions gained new access to national politics. The idea that popular demands were legitimate and should be prioritized by the state was widely disseminated by the actions and rhetoric of the military government. The government similarly validated popular demands as an expression of citizenship within education. As the next chapter reports, education was used by the Velasco government to mold campesinos into its vision of the Peruvian *hombre nuevo.*

CHAPTER 3

Education for Social Change: The Making of the Campesino Citizen

In announcing the agrarian reform law, President Velasco declared that the Peruvian campesino would become "truly a free citizen," whose right to the land finally would be recognized. The campesino would "no longer be, as until now, a diminished citizen, a man to be exploited by another man."[1] As well as being enshrined in the agrarian reform law, this shift in citizenship rights for the peasantry was emphasized throughout the government's educational policies. Alongside a general educational reform to overhaul the formal education sector, the Velasco government invested in a nationwide literacy program and training for agricultural cooperatives. While government-sponsored programs enjoyed moderate success in raising literacy and numeracy levels, more significant was the emphasis placed on education as a means of empowerment. The role of education in forging a new ideology and responding to society's problems was judged to be particularly important in the context of major agrarian reform, as existing social hierarchies were dismantled and a new model of collective farming was introduced.

Throughout the Velasco era electoral participation was confined to specific spheres such as the selection of cooperative representatives. Provincial and departmental representatives were either retained from the previous administration or replaced through government nomination rather than a popular vote. However, the Velasco government stressed that true citizenship comprised a number of social and economic rights that extended beyond those upheld by formal democracy. In a speech delivered in October 1969, Velasco proclaimed: "There is no authentic democracy without social justice. . . . There is no authentic democracy when the people continue in misery; when the campesino has no land; when the powerful dominate everything. The pure formal democracy of periodic votes, which are negotiated over behind the backs of the people, is not democracy!"[2] The "true" democracy that the Velasco government aimed to bring about encompassed access to basic education, health care, and legal representation and freedom to express a voice in public affairs. Against this backdrop, the educational reform and training programs that accompanied the agrarian reform were designed to raise consciousness among the whole population and enable peasants—and other marginalized groups—to challenge their historic exclusion from formal democracy and demand greater recognition as Peruvian citizens.

Yet this position was not without its tensions. When asked why elections were considered a good idea for the agricultural cooperatives and not for the country as a whole, SINAMOS chief General Rodríguez Figueroa responded: "One should not forget that we are talking about an electoral process in cooperative organizations. Therefore it is not about, strictly speaking, political elections and much less political party elections. Here there are no political flags in conflict. The other elections, to which you refer, those that you call elections 'for the country' are events of an exclusively political character."[3]

Whereas party politics was seen as a game that had historically played out among the elites at the cost of ordinary citizens, cooperative elections were presented as a case of direct democracy that would have immediate benefits for the cooperative members. The majority of campesinos had been excluded from electoral democracy on the grounds of illiteracy, but during the Velasco government they made up the majority of those electing directors and delegates within the CAPs, SAIS, and agrarian leagues. These elections set an important precedent for the inclusion of illiterates in electoral proceedings. Armed with the language of emancipation and citizenship that was disseminated through the government's educational initiatives, cooperative members ultimately pushed the limits of political participation beyond those envisioned by the Velasco regime.

Education was used to promote social change in a variety of contexts across the world. By the mid-twentieth century, education was widely understood to be a crucial aspect of national development. The parallels between Peru and other so-called Third World countries are evident, yet the particular significance of the historical relationship between literacy and the exercise of citizenship in Peru is noteworthy. The Velasco government's educational philosophy merits analysis along with its interventions in three key areas: educational reform, rural education programs, and literacy training. While many areas of education policy are left out of this discussion, this chapter focuses on those that bear most directly on the agrarian reform and the dynamics of citizenship in rural areas. These educational policies were not inconsequential for political participation and citizenship in Peru. The government's efforts to forge an *hombre nuevo* interacted with—and were challenged by—regional conceptualizations of education and citizenship.

Education for Social Change: A Global Perspective

Debates on the social role of education developed in many parts of the world during the late nineteenth century. In China, toward the end of the Qing dynasty, the national government ordered communities to establish, manage, and fund their own schools, believing this would help create a modern nation-state.[4] Similarly, in early twentieth-century Mexico, President Porfirio Díaz introduced the Law of Schools for Rudimentary Instruction, which ordered the creation of basic schools throughout the republic to teach children to read, write, count, and speak Spanish to promote national integration.[5] After 1910, education became an important vehicle for the consolidation of the Mexican Revolution. As rector of the national university during the 1920s, José Vasconcelos launched a mass literacy campaign that over 10 years affected 6,973,855 people, more than 66 percent of the population. He drew inspiration from the educational activities of Maxim Gorky and Anatoly Lunacharsky in Russia and argued that literacy training should be approached like a military campaign, with all citizens coming together to "save" the country from ignorance.[6]

In Cuba, Fidel Castro described illiteracy as a national enemy and declared 1961 the "Year of Education." He instigated an innovative literacy campaign that dramatically reduced the country's illiteracy rate from over 20 percent to just 3.9 percent in a single year. This was achieved by sending over 100,000 young volunteers into rural areas to live with illiterate peasants, where they taught their hosts to read and write in return for food and board.[7] The Cuban government saw literacy as a major part of modernization, believing it would contribute to agricultural and industrial production and aid communication among the population.[8]

Literacy was also viewed as an important foundation for the development of social equality. In the case of China, the mass literacy campaigns of the 1950s were promoted as a means to politicize the masses and challenge the domination of a literate elite.[9] In Tanzania, President Nyerere (1964–1985) introduced a series of mass literacy campaigns in line with his policy of Ujamaa socialism, or "African familyhood." Under Nyerere, improving literacy levels was seen as a way of enabling equal access to social services and economic opportunities in the countryside.[10]

The desire to use literacy programs to boost social equality was not confined to socialist or communist regimes, however. A series of publications by the United Nations Educational Scientific and Cultural Organization urged governments to expand access to education for poor populations, improve teaching standards, and increase literacy levels. From this perspective, education could aid social equality by providing poor people with new skills, which would in turn offer access to greater employment opportunities and social mobility.

The promotion of education has not always come from the government level, however. Grassroots demand for access to education has historically been particularly strong in Latin American countries. Fiona Wilson's research on the central Peruvian province of Tarma found that "in the populous heartland of the province, education was by no means an alien concept foisted on resistant rural people. On the contrary, eagerness for schools in the communities of Tarma during the late nineteenth and early twentieth centuries suggests that education represented an escape from the label of *indio ignorante* (ignorant Indian) and release from forced labor systems."[11] In the case of Tarma, the rate of school building actually decreased after responsibility for education passed from the municipal authorities to the central government in 1904.[12] Throughout the twentieth century Peru's peasants continued to attach immense social and political importance to acquiring education, seeing it as a way to "*salir del engaño*" (escape from deception/trickery).[13]

In the 1960s, modernization theories that treated education as a technical process began to give way to interest in education as a means to raise consciousness. The key proponent of this approach was Brazilian intellectual Paulo Freire, who argued that authoritarian teaching methods should be abandoned in favor of an equal relationship between educator and student. His techniques for literacy training centered on the use of dialogue: "Because dialogue is an encounter between women and men who name the world, it must not be a situation where some name on behalf of others. It is an act of creation; it must not serve as a crafty instrument for the domination of one person by another."[14] Freire argued that for societies seeking greater social equality it was not enough to simply extend access to education among broader sectors of the population; there also had to be a fundamental shift in the style and scope of education so that students were encouraged to think for themselves. This style of education could help raise political awareness or consciousness among the poor and oppressed, ultimately enabling them to exert greater political power.[15] Although Freire was not directly involved in the Peruvian revolution, his ideas were highly influential in the Velasco government's efforts to raise consciousness.

In order to understand why education took on such significance in Peru during the Velasco years, it is worth reviewing the historical development of the country's political system, which placed particular importance on the ability to read and write. As Frank Salomon and Mercedes Niño-Murcia note, after Peru gained independence from Spain in 1821, literacy formed part of a national project to transform "Indians" into citizens: "The desired information regimen was to be monolingual, undivided by ethnic discontinuities, and evenly documented throughout. The new regime would create for any citizen and his or her relations with the state a uniform type of dossier, universal within Peru and recognized to the exclusion of all others. Alleged illiteracy and ignorance of the language in which official literacy had been vested made 'Indians' seem poor prospects for this sort of citizenship."[16] According to this rationale, indigenous populations who did not read or write Spanish could be treated as wards of the state, who needed to be "civilized" before they could become full citizens. The ability to read and write was taken as proof of the capacity for critical thought and increasingly came to constitute one of the conditions for suffrage.[17]

The criteria for participating in elections varied between different levels of government and changed over the course of the nineteenth century. Although literacy often formed one of the requirements, this could be offset by the fulfilment of other conditions, such as being an active member of the parish or being in recognized scientific, mechanical, or industrial employment. Moreover, indigenous communities continued to exert some political influence in return for tribute paid to the state and regional caudillos, a continuation of what historians have termed the "colonial pact."[18] In 1896, however, a universal literacy requirement was applied to all elections. This change reflected a shift in the balance of power from regional authorities to the central state. As Alicia del Águila argues, the traumatic experience of the War of the Pacific (1879–1883) convinced the ruling elites that they needed to forge a more unified and modern nation: "That, in electoral terms, meant forming a central electoral organ away from the pressures of local caudillos, on one hand, and on the other, establishing a single, general suffrage requirement. With that, the great majorities, especially the indigenous, were left without suffrage."[19]

Although suffrage was extended to women in 1956, the literacy requirement remained in place until 1979. This meant that in the decades prior to the Velasco government, formal political participation was restricted to a small minority of the population and was particularly limited in rural areas, especially the southern highlands. For example, in 1963 just 8.93 percent of the population of Cusco was registered to vote, whereas in Lima it was 34.79 percent.[20]

This restriction on citizenship rights was contested in various ways. Salomon and Niño-Murcia make the important point that although often described as "eternal outsiders to the world of letters," indigenous communities continued to be linked to many institutions through the use of scribes.[21] They also developed their own ways of using writing, for example, to enforce labor reciprocity within and between communities.[22] The introduction of the literacy requirement therefore did not deprive indigenous communities of all political agency, but it tended to push them to the margins of electoral democracy. The first political challenge to this situation came in the early 1920s from the Comité Pro-Derecho Indígena Tahuantinsuyo (Tahuantinsuyo Pro-Indigenous Rights Committee), an *indigenista* association. The Tahuantinsuyo Committee championed indigenous leaders and argued that they should have an active role in national politics. It campaigned for more educational provision in rural areas and suggested that literacy could empower indigenous citizens to engage politically while still retaining their indigenous identity.[23]

The Tahuantinsuyu Committee did not question the legitimacy of the literacy restriction on voting rights, but it sought to offset the law's discriminatory effects by using literacy as a means to achieve political ends. For example, the concluding communiqué of its First Indigenous Congress in 1921 stated: "[We consider] the 28th of July of 1921 as the point of departure of a new era, when we should learn . . . to protest and rebel against the oppressive hand. . . . But before being bold it is necessary to be literate. Even if the government has the best intentions, if we [the Indians] do not impel those intentions, we will never ever be able to do anything that will really favor us."[24] The Tahuantinsuyo Committee briefly benefited from a paternalist relationship with President Augusto B. Leguía (1919–1932), who was anxious to secure support for his reforms and a national program of road building that was largely dependent on indigenous labor. However, by 1927 Leguía began building alliances with local landowners and more conservative voices within the *indigenista* movement and no longer needed the support of the Tahuantinsuyo Committee.[25]

In the 1930s, the arguments made by the Tahuantinsuyo Committee in favor of an "Indian citizenship" empowered by literacy slipped off the political radar. Instead, it was argued that illiteracy was a symptom of deeper structural social problems that should themselves be the focus of political activism. In his *Siete ensayos de interpretación de la realidad peruana*, José

Carlos Mariátegui wrote: "The problem of the illiteracy of the Indian is, ultimately, a problem that extends beyond the limited framework of a solely pedagogical plan. Every day it is further proven that to train someone to be literate is not to educate them. The elementary school does not morally and socially redeem the Indian. The first real step toward his redemption must be the abolition of his servitude."[26] According to this analysis, the extension of educational provision would achieve nothing if it was not accompanied by a fundamental reordering of Peru's economic system.

In leftist circles, ideas of indigenous citizenship and the use of literacy as a political tool were abandoned in favor of Marxist arguments that focused on the political activism of the urban proletariat, a trend that continued into the 1960s.[27] Education nevertheless retained crucial importance among the wider population. Some of the most serious protests faced by the Velasco government were those held in Ayacucho in 1969 over the reduction of free education.[28] Significantly, although the protests were started by students, they were soon joined by campesinos, and together they took over the city of Huanta (Ayacucho) on 21 June. In the ensuing confrontation between police and protesters, eighteen people were killed and sixty-six wounded, indicating the strength of feeling that access to education inspired.[29] From the Velasco government's perspective, education could play a central role in transforming Peruvian society by challenging existing patterns of social domination in parallel with its other social and economic reforms. This vision was articulated through educational reform, interventions in rural education, and a mass literacy campaign.

Educational Interventions under the Velasco Government

Education Reform

Efforts to reform the education system began in 1969 with the creation of the Education Reform Commission, headed by the well-known intellectual Augusto Salazar Bondy. The commission's assessment of the existing education system and of the changes that were needed was published in September 1970 as *Reforma de la educación Peruana. Informe general* (Reform of Peruvian education. General report), also known as the Libro Azul (Blue Book). The Libro Azul criticized the education system for preserving social inequalities and argued that education should instead be used to change society, according to what it called "humanistic" values.[30] The report's suggestions were incorporated into the 1972 General Law of Education (D.L. 19326), which became known simply as "the educational reform" and was hailed by Velasco as "a vital necessity for Peru's development and a major objective of our revolution."[31] As Patricia Oliart notes, the education reform was the project that showed most clearly the alliance between the military government and the group of progressive intellectuals that supported it.[32]

The education reform departed from the tendency common across Latin America since the 1950s (heavily influenced by the United States) to see development as a process of reducing poverty through gradual modernization.[33] Rather, the Libro Azul expressed the objectives of the education reform in explicitly political terms:

> Reformed education is an essential way to achieve a new man in a new society. This means creating the original conditions for the development of forms of personal and social behavior that are authentically human and, as such, not subject to the distortions historically produced in underdeveloped and affluent societies, both governed by profit, repression and aggression. It is through the new society and the new education that we may achieve the realization of man's best possibilities, conscious of our specific situation as a country located in the global historical process of the emerging third world.[34]

The aims of the reform were defined as "1) education for work and development[,] 2) education for the structural transformation of society[,] 3) education for self-affirmation and the independence of the Peruvian nation."[35] In practical terms, this meant altering the organization of educational provision, introducing new pedagogical approaches, and changing curriculum content.

A key structural change brought by the reform was the introduction of Núcleos Educativos Comunales (Communal Educational Nuclei), a form of local council that included parents, teachers, and government officials. This policy had been tested in some areas since the 1940s, but the Velasco government made it a comprehensive national system.[36] As well as administering resources and providing advice to local schools, the nuclei were designed to encourage local involvement in the management of educational provision. It was hoped that such participation would encourage Peruvians to see the school as part of their community rather than as an external imposition. In addition, local and regional offices of the education ministry were instructed to establish flexible school calendars that were adapted to the local context, and researchers of adult education were encouraged to involve local populations in their studies (using group discussions and interviews with local residents) so that education programs might respond better to their needs and interests.[37]

These measures reflected a move away from top-down, authoritarian educational models. The philosophy behind the Communal Educational Nuclei policy is captured in a 1974 Ministry of Education report: "We must get away completely from the idea that a person who has studied at university, or has more money, or is 'white' (or is a man) is more 'cultured.' . . . What we should aim to achieve and promote is a real transfer of power in education."[38] Thus, equality was to be established through both equal provision of education and the opportunity to participate on an equal basis in the design and implementation of educational systems.

The education reform also established parity between formal education and other forms of educational provision. It abolished the previous category of secondary education and regrouped its constituent parts, with the lower grades forming part of a new basic education sector and the higher grades merging with the university sector to create new Escuelas Superiores de Educación Profesional (Higher Schools of Vocational Education [ESEPs]). The previous system of night schools was reformulated as a separate system of "basic education for work" that could also provide access to the Escuelas Superiores de Educación Profesional. Significantly, this restructuring placed night schools and work-based training on the same footing as the basic education sector, with higher education no longer reserved for the elites (at least in theory). In addition, the education reform established specialized training centers for the skilled and semiskilled. By increasing the range of educational opportunities, the government tried to overturn what it saw as the elitist and discriminatory character of the existing education system.[39]

In pedagogical terms, the education reform required teachers to adopt methods that would encourage critical reflection rather than rote learning. For example, teachers were instructed to take a global approach to reading that focused on comprehension and engagement, rather than using syllable-to-syllable reading methods. Similarly, the teaching of mathematics was to be based on student participation in hands-on activities involving real objects, replacing the lecture-style teaching of traditional arithmetic.[40] The previous focus on functional skills was to be replaced by work-based training that allowed workers "to realize themselves as people" and build solidarity with their coworkers.

The education system was also to be opened up to allow the accreditation of independent study and education in nontraditional settings. For Leopoldo Chiappo, one of the members of the Education Reform Commission, this implied a fundamental reconceptualization of what education should involve: "The education system, strictly limited to the school model, has resulted in the dropout of the great majority, who have learned from the school itself [to feel] inadequate and frustrated. . . . Those young people from the village, instead of exploring their destiny and their own words through dialogue and mass organization, learn to imitate the upper classes and in doing so they denaturalize their own being."[41] By accrediting education received in nontraditional settings, the reformed education system would place less emphasis on students having to conform to particular cultural norms and instead embrace other ways of teaching and learning.

The reform also introduced a series of changes to the school curriculum, including a focus within the social sciences on issues of sexism, racism, and class inequalities; greater attention to Peru's national diversity and respect for its different cultures; the use of local dialects inside the classroom (rather than academic Spanish); and greater attention to the needs of monolingual speakers of indigenous languages. In addition, all teachers were to learn an indigenous language.[42] The education reform also introduced changes that reflected the Velasco government's popular nationalism: a single gray uniform was introduced for all children, including those attending private schools; folk dancing became a mandatory part of the curriculum for all ages; and the national flag was to be displayed in all classrooms.[43]

Rural Education Programs

Education in rural areas was given priority in the education reform, with programs for rural areas being one of three special programs identified at Title XIX of the legal decree (the other two were national defense and Latin American integration).[44] A 1975 guide for educators produced jointly by the Ministry of Education, Ministry of Agriculture, SINAMOS, and the Inter-American Institute of Agricultural Sciences began by noting that with the passage of the education reform, "adult education receives a vigorous impulse and is reoriented and extended toward new sectors of the population."[45] According to the authors, the government attached particular importance to rural adult education for two reasons: first, the need to support the agrarian reform, which was considered one of its most essential structural reforms, and, second, the moral obligation to give preferential attention to those who had traditionally been marginalized by the education system.[46] The new rural adult education was designed to

- be equivalent in quality and structure to the education provided in schools, but delivered in predominantly non-school settings and driven by communities themselves;

- not be limited to technical knowledge but approached as a means of integral development;
- raise social consciousness and change attitudes to allow political participation;
- enable increased productivity, technological development and the successful management of production;
- be supported by an infrastructure of radios, newspapers and pamphlets to reinforce lessons learnt and avoid education being "lost through disuse"; [and]
- give special importance to literacy training and women.[47]

From the regime's perspective it was essential to create an agricultural workforce that was educated in political as well as technical matters if the agrarian reform was to succeed. Unlike the hacienda system, in which all decisions were made either by the landowner or the estate administrator, in the cooperative system decisions were to be made collectively via the administrative and vigilance councils and the general assembly. Cooperative members needed to be able to make informed decisions about who would represent them in the various governing councils and be equipped to participate in the discussions of their general assembly. This was especially true after 1972, when changes to cooperative electoral procedures ended the practice of government-appointed delegates and gave greater representation to laborers than managers and technical staff within each cooperative.[48]

To that end, the Velasco government aimed to deliver a fundamentally different kind of education to the training that had previously been directed at cooperatives. An article in a SINAMOS staff magazine observed that in the past, "cooperative training was oriented toward the delivery of a series of formal events (courses, workshops, talks, discussions)" that focused on the rules and regulations of the established structure, becoming nothing more than "a task of collective domestication to insert the members within a determined company structure." By contrast, in the Peruvian revolution, training and education were part of "a continuous process . . . characterized by the organization of the population for the realization of their collective project. The population educates itself through change itself and starting from that change."[49]

In that respect it is interesting to compare the Velasco government's educational initiatives with development projects that took place in Peru in the 1950s and 1960s, such as the Vicos Project in the northern highlands (Ancash). This was a joint project between the Peruvian government and Cornell University, which bought the Hacienda Vicos and transferred ownership to the resident campesinos, with the intention of using the former hacienda as a center of sociological study and a pioneering example of development through modernization. Vicosinos were to be taught to behave as modern agriculturalists, able to engage in a global economy. The prejudices inherent in such a project are apparent in its stated objectives, which included "the westernization of clothing" among Vicos inhabitants.[50]

The Velasco government rejected the developmentalist orientation of programs like Vicos and argued instead that it was necessary to proceed with fundamental structural change and fill the educational gaps as required. A special supplement of *El Peruano*, the country's official newspaper, published in October 1969 commented: "[I]t had always been said that first one had to educate the campesino in order to later hand him the land. First education, later the Reform. First literacy, later justice. And Peru remained at a standstill without being able to do either one or the other."[51] If one waited until the population had been educated to the required extent, major change might never happen. Education and training therefore took place simultaneously with the creation of cooperatives, rather than as a preparatory step toward collectivized production.[52]

The education programs that were delivered within Peru's CAPs, SAIS, and peasant communities were similar to those provided in Chile during the Frei and Allende governments as part of their policies of agrarian reform. As Heidi Tinsman showed, rural education projects in Chile often centered much more on promoting particular attitudes than technical training. In particular, rural education programs emphasized certain gender roles within the agrarian reform process, defining men as the protagonists and affirming their authority over women.[53] In the Peruvian agrarian reform, rural education programs emphasized the ethical principles of cooperative management, understood in moral terms that linked cooperative membership to being a "good citizen." A pamphlet on the cooperative system that accompanied training in Tacna characterized "traditional" cooperative models as "another mechanism of domination" and defined the new system in the following terms:

- The constitutive and final element of the Cooperative Society is the Person.
- Entry is voluntary.
- The management is democratic: SOVEREIGNTY RESIDES IN THE GENERAL ASSEMBLY.
- The economic operations are inspired by a social Philosophy with the spirit of Service.

- The distribution of profits will be effected in accordance with the cooperative activity realized.[54]

As this example shows, rural education programs were used not just (or even, primarily) to impart practical information, but rather as an opportunity to project the government's vision for the new Peru. This was to be organized in the interests of the collective good and driven by the "spirit of service," in contrast to the supposedly individualist and alienating tendencies of capitalism.

Beyond formal training programs, a variety of innovative methods were employed to inform rural populations about the agrarian reform. Puppeteers Gastón Aramayo and Victoria Morales were recruited specifically by Carlos Delgado, one of the leaders of SINAMOS and a member of the Education Reform Commission, to produce and present a traveling puppet show, promoting the agrarian reform in rural areas across the country.[55] Filmmaker Francisco Salomon was employed by the Ministry of Education to produce films about the problems of particular cooperatives and use these films to generate discussion within the cooperatives and peasant communities. Salomon recalled that "there was a certain identification in some cases. They said: 'That is the same as our problem, no? How have they resolved it? How do they want to resolve it? We could resolve it in that way.'"[56] Such practices owed a clear debt to Paulo Freire and his philosophy that education should be a collective endeavor that encouraged people to propose their own ideas rather than simply receiving information from a preestablished curriculum.

Literacy Training

In addition to education reform and rural education programs, the Velasco government viewed literacy training as a means to alter the balance of power in the countryside. According to the 1961 census, some 38.9 percent of Peru's adult population older than 15 years of age was illiterate, and rates of illiteracy were concentrated in rural areas: 59.4 percent of the rural adult population was illiterate, more than three times the percentage in urban areas (17.7 percent).[57] It is likely that these figures had fallen somewhat by the time Velasco took power in 1968, but high rates of illiteracy and poor access to education continued to be an entrenched problem. In 1973 Velasco launched a program of literacy training called "Alfabetización Integral" (Integrated Literacy [ALFIN]), which aimed to teach 1,260,000 people to read and write.[58] Directed from Lima, the program relied on hundreds of literacy promoters who worked among remote rural populations in a manner similar to workers in Cuba's 1961 literacy campaign.

The ALFIN program placed literacy within the wider process of gaining consciousness and used a methodology inspired by Paulo Freire. ALFIN staff were instructed to begin by studying the social context in which they would be working in order to understand their students' perspective. They would then begin teaching a "generative vocabulary"—a list of words that held immediate significance for the learners and could be used to generate a political discussion. For example, introducing the word *pala* (an instrument used to rake or dig the land) could be followed by questions: "What is a *pala* for?" "Who works the land?" "How much do they earn from this work?"[59] As Anthony Burton, an anthropologist who participated in the program, commented: "ALFIN was thus a quite remarkable experiment. It was, after all, attempting to bring about, on a large scale and by official state means, the very effects for which Freire and others had been ejected from Brazil for achieving in a small way. Here was a government offering to promote consciousness change at the level of the masses through approaches that were clearly of a different order to the mechanisms of thought control that are often practiced in revolutionary regimes."[60]

Consequences of Educational Policy

As intermediaries between the state and society, teachers have often been entrusted with championing government agendas. This is particularly true of Latin American countries, where the territorial reach of other state institutions has not equaled that of the education system. In the case of Mexico, Mary Kay Vaughan showed how, during the Cárdenas government (1934–1940), federal teachers became "explicit political actors" who were instructed to organize peasants and workers to press for the implementation of the government's reforms, as well as to lead "civic ritual" to help consolidate the state and ruling party.[61]

Educational change followed a more peaceful path in Peru than in revolutionary Mexico, where the state's controversial policy of excluding the Catholic Church from the provision of public education resulted in high levels of social agitation and violence, with 300 teachers killed during the 1930s.[62] In Peru, although associations of parents from private Catholic colleges protested against the education reform, tensions between the Catholic Church and the state were mediated by the creation of a mixed commission, comprising representatives of the government and the Consortium of Church Schools.[63] Although the open agnosticism of some members of the Education Reform Commission angered church authorities, the Velasco government as a whole was not anticlerical and indeed frequently turned to Catholic educators to help implement its educational policies.[64]

On the other hand, the education reform faced substantial opposition from teachers, the very people who were expected to implement it. Although Peru's General Law of Education was not promulgated until 21 March 1972, efforts to persuade teachers of the need for change began much earlier. The Libro Azul, numbering almost 200 pages, formed part of this campaign. The reform commission also recruited 400 *entrenadores*, young teachers selected for their strong commitment to the government's revolutionary goals who went out to schools across the country to discuss the proposed reforms with teachers and the public.[65] These efforts had limited impact, however. While policies such as the national uniform and displaying the flag were widely implemented, efforts to direct the school curriculum toward the government's revolutionary objectives were strongly resisted. Matthias vom Hau observes: "Both rural and urban teachers portrayed the top-down character of the Velasco educational reforms as an offense against their professional autonomy and resisted the implementation of new educational materials, even when the new textbooks were in sync with their own conceptions of nationhood."[66] Resistance often took indirect forms, such as refusing to use new government textbooks or using them in combination with other sources that put forward an opposing view.[67] Open political opposition came in the form of strike action organized by the Sindicato Unitario de Trabajadores en la Educación del Perú (Unitary Trade Union of Education Workers of Peru [SUTEP]).

Founded in 1972, SUTEP brought members of the primary and secondary education sectors into a single union for the first time and created a powerful political movement. It is estimated that some 100,000 teachers (70 percent of the profession) were members by the mid-1970s.[68] SUTEP regarded the armed forces as a conservative, repressive institution and was skeptical about the prospects of real change under a military government. Direct action led by SUTEP became a frequent occurrence, particularly once the PCP-PR had become dominant within the SUTEP leadership. At a time when the legitimate presence of political parties had been severely reduced, control of the major trade unions served as a proxy for partisan activity.

However, strike action was not motivated solely by party political concerns. In the 1970s Peruvian teachers came overwhelmingly from the poor and lower middle classes. They strongly opposed the Velasco government's repeal of a 1967 law that had guaranteed career progression for teachers and consolidated their labor rights, and they had legitimate complaints about how the reform would affect their income and social status.[69] The education reform became a major source of tension between the government and the teaching profession, which was periodically subjected to intense government repression. In 1973, for example, following a national strike organized by SUTEP, some 500 teachers were removed from their positions.[70] The Velasco regime's creation of the rival Sindicato de Educadores de la Revolución Peruana (Union of Educators of the Peruvian Revolution) served only to worsen its relationship with teachers.[71]

The radical changes proposed by the education reform also produced considerable debate outside education circles. José Rivero, a specialist in education policy who worked in the Ministry of Education during the Velasco years, wrote: "From September 1969, when the Commission was established, until March 1972, when the new General Law of Education was promulgated, there was an intense debate in Peru about the current education [system] and that which was proposed to the country; education ceased to be something that corresponded exclusively to the Ministry of Education, the schools, and the teachers, and became a center of collective interest."[72]

For the Marxist PCP-PR, the government's educational activities were a cynical attempt to control peasant organizations and prevent the "true" revolution. In response to the government's rural education programs, members disrupted cooperative meetings and encouraged peasants not to attend. The filmmaker Francisco Salomon recalled how training sessions were frequently obstructed by left-wing radicals: "They wanted to convince [the cooperative members] that what we were saying was wrong, that the government was wrong, and [that] it was going in the wrong direction. That the revolution was being delayed, that it would be better to have a direct confrontation . . . that . . . revolution is not done peacefully, but with arms."[73]

The numerous training meetings organized by government agencies up and down the country provided a context in which radical groups could intervene and introduce their own ideology in opposition to the government's discourse. While these discordant voices were viewed with irritation by government agencies, their presence was broadly tolerated and arrests for "counterrevolutionary activity" were made on a selective and sporadic basis. Rather than closing down debate, as was often the case in the educational programs of the Chinese and Russian revolutions, the educational activities that accompanied the Peruvian agrarian reform tended to stimulate discussion and increase political awareness in rural areas.

However, the discourse of liberation through education that was reiterated throughout the government's educational initiatives was always in tension with the armed forces' preference for order, efficiency, and tangible results. In the case of ALFIN, the teams of promoters tasked with delivering the program faced competing demands of quality and quantity. A 1975 study noted: "This anxiety leads to the risk that they limit themselves to an *alfabetista* action [a focus on the alphabet and orthography] even if—no easy thing—they achieve a regular and adequate attendance of the learners to the majority of literacy meetings."[74] After witnessing the program in action in Cusco and Puno, the anthropologist Anthony Burton wrote: "The teachers were fine people, young, full of enthusiasm for their task. However, what they were doing had nothing to do with the Christian existentialisms of ALFIN in Lima under Salazar Bondy. They were traditional literacy programs, run by teachers with deep involvement in their task."[75]

At an organizational level, ALFIN suffered from the obstructive actions and indifference of conservative elements within the state bureaucracy. The sudden death in 1974 of Augusto Salazar Bondy, the program's chief advocate, left ALFIN without sufficient support and representation within central government. The program was ultimately shut down in 1976, judged to be ineffective and inefficient. Over the four years of its existence (1973–1976), ALFIN did succeeded in teaching 241,216 people to read and write, but this represented a mere 20 percent of its target.[76] Part of the problem was that ALFIN was conceived from a highly theoretical perspective that gave little credence to the existing knowledge and priorities of the campesinos it aimed to benefit. In particular, lack of enthusiasm for literacy classes among the population of interest was treated as an absence of "consciousness" rather than a rational assessment by peasants of the likely benefits that basic literacy would bring them in their daily lives.

Nevertheless, the program did play an important role in opening up space for alternative literacy programs run by recently formed nongovernmental organizations, and it reinforced the rhetoric of campesino empowerment being articulated by the education reform and cooperative training programs. Moreover, the impact of the government's educational interventions varied according to the regional context. Educational initiatives within the cooperatives have long deserved particular attention since these have been neglected within the literature on Velasco's educational policies.

Cusco

In Cusco there was strong local enthusiasm for education and the application of the education reform. At the first Provincial Congress of Calca Peasants in January 1972, delegates agreed to a series of demands related to education, including the creation of nine new schools and two new agricultural colleges, the provision of new school buildings, and the reorganization of the regional education authority. In particular, they called for the director and "bad functionaries" to be changed because of their affiliation with political parties that obstructed the revolutionary process. In addition, the delegates vowed to support the implementation of the education reform "in all its aspects" and called for the government to implement it as soon as possible.[77]

At the same time, they criticized the province's educational establishment as unsympathetic to the government's revolutionary goals and the rural population's educational needs. The delegates asserted that "the Director of the Education Region V is an open enemy of the dissemination of the content of Law 17716 [the agrarian reform law], even taking repressive actions against the educators who want to collaborate with this dissemination."[78] Resolutions calling for teachers who worked in the countryside to live there on a permanent basis and to be "selected for the peasant zones depending on their affection and commitment to serving the peasantry" implicitly criticized the current teaching staff for a lack of dedication.[79]

This enthusiasm for accessing education is similarly evident in relation to the rural training programs offered to agricultural cooperatives. For example, the annual reports of the Central de Cooperativas Té Huyro, the umbrella organization for tea- and coffee-producing cooperatives in La Convención valley, show that in 1973 the center reserved three thousand soles per month to pay for the transport and accommodation costs of periodic visits by promoters who were specialists in cooperatives. It also requested training from SINAMOS and approached the Konrad Adenauer foundation regarding talks on cooperative practice.[80] The center also put aside money to allow the daughter of one of its members to study accounting in Cusco on the understanding that she would come back and work for the cooperatives as a trained accountant.[81]

In addition to being seen as necessary for the technical advancement of the cooperatives, access to education formed part of a wider set of social aspirations. Hilario Pérez Jaro, a former president of the center, described how, as a member of the cooperative, he became interested in the history and philosophy of the cooperative movement and later went on to complete a correspondence course on the subject.[82] This achievement was particularly significant for someone who, as a child, had been forbidden from receiving a secondary school education. He recalled how his father, a *feudatario* (sharecropper) had wanted him to be a professional and had sent him to study in the town of Urubamba, some 120 kilometers (75 miles) away: "So when I finished my primary, the hacendado forced me to go and work on his hacienda . . . [t]hat is, to prevent me from continuing to study. . . . [H]e didn't want us to study, to become professionals. . . . There was no choice. Otherwise, he would take that piece of land, he would take it if we didn't do it. Without wanting to I had to leave school to serve the landowner and defend the *chacra* [small farm]."[83] Until 1964, landowners were at liberty to evict campesinos from the land that they leased to them. In the case of Hilario Pérez, refusal to work for the hacienda could have resulted in the loss of the family's land.

This situation began to change with the introduction of Law 15037, the agrarian reform passed by President Belaúnde in 1964. Among other things, it guaranteed that land could not be arbitrarily withdrawn from those who were cultivating it. For Pérez, this legislation came too late. He cites the forced abandonment of his studies as a major reason for his subsequent involvement in peasant unions and the campesino campaigns of the 1960s: "I started to participate for vengeance. Why? Because he stopped me from becoming a professional. That was my revenge."[84] An only child, he deeply resented that the hacendado had had such control over his prospects.

However, such enthusiasm for education was not universally felt by the members of Pérez's cooperative center. After contracting three teachers dedicated to literacy training for cooperative members in 1973, the center's 1974 report noted with palpable frustration: "Once again we must say that this task is very important, but that it does not find support from the base Cooperatives and even less from those directly concerned [i.e., the beneficiaries]. Very little has been gained in this aspect despite the money spent on this literacy campaign. This should be continued in 1974, until a better result is achieved."[85] While the reasons for the low uptake of literacy training are not stated, this comment suggests a divergence of perspective between the cooperative leaders and the rank and file. Among the latter group there was a degree of mistrust toward educators who came from outside the community or local area, particularly if they did not speak Quechua.

This mistrust became critical when it came to the delivery of cooperative training programs. A 1972 report on the center by government agency CENCIRA commented: "*The Quechua language is being taken as a symbol of identification by the campesino*[, and] demanding communication in Quechua despite understanding Spanish seems to be the instruction formulated by the union leadership. *Officials from various state agencies are repeatedly criticized precisely because they do not know the Quechua language.*"[86] In a context in which the majority of the cooperative members spoke both Quechua and Spanish, the ability to speak Quechua came to be used as a test for newly arrived officials: "what happens is that when the campesino confirms that the external agent speaks Quechua, the demand for this language to be used reduces[;] it seems that having confirmed this fact they paradoxically tended to prefer [using] Spanish."[87]

Given the difficulty of building trust with the cooperative members, government officials and promoters often focused their attention on cooperative leaders and used them as a catalyst within the cooperative. This made training and administrative procedures easier, but as CENCIRA observed, this had two negative effects: the functionaries became closed off to other categories of *socios* (young people, women, men with no experience of group leadership), and it created a relationship of dependency between the leaders and the base membership. The leaders were regarded as the only ones who were knowledgeable about the cooperative, at times breeding anxiety and resentment among the *socios*.[88] Since cooperative leaders ordinarily gained their position on the basis of already holding higher social status, the fact that government trainers focused their attention on the leaders rather than the members tended to compound existing social differences within the cooperative.

Those delivering education and training in rural Cusco also encountered difficulties in explaining the government's cooperative model in locally meaningful language and concepts. In the case of Té Huyro, CENCIRA researchers found that despite receiving training on the cooperative system, the idea of the cooperative as an organization had failed to take root among the *socios*. They tended to refer to the cooperative either as the institution that provided their livelihood or as a building or a collection of resources: "[I]n some cases [they perceive it] as the building (office), they say it like that—I'm going to the cooperative—in other cases the cooperative is conceived as a collection of goods, plots or fields of produce and physical plants. There is little or no idea that the cooperative may be a group of men, that is, that they (the *socios* [the members]) are in the ultimate instance the cooperative."[89]

Huyro is located in the valley of La Convención, an area of Cusco that, as noted in chapter 1, was at the center of the peasant-led hacienda occupations that swept the southern highlands 1963–1964. It seems, however, that this kind of collective political action did not translate easily to the more everyday forms of collective organization required by the cooperative system.[90] In the Marxist language of the era, CENCIRA staff attributed this to the "residues of individualism" associated with the hacienda system: "This individualism comes from the time of the exploitation by the owners of the former hacienda, an era in which everyone had to ensure their own subsistence. Now the cooperative member tends to demand more of the Cooperative than he demanded of the master."[91]

Part of the problem was that so-called ideopolitical training courses tended toward indoctrination rather than intellectual engagement with existing local knowledge and systems of organization. A 1972 government evaluation of the training delivered at the CAP Lauramarca Ltda., no. 56, in Quispicanchi provides important insights on the weaknesses of government education efforts in this area. For example, the information provided to the *socios* in Lauramarca covered the following points:

> a. With the Cooperative the campesinos would enter a better way of life;
> b. With the Cooperative the *patrón* would disappear forever;
> c. From now on the campesinos would work for their own benefit;
> d. With the Cooperative the campesino would no longer have reason to humble himself before the "*misti*";
> e. They would work as a single man, with a single heart;
> f. The cooperative would bring an end to unpaid work.[92]

As the authors of the report commented, "This information is superficial and incomplete[;] the how and in what form are absent, contributing to a partial understanding of the model."[93] In particular, it was not made clear how the system of cooperative production differed from the principles of mutual help that had long subsisted in the region, within a system of individual production and private ownership.

This created serious practical difficulties for managing the cooperative's resources. For example, the CAP Lauramarca owned a small truck. All the *socios* were entitled to use it, but the absence of prior coordination or compromise regarding its use meant that at times more than twenty people piled in to make the journey from T'inke to Cusco, often at risk to their own lives. While the *socios* clearly needed the truck for transport, CENCIRA suggested that this situation also reflected their broader perception of cooperative property: "It seems that the reasoning works in the following way: if I am the owner of a good I have the right to use it[;] if I cannot use it as I see fit it is because either I am not really the owner or I am not acting as such. . . . [W]hen the President [of the cooperative] limits the number of passengers on the vehicle, the *socios* think that he is restricting a right inherent to their status as *socios*."[94]

The broad message of the training was that "the indigenous peasant has the right to occupy the same human status as any other citizen of the country." However, this had unanticipated consequences in fueling a combative attitude on the part of the cooperative leaders, particularly in their relations with the mestizo population of the district capital, Ocongate. This was manifest in actions such as the refusal to provide labor for public works in Ocongate and treating the cooperative (rather than the town authorities) as the deciding body in the event of conflicts between the *socios*.[95]

One of the earliest bases of the FDCC, Lauramarca was also one of the first haciendas in Cusco to be expropriated by the agrarian reform. A testy relationship developed between the former hacienda workers and the Velasco government: in 1970 five campesinos of the hacienda were detained by the police for denouncing the agrarian reform as a con (*una estafa*) and mobilizing others to boycott it, while in February 1971 campesinos of Lauramarca were "violently repressed" by civil guard officers as they demanded the immediate handing over of the hacienda and the release and suspension of charges against their leaders.[96]

An added problem with the training provided to agricultural cooperatives in Cusco was their brevity. In Lauramarca, CENCIRA researchers questioned the tendency for government promoters—particularly those from SINAMOS and the Ministry of Agriculture—to focus on the administrative milestones of establishing a cooperative, rather than building its organizational capacity in a broader sense:

> What should be the indices or parameters that allow one to declare that a cooperative has progressed or not in its organization? Undoubtedly it will not simply be the facts of inscribing members and achieving the election of the members of its different administrative organs, nor even having secured the basic understanding of the management; what is more, we would venture to say that the moment at which a cooperative is "up and running" is the least propitious time to abandon it to its fate, the moment at which it most needs genuine advice.[97]

While the CENCIRA researchers advocated a permanent or long-term advisory presence to support new cooperatives, those in charge of delivering training saw their role as a short-term one concerned primarily with the early stages of a cooperative's life.

In summary, there was a strong popular appetite for education among Cusco's rural communities. This was evident in the requests made by cooperatives and agrarian leagues for greater school infrastructure and the provision of targeted agricultural training. Campesinos seized on the education reform as an opportunity to get rid of bad functionaries and demand greater attention to their educational needs. For those previously denied access to education because of the actions of the hacendados, it was also seen as a means of individual and collective empowerment. On the surface this resonated with the Velasco government's discourse on education as a tool of social change. Yet government promoters encountered resistance as outsiders—particularly if they did not speak Quechua—and the concepts they sought to embed through ideopolitical training were challenged by preexisting ideas about property and collective management.

Tacna

In Tacna, as in Cusco, rural inhabitants complained of inadequate attention to their educational needs. At the second convention of the Agrarian League "Eugenio Flores Q." in 1975, delegates asserted that in their experience teachers did not comply with their requisite hours, and some did not identify with the education reform. They called for the immediate dismissal of particular teachers in the highland districts of Huanuara and Chucatamani for being "disruptive and counterrevolutionary elements" and dedicating themselves to "other activities like agriculture."[98] Similarly, delegates of the Agrarian League "José Carlos Mariátegui" denounced the fact that "some teachers do not comply with [their] working hours resulting in delays in the education of our children" since they worked three or four days per week only. In addition, the delegates called for promoters employed by ALFIN and Educación Básica Laboral (Basic Work Education), a branch of the education ministry, to be made available to the peasantry of Moquegua and Torata (Tacna) on the grounds that "[a] large part of our adult peasant population is illiterate, or has a low cultural level."[99]

Coming over three years after the promulgation of the education reform and two years after the start of the ALFIN program, these comments reflect the widely experienced limitations of the Velasco government's efforts to overhaul the education system, discussed earlier in this chapter. They also reflect the particularly antagonistic position taken by Tacna's teachers in relation to the government's reform agenda. The region was a stronghold for the national teaching union SUTEP, which opposed the education reform. In July 1975, the local SUTE candidates won 83 percent of votes in the elections for the Tacna and Moquegua teachers' cooperative.[100] According to local newspaper *La Voz de Tacna*, this was the only place in the country where SUTEP candidates won all of the cooperative positions that were up for renewal.[101] Consequently, SUTE was able to mobilize large numbers of teachers to participate in strikes, which were interpreted by SINAMOS as "open opposition to the [revolutionary] process."[102] The regional SINAMOS office identified the political parties PCP-PR (radical left) and APRA (conservative right) as the chief organizers of SUTE strike action, with APRA holding the greatest economic and political control.[103]

According to a SINAMOS report, SUTE opposition was particularly strong in Tacna's rural areas, where "the teachers have become not just another group of leaders but rather they speak or act and decide in the name of the population." This was problematic because, owing to their subordinate position in relation to their "metropolitan" colleagues, "they find themselves obliged to align themselves and mechanically apply the dispositions that generally emanate from SUTE. This is the basis on which the teachers of the countryside oppose the work of SINAMOS."[104]

In addition, Tacna's "elite-classist education centers" were identified as an obstacle to the education reform, and the (private) University of Tacna was described as a center of antigovernment meetings, where students with "insufficient political training and little or no perception of the reality . . . are used by sects led by leaders of known trajectory at the level of the Peruvian university."[105] There is an air of paranoia to these statements, but they nevertheless indicate that in Tacna teachers did not play the revolutionary role that had been assigned to them by the education reform and in fact represented a key source of opposition to the Velasco government.

In response to this resistance from students, the regional SINAMOS office sought to influence students directly through literary competitions that focused on revolutionary themes. In June 1973 secondary school students were invited to submit poetry, compositions, and works of art and theater on the theme of the agrarian reform and the Peruvian campesino. The rationale behind the competition was to develop in the students "interest in the literary and artistic disciplines and stimulate the creative faculties of the child and young person of the region, which will permit the reordering of the concept of national and popular culture."[106] While broadly tallying with the aims of the education reform in challenging elite culture, the propagandistic nature of the exercise is apparent in the two submissions selected for publication: a poem that called on peasants to take action—"Fight now for your land/ Defend it with your blood"—and a composition that described an urban sophisticate who visited the countryside before and after the agrarian reform and praised the revolution—"A miracle has been made and a great Peruvian triumph has been realized."[107]

In terms of education for the cooperatives, SINAMOS archives indicate that Tacna's cooperatives and agrarian leagues made substantial efforts to increase access to training and modify the training that was offered. At a 1974 meeting with the SINAMOS technical assistance unit, representatives of various agricultural organizations suggested increasing the length of agricultural training programs, extending access to the wives and children of *socios*, allowing the bases to suggest what type of training they required, and pitching courses "at the level of the peasants' understanding."[108] Moreover, they expressed their dissatisfaction with "so many meetings, which do not give them any benefit."[109]

Cooperative members also used educational opportunities to strengthen their involvement in peasant networks at the regional, national, and international levels. For example, a 1973 SINAMOS report on the CAP "28 de agosto" Ltda. 135 noted that one of the *socios* was attending an international summit on agricultural matters in the city of Quito, Ecuador. A further two *socios* had been awarded a scholarship to enable them to attend an educational conference on "peasant companies" in Arequipa. The cooperative had also sent delegates to preparatory meetings for the creation of the Central de Cooperativas de Tacna-Moquegua.[110] These opportunities for the exchange of ideas were an important aspect of the rural training programs established during the agrarian reform, expanding the horizons of the cooperative members and enabling them to engage with wider political debates.

At the same time, trainee agricultural technicians were given the opportunity to visit the region's agricultural cooperatives in order to gain contact with the "zonal reality" and "dialogue with cooperative leaders." In an interview with *La Voz de Tacna*, agronomy students reported that the visits had allowed them to see how "the marginalized sectors of the Prerevolution" were beginning to "constitute a great social base that really decides and has power." They added that in coming weeks they would be visiting the comunidades campesinas and other base organizations to "internalize their problems and help them to the best of our ability."[111] While this attitude was clearly given a positive spin in the article, the fact that trainee technicians talked about dialogue with cooperative and community leaders rather than a unidirectional application of expertise represented an important shift away from the developmentalist discourse of the 1960s (discussed in the first part of the chapter).

The limitations of the educational change achieved in rural Tacna are made clear in the complaints raised during the second regional convention of Tacna and Moquegua agrarian leagues in August 1975. These included teachers' absences, their lack of commitment to the education reform, deficient school infrastructure, and insufficient commitment on the part of SINAMOS promoters working with the cooperatives and peasant communities.[112] However, the minutes of the convention also reveal the extent to which the delegates now expected their teachers and other government functionaries to be committed to the aims of the revolution and felt democratically empowered to denounce those individuals they saw as counterrevolutionary. For example, delegates from Torota province argued that the members of its Agrarian Association of Direct Conductors, Revolutionary Female Nucleus, Youth Brigade, and Services Precooperative were "representatives of the feeling of the people of Torota." As such, they called for the dismissal of the mayor of Torota, who had been "acting in a presumptuous and discriminatory way toward the mentioned organizations, calling their members *indios* [and] *cholos* and marginalizing them from village matters and denying them use of the council building."[113] Thus, the government narrative regarding peasant empowerment and the representative role of the cooperatives and other local associations—a key theme of SINAMOS training programs—was seized upon to demand change in the face of discrimination.

Piura

As one of the first regions to be declared a zone of agrarian reform, Piura became a key site of intervention for literacy training. As an article in the journal *Educación* commented in 1970, in the context of the new cooperatives it was important that illiterates did not become exploited once again because of an inability to engage with the organization's written documents and bureaucracy.[114] In addition, Miguel Zegarra, who worked as an ALFIN promoter in Piura between 1973 and 1976, described how the program mediated in government efforts to disseminate the cooperative model among rural inhabitants. Since its methodology focused on the nature and use of knowledge, it was seen as a good way to generate engagement with cooperative principles. In practice, however, Zegarra found that the program could only touch the surface. Participants were expected to learn to read and write in just three months, and some teachers were not sufficiently well trained or open to new methodologies and continued to use traditional techniques of rote learning.[115]

In addition, the program was beset by a lack of coordination between the different institutions that were involved in campesino education. In September 1973 a two-day conference was held in Piura that brought together more than two hundred adult education promoters from ALFIN, Basic Work Education, the Ministry of Agriculture, SINAMOS, and other organizations operating in the departments of Piura and Tumbes. According to Rafael Menacho Jaramillo, an observer, the meeting revealed noticeable differences in attitudes among the participants, who "did not have shared criteria regarding technical and practical aspects that would allow for good work in the field."[116] He went on to note that the traditional and conservative attitudes of government functionaries were largely to blame for the slow pace of implementation of the revolutionary government's policies and that they were creating a negative impression on the public. In Piura, communities that were experiencing the education reform recognized the importance of ALFIN for accelerating the process of change, but they also identified a lack of commitment and identification on the part of ALFIN promoters. Menacho called for a reevaluation of all ALFIN personnel by an intersectoral team, using information provided by the base organizations (cooperatives, peasant communities), to improve the functioning of the operation.[117]

In parallel with ALFIN, the Centro de Investigación y Promoción del Campesinado (Center of Research and Promotion of the Peasantry [CIPCA]), which was established in Piura in 1972, developed another literacy campaign. CIPCA is an interesting example of the kind of development organizations that emerged in Peru during the military government. CIPCA's founders were a group of French and Spanish Jesuit priests who were influenced by evolving currents of "liberation theology" and inspired by the historic opportunity that the Peruvian agrarian reform represented. They chose to base their activities in Piura because it was a region where the agrarian reform had good prospects to achieve economic and social success and where the population overwhelmingly spoke Spanish.[118]

During its first two years, CIPCA focused on providing literacy and other forms of training to newly formed cooperatives and other beneficiaries of the agrarian reform. Óscar Jara Holliday, who has written about his experiences as a CIPCA educator, was 21 years old when he started working on the program as one of eight literacy trainers. Classes, in groups of eight to 15 students, began before the *socios* started work and took place wherever there was space: under the trees, in the administrative offices, or in the storerooms for tools and machinery. In the evenings the trainers went to the local *caseríos* (settlements) to teach women and older people who did not work in the cooperatives.

Before they started teaching, the literacy trainers spent time in the villages to establish contact. They then created a "vocabulary universe" based on the terms and phrases they had heard people say. From this they constructed a "thematic universe," which helped identify the *temas generadores* (generative themes) that represented significant situations within the local economic, social, and cultural context. Teaching began with group discussions based on images that represented these themes, later moving on to the written form of the word and breaking it down to form new words. After class each day the teachers made notes on the class's discussion, writing down the exact phrases and reflections expressed by the group members. These phrases were later used as the basis for "*post-alfabetización*" texts: "It was a way of giving back to them in a structured and thematic way their own thoughts, their own phrases spoken individually, returned now in written form, after being shared and socialized."[119]

As these comments indicate, the approach used in CIPCA's literacy program was remarkably similar to that of ALFIN. However, implementation of the program differed in two important respects. First, the local nature of CIPCA's activity allowed personnel to invest more time and resources in particular locations, rather than moving on every three months as the ALFIN teams did. The program involved long-term placements for promoters (between eight months and one year), who established close relationships with the communities where training was to take place. They read books on the history and literature of the region and made recordings with the elders about their history of peasant struggles. This type of connection strengthened the possibilities for dialogue between educators and students.

Second, CIPCA had greater freedom (and desire) to review the success of its activities and revise its approach. At the end of its first phase of operations, the organization observed that "both the interest of the potential learners and the precariousness of the results did not justify the emphasis on learning to read and write."[120] Many people were more interested in learning basic numeracy than in literacy. In the second phase of its operations CIPCA responded to the needs expressed by the communities and provided literacy training only if it was expressly requested by participants.[121] This change in emphasis did not mean that there was no value to providing literacy training but rather that its significance for participants was somewhat different from the ideological role that Paulo Freire and others attributed to it. Juan Hernández Astudillo, one of the first priests to work for CIPCA, observed that for many campesinos, learning to sign their name was a great achievement and made them feel that they were citizens.[122] To be sure, this was not the politically engaged, pro-reform citizenship that the Velasco government envisioned, but it nevertheless represented a form of empowerment.

In addition to literacy training, between 1972 and 1980 some two thousand campesinos attended CIPCA's administrative training courses. Evaluating their success in 1980, former CIPCA director Vicente Santuc commented: "While the time [spent] and level of implementation eliminate all pretensions of creating 'administrators', an informed awareness of the management problems that a cooperative faces was achieved. The graduates [of the course] leave with some criteria that can inform their practice. In fact, in the CAPs they often regroup as "the CIPCA ones" (*los del CIPCA*)."[123] This development of an esprit de corps among the course participants could be a valuable asset within a recently formed CAP.

A similar state-led cooperative training program was provided by the Oficina Nacional de Desarrollo Cooperativa (National Office of Cooperative Development). Mariano Fiestas Chunga was the office's regional director in Piura throughout the Velasco government. He recalled that a major difficulty he encountered was resistance from landowners, as training was delivered to the prospective *socios* in advance of the expropriation and adjudication of the haciendas:

> It wasn't easy to organize a cooperative. When we had to train [the *socios*] they went the first day. On the second, third, fourth they no longer went. And when we asked them for what reason they didn't attend the classes, they said, "Well, the master won't let us come. And if we come he'll evict us." They were threatened that he was going to throw them out, and not only from work, but from their houses with [their] family and everything.[124]

Since it was common for hacienda employees to live in housing provided by the landowner, they were particularly vulnerable to such threats. When news of this kind of resistance reached the central government, Velasco ruled that training should no longer precede adjudication and the new cooperative members should instead be supported to "learn on the way" (*en el camino aprenderán*).[125]

Miguel Zegarra, the ALFIN teacher cited earlier, also pointed to the cultural barriers involved in communicating the new cooperative model. The concept of a CAP did not tally with people's previous experiences or understanding of property. Whereas there was some awareness of service cooperatives (a model that has also regained popularity in the region in recent years), production cooperatives "belonged to everybody and yet to nobody." Zegarra recalled that a common question raised by the new cooperative members was, "When is it going to be mine?" adding, "The government did not understand that difficulty, the cultural part."[126]

Mariano Fiestas Chunga similarly conceded that the impact of cooperative education was limited, commenting that the *socios* "understood something. They learned to sign their checks." However, he argued that the practical experience of the cooperative system had had an important political legacy in the region. For example, the emphasis placed on recording the proceedings of cooperative assemblies through written minutes has persisted among peasant communities and associations: "Even now 'may it be recorded in the minutes' is a phrase that is used. Where did they learn that? In the cooperatives."[127] He further pointed to the democratic legacy of the elections that were held within the cooperatives, arguing the *socios* "became conscious of what democracy is. To elect a government through their direct vote. Because they were worth something as a person, not for what they might have in their pocket, not like in the other companies, which were [organized] by shares."[128]

Partly as a consequence of this emphasis on cooperative democracy, there emerged a generation of politically active campesino leaders who used the cooperative system as a basis for peasant-led development and politics. Throughout the 1970s they repeatedly organized protests across Piura on issues such as the defense of cotton prices and the commercialization of agricultural produce.[129] Such actions continued well beyond the end of the Velasco government. For example, the former president of the CAP "Negri Ulloa," César Zapata, described how, during the 1980s, his cooperative developed new systems of member participation and collectivized the purchase of fertilizers and the marketing of its produce. Zapata recalled the 1980s and 1990s as a time when the cooperative was "*pujante*" (forceful), proposing various changes to achieve social justice and wealth distribution.[130]

As these comments indicate, agricultural cooperative members developed an autonomous political and economic presence in Piura. In part this was a result of the new economic power at their disposal as landowners and agricultural producers. Yet it also owed a debt to the political terms in which the cooperative system was presented through rural education programs. Ironically, a former regional SUTEP leader, who vehemently opposed the Velasco government's educational policy at the time, commented that after receiving what he described as "an emancipatory education," the region's campesinos "discovered that they could enter and fight not only for the land, not only for water, but also that they had to fight for better prices." This was a generation of campesinos and agricultural producers who "became actors in the political scene" and "had an impact particularly in the regional political economy of cotton."[131]

Conclusion

The Velasco government approached education as a key battleground of its revolution. Through education reform, literacy programs, and cooperative training it sought to build a new consensus around ideals of equality, cultural diversity, and cooperativism. This agenda took on particular importance in relation to the agrarian reform, where it was understood that a reordering of social relations was a necessary complement to land expropriation. Yet the government's educational interventions were marked by persistent tension between political idealism and expediency, between the dialogue and emancipation promoted by Paulo Freire and the authoritarian and paternalist expectations of a military-led administration.

Comparing the application of educational policy in the rural areas of Cusco, Tacna, and Piura has revealed similar difficulties in using education to communicate the regime's vision for a modern rural society. In Cusco, the cooperative model did not sit easily with either the reciprocal traditions of *ayni* and *mit'a* labor or established practices of private property and contracted labor. In Tacna, training was not presented in terms that resonated with local communities and tended to exclude women and children. And in Piura, the idea of a production cooperative held little meaning for a region whose primary experience of cooperative practice was through service cooperatives. In all three cases, educators involved in cooperative training pointed to the brevity of the courses, insufficient attention to technical rather than ideological issues, and the cultural barriers to establishing the cooperative system.

On the other hand, the government's emphasis on education as a means of emancipation created spaces for peasants in all three regions to increase their political profile. Piura's CAP "Negri Ulloa" used the government's discourse on the power of the collective to push for changes to the marketing of its produce. Tacna's agrarian leagues seized on the principles of the education reform to demand the dismissal of "counterrevolutionary" teachers and local government officials. In Cusco, the simple fact of having access to education and the ability to educate one's children was seen as a key ingredient for social progress and a form of revenge against the hacendados.

Important differences also characterized the experience and consequences of education reform. In Tacna, the strength of opposition from SUTEP and conservative teaching establishments limited the scope for change. The fact that Tacna did not become an agrarian reform zone until 1975 also meant there was not the same push for cooperative training as in northern regions like Piura. Whereas in 1975 the delegates of Tacna's agrarian leagues continued to press for more sustained and targeted educational input, in Piura the participants of training courses had developed an esprit de corps and assumed a prominent role in the regional economy and politics. In Cusco, marked social differentiation within the cooperatives meant that leaders benefited from new educational opportunities to a much greater extent than ordinary members, further exacerbating existing social divisions. If the government's educational interventions were designed to produce a "new man" with a national identity and shared engagement with the cooperative system, in practice the results were varied and contradictory. The impact of educational policies continued to be guided by the local political dynamics of each region.

Yet taken as a whole, the Velasco government's educational policies were fundamental in reframing the terms of Peruvian citizenship. Since 1896 the vast majority of Peru's campesinos had been denied the vote on the grounds of illiteracy. By the time of the 1978 constituent assembly, as the country prepared for a return to electoral democracy, there was a consensus among all the political parties that the new constitution should incorporate suffrage for all citizens over 18 years whether or not they could read or write.[132] Interventions in literacy training and cooperative education succeeded in propelling a generation of campesino leaders into politically prominent roles at both the regional and national level. Ultimately, it was the independence and political ambition exercised by the popular sectors themselves that caused this dramatic shift in the status quo. However, the Velasco government's education policies played a critical supporting role. More inclusive ideas of Peruvian citizenship were also consolidated by developments in mass media and public discourse, as the next chapter reports.

CHAPTER 4

The Agrarian Reform in Public Discourse

The 1969 agrarian reform was characterized by the government's extensive and innovative use of mass communication. During the course of the agrarian reform, mass communication became a locus of intense political struggle. The Velasco government recruited communications professionals and used the mass media in innovative ways to inform and persuade the population about the agrarian reform. Operating on the premise that the creation of a "new Peru" depended on the simultaneous transformation of the country's economic and cultural systems, it also expropriated the national press, expanded government communications in rural areas, and provided state sponsorship for creative projects in radio, film, magazines, and newspapers.

As military men, leaders of the Velasco government had little experience in mass communication, prompting President Velasco to turn to journalists, artists, and intellectuals to publicize the government's reforms. The government's distinctive approach to mass communication and use of media stimulated a surprisingly strong reaction among left- and right-wing opponents, motivating different opposition groups to try to counteract the government's propaganda and reframe the debate on agrarian reform. Examining these media wars at the regional level and comparing government interventions in the media and local responses in Tacna, Piura, and Cusco shows how, in the long term, the government's use of the mass media set important precedents for peasant participation in the public sphere. By placing rural politics and peasant interests at the heart of national political discourse, the agrarian reform ruptured the status quo and enabled campesinos to demand greater representation within national politics.

The Mass Media: Government Interventions

The Velasco government attached considerable importance to mass communication as a way of generating support for its reforms. Even before the agrarian reform law was announced, the government requested the assistance of experienced journalist Efraín Ruiz Caro. As well as writing President Velasco's speeches, Ruiz Caro was tasked with establishing the DPDRA, a small team of publicists, artists, and writers who produced posters, leaflets, and fliers that were distributed across the country to publicize acts of land expropriation and adjudication. Answering directly to the head of the DGRAAR, the DPDRA was given substantial autonomy and resources to promote the agrarian reform.

The Velasco government was often divided about how best to generate political support, however, and about mass communication's role in the process. SINAMOS, which played a vital role in coordinating political activity across the country, was created some three years after the 1968 coup. It is therefore important to consider the tensions that surrounded particular communication strategies and the volatile nature of the military government's relationship with its sponsored artists. Jesús Ruiz Durand, one of the chief artists of the DPDRA, for example, ceased working with the government in 1972 after becoming disillusioned with its approach to popular mobilization and feeling constrained by the loyalty demanded by senior government figures.[1]

In broad terms, 1968–1972 can be seen as a time of experimentation and relative artistic freedom, as artists and intellectuals were drawn to collaborate with what they saw as an unusually progressive military regime that offered the chance to put into practice their long-cherished ideas about politics and art. Following the creation of SINAMOS in 1972, these artists and intellectuals were subjected to greater institutional oversight. In the context of Peru's declining economic fortunes and the president's ill health, the government also became more combative and intolerant of opposition from 1973 onward. This trend is reflected in the extent of government interference in the mass media and the large number of journalists that were exiled by Velasco toward the end of his premiership.[2]

Pamphlets were a key method the government used to inform the population about the agrarian reform.[3] For example, a leaflet addressed to *feudatarios* (sharecroppers) highlighted that the agrarian reform law guaranteed them preferential treatment in the adjudication process. Given the low levels of literacy in rural areas, this leaflet was intended to form the basis of a discussion, with those able to read passing on the relevant information to those who could not. The accompanying text instructed the reader: "Do not throw this leaflet away, do not keep it, show it to your brother *feudatarios*. Inform them about their responsibilities and rights in relation to the new Law of Agrarian Reform."[4]

Similarly, a leaflet entitled "*ABC de la reforma agraria peruana*" took a question-and-answer format, setting out what the reform offered to peasants. Printed on brightly colored paper and featuring bold, modern typesetting, the leaflet presented a somewhat utopian vision of the agrarian reform. Read, for example, the response to the question "How does the law affect the peasant communities?":

> It benefits, invigorates and modernizes them. It returns to them the land that was taken from them; it gives them new land, in the case that what they have is insufficient[;] it defends them from any threat from the *gamonal* [landowner]; it promotes their transformation into cooperatives, if that is what the *comuneros* wish; it sets them up in the predominant form of *serrano* agriculture; and it simultaneously provides them with all the technical assistance necessary to increase their productivity.[5]

Using recently developed offset printing techniques, the DPDRA frequently adapted or embellished photographs taken in the agrarian reform areas. For example, figures 4.1 and 4.2 show how the artist Jesús Ruiz Durand adapted a photograph of a sugarcane worker taken outside the CAP Laredo, in the La Libertad department, for use in an agrarian reform poster. The poster's psychedelic color scheme transforms an ordinary worker into a figure imbued with vibrant energy, while the removal of the Laredo sign serves to universalize the image, producing a general statement about the agrarian reform. In this way, the DPDRA produced iconic images that resonated with the public much as the imagery of the Cuban Revolution had done.

Government posters and pamphlets also articulated the regime's expectations of the public. A leaflet targeting the urban population, for example, gave instructions on how best to assist the agrarian reform process: "If you are thinking of [offering] training in the countryside REMEMBER that your most valuable support will be in the personal and human aspect. If you are working for the Agrarian Reform DO NOT FORGET that the protagonist of the Agrarian Reform is the campesino" (figs. 4.3 and 4.4).[6] Similarly, a newspaper advertisement targeting students and young people carried the slogan: "There is no revolution without [the] youth. Because there is no youth without revolution." Inviting students to become involved in the gov-

Figure 4.1. A sugarcane worker carrying a shovel at the CAP Laredo; photograph published in *El agro peruano: Una nueva estructura* (Lima: Ministerio de Agricultura, 1972): 18. ISA Pamphlets, Special Collections, Senate House Library, London.

ernment's reform program, it asked: "Who can allow themselves the luxury to continue being a spectator, to be swept along by history and remain at the margin of the Peruvian revolution?" (fig. 4.5).[7]

According to Hugo Neira, one of the key intellectuals who worked for the Velasco government inside SINAMOS, this urban, nonpeasant audience was given high priority at the time:

> Our propaganda was rather directed at the middle-sector workers, middle class, popular [class], students in order to convince them that we were doing something realistic, that was necessary, that was good for Peruvian society, well, to get out of the colonial period, the preindustrial period, right? So the posters and all that were not so much for the campesinos, because the campesinos were managed in another way. We had Quechua translators and Quechua radio. We gave a lot of importance to Quechua.[8]

Neira argued that the campesinos were convinced by the act of agrarian reform itself and did not need further persuasion. A more pressing concern

Figure 4.2. Agrarian reform poster designed by Jesús Ruiz Durand (ca. 1970) for the Dirección de Promoción y Difusión de la Reforma Agraria. Jesús Ruiz Durand, private collection.

Figures 4.3 and 4.4. *Al hombre de la ciudad peruana: ¿Cómo ayudar a la reforma agraria?* (Lima: DPDRA, 1969). ISA Pamphlets, Special Collections, Senate House Library, London.

Figure 4.5. Advertisement placed by Dirección de Promoción y Difusión de la Reforma Agraria, published in *El Comercio* (8 October 1969). Biblioteca Nacional del Perú, Lima.

was to defend the agrarian reform from the criticism of the urban classes. On the other hand, Héctor Béjar, who also worked in the SINAMOS leadership, suggested that although the campesinos were certainly convinced that something needed to be done, they were not necessarily persuaded that it should be done in the way that the agrarian reform proposed:

> To start with, for many of them the reform descended on them by surprise; they had never asked for it. That has to do not necessarily with the campesinos but with the agricultural workers of the sugar mills that were the most advanced organizations. . . . But that was a particular case, quite singular. In general, let's say, in the rest of the countryside it was a rurality of the sierra latifundio kind. Yes, of course, the campesinos wanted—they wanted the agrarian reform so much that in many cases they began to invade the land before the reform, but they didn't want it in the manner of the reform. The reform proposed collective systems of production, and many of them wanted the land for themselves, for their families.[9]

In fact, communicating with this latter group of campesinos—politically mobilized but in pursuit of their own vision of agrarian reform—proved particularly difficult.

Much of the propaganda produced by the Velasco government contained contradictory messages about campesinos' role in the agrarian reform. Despite insisting that the protagonist of the agrarian reform was the campesino, the Velasco government, in the leaflet directed at urban Peruvians (figs. 4.3 and 4.4), pictured campesino children in threadbare clothes who had an air of desperation. A sharp visual contrast is drawn with the leisurely, well-dressed urban Peruvians, and the overall effect is to produce feelings of empathy, rather than encouraging a particular action. While explicitly referring to campesinos' protagonism, the implicit message is that the agrarian reform is to be coordinated by the government, not imposed by urban do-gooders.

The guiding power of the state is similarly hinted at in the photograph of a campesino holding two DPDRA leaflets (fig. 4.6). The campesino holds one of the leaflets aloft in the manner of a flag or placard and appears to be looking at it rather than reading it. The scene is extremely staged and seems to celebrate the information being imparted from above rather than the campesino's active engagement with the reform. At the same time, however, it is the apparent authenticity of the campesino pictured that gives the image and its accompanying text legitimacy. Across Latin America, photographers had begun turning their attention to rural subjects and social conditions in the countryside since the 1930s, with the argument that such scenes represented "real life" for the majority of Latin Americans. The publicists working for the government were conversant with this trend and used it to project the idea that the regime represented "the people." [10]

In 1972 the DPDRA was incorporated into a new organization: SINAMOS. The directors of SINAMOS thought carefully about the task of "raising consciousness," including among the organization's staff. In 1972 the national training division of SINAMOS began producing pamphlets that were designed to initiate dialogue and facilitate group discussion among the organization's personnel. As an internal magazine noted, this was a novel form of training within the state bureaucracy: "Now the means are being given to the functionary so that he may be conscious of what he is doing; he is being allowed to judge our reality. In this way, we at SINAMOS not only promote popular participation, but we are ourselves participating, and with great commitment, in our revolutionary process."[11]

As demonstrated in chapter 2, SINAMOS staff frequently encountered indifference and opposition from other sectors of the state bureaucracy,

Figure 4.6. A campesino holding agrarian reform leaflets; photograph published in the DPDRA pamphlet *Del latifundio a la cooperativa* (Lima: DPDRA, ca. 1969). ISA Pamphlets, Special Collections, Senate House Library, London.

such as the Ministry of Agriculture. Through propaganda directed specifically at its own staff, SINAMOS tried to forge a new generation of state functionaries who would be both ideologically committed to "the revolutionary process" and capable of defending government reforms from sabotage. The visual style used in this propaganda was brightly colored and conveyed a sense of youthful optimism. Government ministers, the majority of whom were military generals, were portrayed as being down to earth, without the formal regalia usually associated with the armed forces (see figs. 4.7 and 4.8).

In addition to the activities of the DPDRA and SINAMOS, the Ministry of Agriculture's Office of Public Relations used various tactics to confront the government's critics. Pedro Morote, then Director of the Office of Public

Figure 4.7. Front cover of the Sistema Nacional de Apoyo a la Movilización Social internal magazine, *SINAMOS informa* 2, no. 12 (1973).

Figure 4.8. *SINAMOS informa* 2, no. 15 (1974): inside cover. The text reads, "Our work is risky, tense, hard, difficult. It is the work of those that fight on the front line of the revolution."

Relations at the Ministry of Agriculture, described a marked change in what was understood by "public relations" at that time. Coming from a background in journalism, he engaged in news management and urged his staff to abandon the view that public relations was about organizing champagne receptions and ordering flowers for dignitaries' birthdays: "It became like a newspaper. Everyone was like a reporter there. And those who could not fit in with that, I got rid of them."[12] The majority of the national newspapers were not supporters of the government (although they welcomed some aspects of the agrarian reform). Maintaining a positive image of the agrarian reform in the press therefore involved a combination of paid advertising, public persuasion, and coercive treatment of the newspapers.

Beyond the communication of a specific message, the Velasco government sought structural change to the power and role of the mass media. Ministers argued that the media should serve the development needs of society as a whole, rather than the private interests of media owners. The government introduced a series of laws to increase state control of the communications infrastructure and reduce the power of private media owners. For example, the 1969 Press Freedom Statute (D.L. 18075) banned newspaper ownership by non-Peruvian nationals and required media companies to publish twice annually a list of their shareholders and board of directors.

This was followed by the 1970 Law of the Journalist (D.L. 18139), which strengthened the rights of journalists vis-à-vis newspaper owners, and the 1971 Telecommunications Law.[13] The latter permitted the state to take control of radio and television stations in which it held more than a 25 percent share and limited private media ownership by any single individual to one TV license and one radio license per department, up to a total of seven licenses across the whole country. The law also required radio stations to fill 60 percent of weekly programming with content produced in Peru and made provision for the creation of "telecommunications communities"—groups of employees who were entitled to a share of the company's profits and participation in decision making.[14] For Velasco, these steps were evidence of the regime's refusal to cower to imperialist interests; they defined a new era of media with a social purpose.

The most emblematic of the Velasco government's media interventions was the 1974 expropriation of the national newspapers. While state control of the press is often considered a typical act of dictatorship, the reality in this case was more complex: the government and its intellectual supporters imagined a different kind of mass media, not simply one in which opposition was silenced. Following expropriation, each of the national dailies was to be placed in the hands of a sectoral organization and redirected to reflect workers' interests. Thus *El Comercio* would be assigned to the peasant sector, *La Prensa* to the industrial workers, and so on.[15] The policy attracted international interest. The *Guardian* described it as "one of the most interesting experiments in the history of journalism."[16] The Inter-American Press Association condemned it as "an arrogant abuse of power based mainly on the persuasive use of guns."[17] Yet as Hélan Jaworski observed, the Velasco government's discourse rejected the monopoly of communication and proposed an alternative to the liberal model of press freedom by placing media power in the hands of representative organizations. This was "something radically different" from the usual pattern of media control under a dictatorship.[18]

The Velasco government's conceptualization of the mass media reflected a global trend known at the time as the New World Information Order. This emerged from the discussions of the United Nations Educational, Scientific and Cultural Organization (UNESCO) at its Sixteenth General Conference in 1970.[19] The basic argument of the New World Information Order was that the superior publishing power and media infrastructure of western or developed nations had resulted in the cultural domination of Third World countries. It was therefore necessary for Third World countries to strengthen their own communication and information infrastructure in ways that were attuned to their development needs. These ideas crystallized in a study presented to UNESCO's International Commission for the Study of Communication Problems by Mustafa Masmoudi, the Tunisian Secretary of State for Information. Masmoudi observed a "profound imbalance between developed and developing countries" in the international information system and argued that "the right to communicate should guarantee not only the right to be informed but also its corollary, the right to inform, to complete mutilated information and to correct false information."[20] In the Peruvian case, the Velasco government's commitment to these principles facilitated important, if short-lived, media innovations.

One such area of innovation was film: the government established tax incentives for Peruvian productions and mandatory distribution and exhibition for approved productions. The government was particularly keen to sponsor mass communication initiatives connected with rural themes. For example, SINAMOS sponsored the production of short documentaries related to the agrarian reform. *Runan Caycu* (Quechua for "We are people"), directed by Nora de Izcue in 1973, tells the story of Saturnino Huillca, a Cusco peasant leader. The 38-minute documentary describes his progression from a poor peasant background to growing political activity and union leadership. Another film, titled *Niños* (Grupo de Cine Liberación Sin Rodeos/SINAMOS, 1974), focuses on the daily lives of a group of schoolchildren in Ollantaytambo (Cusco). In a classic cinematic trope, the children are presented as the new hope of Peru. During a classroom scene the students are urged by their teacher "to learn history outside the school" and be vigilant against the former landowners, who seek to recover their lands.

The Cusco landscape plays an important role in both films, reflecting what Jeffrey Middents has identified as a shift in cinematic representations of the Andes between the early 1960s and the 1970s. Whereas the entries to a Peruvian short-film contest in 1965 "generally regarded areas outside Lima with something akin to a 'tourist's eye,'" those produced ten years later "tended to be more ethnographic than archaeological in orientation, delving into everyday situations of Andean culture."[21] The Velasco government's interest in supporting this kind of filmmaking provided an important boost for avant-garde productions and encouraged efforts to capture rural life on screen.[22]

The government also sponsored a number of initiatives in the print media and radio. In 1975 (after the expropriation of the newspapers), the national daily *La Crónica* began producing a separate weekly newspaper written entirely in Quechua, entitled *Cronicawan* (*With the chronicle*). Engineered by the prominent journalist Guillermo Thorndike, *Cronicawan* was varied and visually interesting. Sold to the public at the subsidized price of four soles, the real cost of producing each edition was fifty-two soles.[23] This was the first time in Peru's history that a national newspaper had been produced in Quechua. Following shortly after Quechua had been declared an official language in Peru, the newspaper reflected a new optimism about the language's role in contemporary society. Its editorials struck up a horizontal (rather than paternalistic) relationship with the reader: "As a communal labor, *Cronicawan* begins this work after 450 years of oppression and hegemony, recovering *Runa Simi* once more and placing it within the reach of the people."[24] As well as peasant issues and the progress of the agrarian reform, articles covered general current affairs, including developments in Cuba and Mozambique.

After its eleventh issue, the newspaper began publishing Quechua and Spanish texts in parallel, but it remained committed to writing from an Andean perspective.[25] The editorial introducing the new format stated: "[W]e write first in Quechua, afterward in Castilian[;] we want everyone to read us[;] we want everyone to know us, the things we say, where we carry our injuries, where we carry our happiness—it's like that for us—we don't hide anything. . . . [Y]ou will tell us if we are mistaken or we are walking on the right road, you will tell us."[26] *Cronicawan* was discontinued shortly after General Morales Bermúdez took power in 1975, probably due to financial constraints and changed political priorities. Although short-lived, the newspaper stands apart for its radical use of Quechua and the scale of its ambition; to my knowledge there has been no subsequent attempt to produce a national print newspaper in Quechua.

The Velasco government's commitment to what it considered the right to communicate was also reflected in its support for new forms of participative media. For example, the agricultural cooperatives were encouraged to publish their own bulletins. A government pamphlet advising cooperatives on how to produce a bulletin argued that such publications could contribute to the training and education of the *socios*, help form a spirit of solidarity, provide reading material for those learning to read, and disseminate news and culture between cooperatives. Significantly, it also claimed that following the expropriation of the newspapers, new opportunities had opened up for popular expression: "The campesinos have a responsibility to use those media made available to them. Their company's bulletin gives them the opportunity to learn to express their opinions and their ideas through the written word."[27] Of course, this would not be the first time that campesinos had expressed themselves using the written word; Peru's local and national government archives are filled with petitions written by or on behalf of peasants throughout the country's colonial and republican history. It was, however, unprecedented for campesino organizations to be actively encouraged by the state to produce their own publications and assert a political presence in the public sphere.

Alongside new forms of print media, the Ministry of Agriculture pioneered the use of the radio forum, a method of group discussion that involved audiences listening to a radio program together and discussing it as a group. The participants' discussion of the program was recorded, and this information was then fed back to the radio production team and incorporated into subsequent programs. This was a national project with various teams based in different regions. Radio programs featuring campesino correspondents also formed a part of the communications strategy deployed by the regional and zonal teams of SINAMOS promoters, as will be discussed in more detail.

Responses to Government Propaganda

Both the scale of the government's media campaigns and the extent to which these penetrated rural areas are indicated in a photograph taken in 1974 by Swedish photographer Mikael Wiström in the community center of Ranra-

Figure 4.9. An array of posters, newspapers, circulars, and other materials in the office of the Comunidad Campesina de Ranracancha, Chincheros, Apurímac (ca. 1974). Photo by Mikael Wiström. © Mikael Wiström.

cancha, a village in the department of Apurímac (south-central highlands). The photograph (fig. 4.9) features a striking array of propaganda pinned to the bare walls, from agrarian reform posters to local newspapers and circulars. Wiström commented: "The particular and interesting [thing] about this photo and the village is that it has always been a community without any relation to an hacienda. But the [community] leadership in those times was very politically conscious and took a big part in everything that was happening in the countryside."[28] Thus agrarian reform propaganda and publications reached even areas that were not targeted by the agrarian reform process and fed into other forms of political activism.

As I noted in the previous section, a number of left-wing intellectuals, artists, and activists lent their support to the Velasco government and went to work for government agencies such as the DPDRA, SINAMOS, and CENCIRA. While many of these individuals had a conflictive relationship with the regime—particularly on questions of artistic freedom and methods of social mobilization—they ultimately decided that they could have greatest impact by working inside the government. More radical leftists rejected altogether the government's "reformism" and the political interventions of SINAMOS. Newspapers and fliers produced by agricultural federations and unions, often with the backing of left-wing parties such as VR or the

Figure 4.10. *La voz del campesino*, cartoon produced by the Confederación Campesina del Perú (ca. 1972). Central archive, Confederación Campesina del Perú, Lima.

MIR-CE, made frequent references to SINAMOS and the Ministry of Agriculture bureaucrats, whom they accused of trying to manipulate and mislead the campesinos.

For example, a cartoon (fig. 4.10) produced by the CCP portrays the government functionary as a pompous bourgeois figure, wearing a jacket and bow tie and sporting a carefully molded quiff hairstyle. The speech bubble extending from his mouth is left open, as if unable to contain the quantity of "bla bla bla" spilling out of it. In the scenes below, SINAMOS is represented using the Túpac Amaru logo, but the words spoken by this supposed icon of revolution are labeled "demagogy." These illustrations show just how visible and familiar SINAMOS had become to a rural audience: without this familiarity the satire would not work. They also indicate the strategies used by the Left to discredit the government's "third way" arguments. In particular, the government's rhetoric of social harmony and its promotion of cooperative forms of agricultural management are portrayed as pious and false, a veil for more sinister motives of political control and capitalist exploitation. Hence the closing argument of the sketch: "The people respond: there can only be union, harmony with those of your own class: poor with poor, rich with rich. Long live the struggle!"

In addition to criticizing what they saw as the government's co-opting of peasant movements, leftists accused SINAMOS of using propaganda to coerce peasants into accepting the agrarian debt and the cooperative system.[29] A report presented at the CCP's Second National Extraordinary Congress in 1975 criticized the government's attempts to launch what it called a "cooperative ideology": "That is to say, the bourgeoisie, through its newspapers and talks, tries to make us believe that with the cooperative we are no longer exploited and for that reason we no longer need trade unions nor lists of demands; that we must make sacrifices in order for the company to make greater profits."[30]

In the context of the agrarian reform and the political change occurring in rural areas, the government and left-wing activists viewed the peasantry as a key support base. VR had started in the mid-1960s as an essentially urban political party of students and intellectuals; after the passage of the agrarian reform law the party shifted its focus toward building a campesino base. This involved targeted operations to neutralize the government's media campaigns, such as that launched in June 1975 to counteract official celebrations relating to the anniversary of the agrarian reform law. A VR circular stated that this day should instead be "exploited by the revolutionary proletariat and the classist peasantry to . . . continue the fight against semi-feudalism, imperialism, and the conciliatory policy of reformism with those enemies and particularly the landowners."[31] The party instructed the "comrades of each front" to produce fliers promoting the struggles of the rural poor and urged them to make contact with the community leaders who would be attending the government's commemorative activities on 24 June: "They should give them informative materials and seek a contact conversation to expand on the information. At the same time they should distribute the fliers about the current struggles, including the land occupations that are planned in Cajamarca for that same day."[32] These comments offer some insight into the political strategies used by organizations like VR. What is more important is that they reveal how the success of the government's media campaigns prompted such organizations to respond in kind, seeking new ways to generate peasant support.

Press reports also played an important role in struggles between the CCP and the government. *La Nueva Crónica*, which was government-controlled from 1970 onward, portrayed the CCP and parties such as VR and MIR as "dogmatic extremists," hoping to undermine their criticisms of the agrarian reform. In August 1973 the CCP lashed out at what it saw as misreporting and distortion that was designed to "create tensions in the heart of the campesino movement, confuse, divide and liquidate the class organizations, favor the opportunist currents within the peasant movement, deform before public opinion the classist line of the CCP struggle and favor the feudal landholders, the greater bourgeoisie and imperialism."[33] Citing the Freedom of the Press Statute, the general secretary and communities secretary of the CCP demanded that their letter be published in full by *La Nueva Crónica*, together with the CCP manifesto that the newspaper had supposedly misreported. If the Velasco government saw public opinion as a major factor in sustaining its revolution, peasant activists were equally concerned about controlling how they were portrayed in the mass media and using the media to shape public opinion.

Those on the right of the political spectrum also tried to shift the terms of the debate established by the Velasco government's mass communication. The Sociedad Nacional Agraria (National Agrarian Society [SNA]), the body representing large landowners, used its influence with the national newspapers to criticize the agrarian reform publicly. In the days following the announcement of the agrarian reform, SNA President Alberto Sacio told a press conference that the new law contained "disadvantageous mechanisms" that would go "against the increase in production and productivity of agriculture, if not corrected."[34] He criticized the fact that no funds had been specified for the provision of technical assistance, and commented that expropriation of land should take place on "poorly exploited" land rather than "productive" lands. These were the same arguments that the SNA had used against the Belaúnde government's agrarian reform in 1964. By concentrating on the agrarian reform's technical aspects, the large landowners sought to divert attention away from the political implications of land redistribution and focus the debate on a much narrower set of issues, such as the availability of credit and the impact on agricultural productivity.

In a slightly different strategy, landowners also paid for advertising to portray themselves as participants in, rather than targets of, the agrarian reform. Shortly before the announcement of the reform, a group of landowners' associations published a notice in *La Prensa* that called on the government to listen to their opinions: "The private agricultural sector, constituted by those of us who exert ourselves directly in agriculture and livestock production as a way of life, confront daily the problems of the peasant situation. To this activity we dedicate our capital, lands and permanent work. These actions give value to our opinions; we have the obligation to give our opinions and we have the right to be heard."[35] Echoing the government's own rhetoric of "land for those who work it," the landowners tried to include themselves within the moral category of those who worked the land. The statement that the landowners "exerted" themselves daily suggested an equivalence between their role as managers of production and the physical labor of the campesinos. The subtext of this discourse was to blame rural poverty on inefficient production rather than inequitable wealth distribution.

Among the national newspapers, a particularly critical position was taken by *La Prensa*, which was owned by Pedro Beltrán, a major landowner and member of the SNA. Beltrán himself published an editorial in the paper during the week following the announcement of the reform, in which he attacked the policy of expropriating the "efficient" sugar estates as unjust and contrary to the government's stated aim of promoting industrialization:

> Of course, it is easy, comfortable and above all fashionable to argue and speak today of the "exploitation of the campesino" and of "social justice." It is easier still to refer to the law, without distinguishing its two sides, as an "instrument of justice." But for anyone who knows the reality of the social work that has been carried out by estates such as Tumán, Pucalá and Casagrande, among others, such declarations are absurd, demagogic and out of touch.[36]

La Prensa also expressed skepticism about the ways that the agrarian reform was being promoted. An editorial published in February 1970 argued that the "propagandists" of the agrarian reform should cease their activities in the capital and focus their efforts in the countryside instead:

> Urban propagandists should join the instructors and indoctrinators, giving up, if only for a time, the comforts of the big city to go to the centers of implementation of the agrarian reform, stay there as long as it takes, and in that way have the opportunity to learn about the problems of those workers whom they invoke so much, and put before them solutions and formulas to be confronted with the reality on the ground, and the objections of those—the *cusqueños*, for example—for whom the new agricultural regime is not a mere matter of political rhetoric, but the burning task of every day. Not here

> in Lima, but there, in the countryside, where there are so many questions to be answered, they must demonstrate their devotion and agrarian expertise, the self-sacrificing apostles of renewal. Less comfortable for them, but more useful for the country and for the success of the agrarian reform.[37]

A generous reading of the article might conclude that the author was genuinely concerned about correcting the inefficiencies of government promotion efforts, but the overriding tone of the piece strikes a cynical dig at the promoters' idealism. It also reflects the view that the agrarian reform was essentially a problem for the countryside and not one that should trouble the urban population.

Yet Peruvian newspapers were far from homogenous in their responses to the agrarian reform. *El Comercio, La Crónica,* and *Correo* expressed support for the reform, largely on the basis that it would modernize the agrarian structure and contribute to industrialization. For example, an editorial published in *La Crónica* shortly after the announcement of the agrarian reform law praised the reform for expanding access to landownership and creating a wider market.[38] Similarly, *El Comercio* praised the reform as an expression of "the new spirit of the Armed Forces" and commented that "the integration of vast sectors of the population, previously marginalized from national economic life, will mean they constitute a market sufficiently wide as to allow the industrial development that will benefit all."[39] The newspaper also supported the Velasco government's nationalist policies, such as the expropriation of the foreign-owned oilfields of La Brea y Pariñas in October 1969.

Given *El Comercio*'s reputation as Peru's leading conservative newspaper, it is somewhat surprising to see the degree of support that the newspaper gave Velasco during his initial years in power. For example, during the president's tour of the northern departments of Lambayeque, La Libertad, and Piura in 1970, the newspaper proclaimed jubilantly: "Trujillo witnessed the largest meeting in its history. President Velasco was constantly applauded."[40] A feature in its Sunday supplement described in a positive light the government's propaganda campaign prior to Velasco's arrival:

> During the whole of last week, the people of Trujillo were witness to a fervor and a mobilization without precedent. Posters of the agrarian reform were put up on all the streets of the city. The posters were at once aesthetic and effective. Armed Forces helicopters dropped thousands of fliers. In the haciendas of the valley of Chicama and the other valleys of the zone abundant activity unfolded. The campesinos and now owners of the largest sugar estates of the country, were preparing themselves for the march to Trujillo on Satur-

day. Certain obsolete union leaders tried, in vain, to detain the enthusiasm of the agricultural workers.[41]

One reason for this positive report by *El Comercio* stemmed from its long-standing opposition to APRA, here invoked as the "obsolete union leaders." In the same article, Haya de la Torre is referred to in veiled but scornful terms as "the boss of a discredited political party" who treated Trujillo as "his personal fiefdom."[42] The newspaper's celebration of Velasco's popularity is therefore largely a statement of satisfaction at APRA's declining political fortunes. Yet it is also clear that the scale of the mass meetings in Trujillo, Chiclayo, and Piura at the start of the agrarian reform prompted interest and enthusiasm even from a conservative newspaper like *El Comercio*. This position changed substantially during the course of the Velasco government's tenure, particularly as rumors spread in 1973 of plans for the expropriation of the newspapers.[43]

An additional consequence of the government's intensive use of the mass media was that it prompted peasant organizations to produce their own press notices, fliers, and circulars. As state-supported organizations, agricultural cooperatives benefited from both the resources needed to produce press notices and the increased possibility of having such notices picked up by the regional or national press. In the context of the agrarian reform, what the cooperatives said could make headlines, and they became adept at using the Velasco government's rhetoric to further their own demands. For example, following the Agricultural Development Bank's suspension of credit for the CAP Tambo Real (Santa Valley, Áncash) on the grounds that its salary increases were unauthorized, the cooperative's trade union responded in a press notice: "What do these officials think? Are we not human beings? Or is it that the laws have been made in order to WORK MORE AND EAT LESS. If we contract tuberculosis, would this be the type of man that the Revolutionary process needs to build the New Peru? Or do we really need strong, well-fed men to build, with their work, THE ECONOMIC BASE OF OUR REVOLUTION THAT IS UNDERWAY?"[44] The statement concluded with a direct quote from a speech given by General Velasco, in which he described the agrarian reform as the transfer of economic and political power "from the oligarchy to the working classes."[45] This and other press releases by the CAP Tambo Real were not petitions to the establishment, of the kind received by local and regional prefects and government ministers in the decades prior to the agrarian reform. Rather, they were open appeals addressed to "public opinion and the people in general" that sought to highlight the discrepancy between government rhetoric and the reality on the ground. In responding to the Velasco government's propaganda, peasants asserted a stronger voice in the public sphere.

Regional Media Wars

Debate was not restricted to the national level; evidence from the regions of Piura, Cusco, and Tacna indicates a similar eruption of public discourse on a local level. While in constant dialogue with the actions of central government, both pro- and antigovernment media in each region developed their own communication styles and characteristics. In SINAMOS zonal offices, staff members, although familiar with the designs and iconography produced in the capital, operated with substantial autonomy and used the—often limited—resources at their disposal. Unfortunately, little remains of the publications, posters, and leaflets produced by the regional and zonal offices of SINAMOS. From the items that have survived, it is possible to see quite how artisanal these publications were. A poster produced by the Puno zonal office (fig. 4.11), for example, echoes the pop art style that had been used to particular effect in Jesús Ruiz Durand's designs for the DPDRA, though this one was produced on cheap paper using fairly rudimentary printing technology, evident in the poor color registration (alignment of the color blocks).

It was the job of regional SINAMOS offices to present the agrarian reform in ways that would respond to local expectations and resonate with different regional cultures (see chapter 2). These propaganda efforts were met by varying degrees of resistance from the local press, peasant organizations, and left-wing political parties. Comparing these media wars at the regional level yields not only important differences but also similarities in the cultural impact of the agrarian reform.

Cusco

Two of Velasco's closest political advisers—the journalist Efraín Ruiz Caro and General Leonídas Rodríguez Figueroa, the director of SINAMOS—were from Cusco. The attention they gave to the region and the language and imagery they incorporated into government communications reflect their *cusqueño* origins. Partly as a result of this cultural influence, Cusco intellectuals and artists were inspired to launch their own activities in support of the revolution. The Javier Heraud Cultural Action Group was formed in 1972 as "a space of external support for the Revolution on the cultural plane."[46] Its

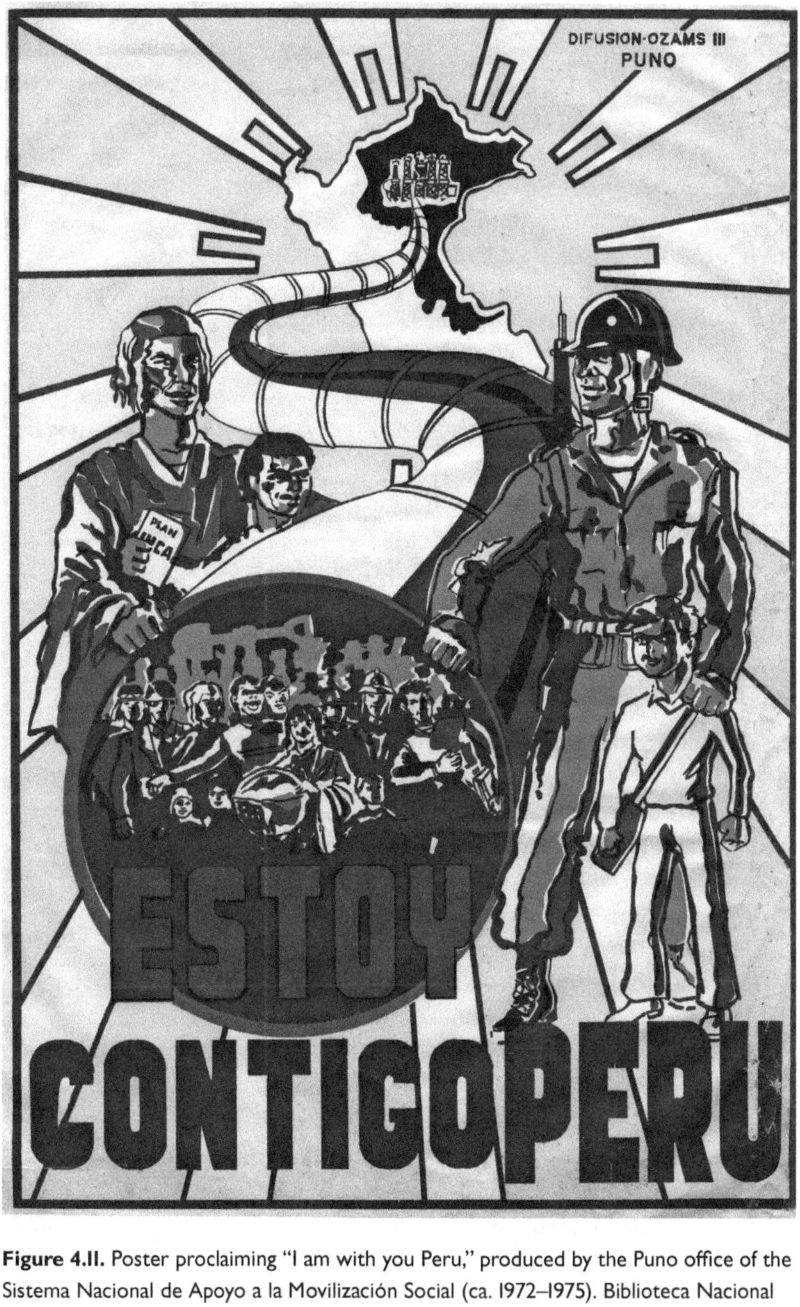

Figure 4.11. Poster proclaiming "I am with you Peru," produced by the Puno office of the Sistema Nacional de Apoyo a la Movilización Social (ca. 1972–1975). Biblioteca Nacional del Perú, Lima.

activities included radio programs, puppet shows, a weekly newspaper, and a mobile cinema. While declaring themselves supporters of the revolution, the group's members maintained a degree of distance between their own activities and the actions of government. However, the Javier Heraud Cultural Action Group was short-lived. According to Guido Guevara Ugarte, a former member, the group soon encountered difficulties in dealing with the state bureaucracy, which "didn't go at the same rate, at the speed with which the cultural action group wanted to progress."[47]

The scale of propaganda activity by both government and opposition organizations in the Cusco region is revealed in the press reports of the era. The newspaper *El Sol*, for example, was irritated by the proliferation of posters and fliers relating to the agrarian reform, and the complaints the activity provoked were part of its roundup of news in Calca province: "It is fine for SINAMOS and other workers' organizations, trade unions and cooperatives to make wall propaganda, but what is really bad is for them to be put up everywhere, even on the front door of the Municipal Palace, spoiling the decoration. In any case those that order them to be put up should learn to respect the institutions and not damage the walls."[48] The newspaper's content was also shaped by those who arrived at its offices wishing to have their story reported, as in the case of the seventy-four campesinos who "on their own initiative and spontaneously" had formed a production cooperative in the district of Ollantaytambo, or the women who had formed their own campesina association to protest against the social and moral rules to which women were being subjected and their treatment as "servile instruments" by men.[49] In addition, the newspaper gave ample coverage of the *cabildos abiertos* (open meetings) that took place in the city of Cusco on a variety of issues of public concern. As Raúl Asensio has noted, these meetings were a well-established tradition in the region, but they took on greater prominence in the absence of electoral politics; the names of key contributors were given and their speeches often reproduced in some detail.[50]

El Sol was founded in 1901 by Ángel Vega Enríquez, a journalist, lawyer, and intellectual who was closely involved in the *indigenista* cultural debates of the early twentieth century. He sought to defend indigenous rights, break with Cusco's isolation as a result of poor transport links, and integrate it into national life in the face of Limeño centralism.[51] By the 1960s, the newspaper had become more informative and less intellectual in its orientation, but it retained the mission of reporting on and representing the region. Although its editors were on the right of the political spectrum, they did not associate themselves with the traditional elites. For commercial reasons, the newspaper aligned itself with the government of the day, a position reinforced by the newspaper's Lima-based holding company. Throughout the Velasco era the newspaper's editorial line remained broadly supportive of government policy. In 1973 SINAMOS did try to interest the company's workers in assuming control as a cooperative, but this appears to have been motivated by opportunism rather than fears of its subversive potential. The attempt was denounced by the newspaper and later abandoned after the workers came out in support of the management.[52]

The government's relationship with local radio producers was more fraught. Radio played a particularly significant cultural role in Cusco, where a limited road network made it difficult to distribute newspapers beyond the principal urban centers. The region also had one of the highest illiteracy rates in the country. In 1970 it was reported that the department of Cusco had the largest number of transistor radios in the country, with approximately one transistor radio for every 1.5 inhabitants.[53] In this context, the government was especially sensitive to opposition from local radio stations. In June 1969 *El Sol* reported that radio coverage had fallen silent during an official ceremony that was part of the municipality's "cultural week." Both the mayor and the president of the organizing commission attributed the failure of radio transmission to sabotage by Radio Tahuantinsuyo, which had the largest transmission range of any radio station in Cusco. Originally founded with the name "Radio Rural del Perú," Radio Tahuantinsuyo had been established in 1948 by Raúl Montesinos Espejo, the son of Cusco landowners.[54] Whether or not the accusation of sabotage was correct, it is indicative of the tense relationship between government authorities and private radio stations at the time.

In 1973 the government radio authority Empresa Nacional de Radiodifusión (National Company of Radio Broadcasting [ENRAD]) announced the closure of Radio Tahuantinsuyo and took control of Radio La Hora, which was owned by the same family. According to the former ENRAD employee Francisco León Farfán, the government chose to intervene in these two stations in particular because they belonged to a national network of radio stations with transmitters in Abancay, Cusco, and Juliaca. Use of this network was an attractive prospect for the government, particularly given the limitations of Radio Nacional—the Lima-based state radio station that had poor coverage outside major urban centers.[55]

While ENRAD Perú retained control of Radio La Hora until the end of the military regime, Radio Tahuantinsuyo remained closed for three months and was allowed to reopen only after successful lobbying by its owner, Raúl Montesinos Espejo. His side of the story is provided in a history of the radio station, *Una vida y un rumbo: Cincuenta años de cusqueñismo, Radio Ta-*

huantinsuyo y Raúl Montesinos Espejo (A life and a direction: Fifty years of cusqueñismo, Radio Tahuantinsuyo and Raúl Montesinos Espejo). In this account, Raúl Montesinos is portrayed as a heroic figure who battled tirelessly to keep his radio station on air. It is suggested that Radio Tahuantinsuyo became a target for SINAMOS attacks because of its popularity, particularly among the campesino population:

> In those hard testing moments, Don Raúl displayed great dignity and strength of personality, he had the firm conviction that everything that signified abuse and outrage would not last, that the manipulation of the peasantry and the popular sectors could for the moment permit the filling of squares and secure apparently multitudinous adhesion to the Velasquista Revolution, but he knew deep down that this had to end; that those who supported the regime did so for personal interest, out of political expectation and pro-Marxist ideological reasons; but the rest, the great masses, had neither real conviction in nor commitment to the process.[56]

This comment indicates the power struggle that occurred between SINAMOS and local radio owners. What was at stake was not just the radio infrastructure and financial assets of private radio companies, but the position of cultural and political authority that came with owning a radio station. Radio Tahuantinsuyo in particular defended its right to exert this cultural authority, seeing itself as "the most *cusqueñista*" of Cusco's radio stations.

Recognizing the importance of finding the right cultural register to influence the local population, the local ENRAD team produced two main programs: one in Spanish called "Avancemos" (Let's make progress) for the city of Cusco and another in Quechua called "Kallpa" (Strength) for a rural audience. Francisco León, who continues to work in Cusco radio, was part of the ENRAD team. In addition to producing programs, he was assigned to work as a journalist, gathering local and regional news that could be used in radio broadcasts. León recalled that the production team was given substantial freedom to pursue what they saw as a more socially committed kind of broadcasting: "to us at that time it seemed excellent, the campesino can have a communication media in his favor and through that communication media he could achieve a better education that would make him more competitive, no? And that he would not be marginalized, no? Because the campesino had never been listened to. . . . In our program we did listen to them."[57]

Alongside ENRAD programming, the Ministry of Agriculture commissioned local DJs to implement the national radio forum initiative (mentioned in the first part of this chapter). Francisco León worked on this program also. He recalled that the radio fora in Cusco centered on a character called "Quri Maki" (Golden Hand):

> He was an almost mythical character, somewhat inspired in what Pachakutiq had done and all that: he was a creator. In the communities we needed there to be an authority. And it had such an impact that this *Quri Maki* was a kind of leader that would draw you to him. So we dealt with specific problems. The case of alcoholism, for example, that was—that is—so rooted in the communities, no? So, through radio theatre, the character intervened and spoke in Quechua, and he made them see, let's say, the havoc that alcoholism causes, etcetera etcetera.[58]

Both the radio program and the discussion were conducted entirely in Quechua. During the discussion, the coordinator took notes in Spanish, and these were later discussed and evaluated by the team in Cusco, which used them as the basis for future programs. León's comment that "we needed there to be an authority" reveals the disciplinarian imperative that underpinned the program. At the same time, however, the methodology of the radio forum project meant that the coordinators were also guided by the issues that participants chose to talk about. For example, Anta community members complained that their sheep had been stolen and that the police took no interest. In these cases, radio forum staff began to intervene on the community's behalf, becoming a kind of advocate between the community and the state authorities.[59]

Piura

In Piura, the local newspaper *El Tiempo* was more open in its opposition to the Velasco regime. It asserted its opposition to the 1968 coup, declaring in its editorial of 4 October: "*El Tiempo* registers its disagreement with this act of force that significantly affects our democratic tradition and places us before the international concert of countries as elements incapable of governing ourselves in a civilized manner through the Constitution."[60] The newspaper similarly denounced the closure of the newspapers *Expreso* and *Extra*, the magazine *Caretas*, and the radio stations *Continente* and *Noticias* in November 1968 as opening the door to "a horrid dictatorship that, with all certainty, does not favor the prestige of the armed forces, nor the citizenry who, rather, call for freedom and unity to resolve the important problems that afflict them."[61]

El Tiempo belonged (and still belongs) to the wealthy Helguero Seminario family, whose own 398-hectare hacienda was expropriated by the agrarian reform. In the days leading up to Velasco's first presidential visit to Piura in October 1971, *El Tiempo* was filled with notes of welcome and praise for the president from private individuals and companies such as Calixto Romero SA, one of the largest landowners in the department.[62] In the editorial "Bienvenido Presidente" (Welcome, President), *El Tiempo* commented, in a veiled allusion to the prospect of Piura being declared an agrarian reform zone, "Piura has great hopes in the security that it will be heard and not disappointed during the visit of the soldier, statesman and piuran Juan Velasco Alvarado. It knows his concern and desire to solve the very serious problems that have halted [Piura's] progress, paralyzed its development, postponed the achievement of a dazzling future, based on the rich potential of its natural wealth and the high quality of its ruling classes and the piuran worker."[63] This was a call for the region's power structures to be maintained, rather than dismantled in the name of reform. Such lobbying efforts were in vain however; just six days after the presidential visit to Piura the department was declared an agrarian reform zone.

Responding to the declaration, *El Tiempo* published an editorial that tacitly criticized the decision. Although it claimed to agree with "the promotion of social justice in the countryside," it cautioned that the reform would not be a success in Piura without adequate irrigation and other resources. Echoing the argument made in the national newspaper *La Prensa*, the editorial called for fair treatment for the landowners as individuals who had contributed to the country's wealth, urging the government to "contemplate impartially and justly the situation of the current owners, those men who throughout many years of struggle and hardship, putting up with the fury of nature, worked the land, leaving their energies there and supporting the state, through tributes and taxes, contributing to the well-being of Peru and all Peruvians."[64]

The newspaper also published a statement by the Departmental Agricultural and Livestock League, which cautioned the government against unleashing a class war in the department, adding: "The process of agrarian reform carries a message of justice for the campesino masses without land and should not necessarily imply the announcement of punishment for the current landowners, as one could deduce from the flippant declarations of some functionaries that arrive in the department, and, with 'tele-publicist' desires for the agrarian reform, allow themselves to make threatening warnings, completely against the spirit that we know animates the Revolutionary Government of the Armed Forces."[65] Such statements reveal the polarizing nature of official propaganda, with Piuran landowners concerned that they would become the targets of political attack.

Piura's second largest newspaper, *La Industria*, provided more favorable coverage of the agrarian reform. Although also owned by a landowning family, the newspaper was one of a chain that included newspapers in Trujillo and Chiclayo. It presented itself as a force for modernity rather than aligning itself with traditional elites. Following the announcement of the reform, the newspaper led with the headline: "End of the latifundio (and the minifundio) announced president." In outlining the motives and content of the reform, it stuck closely to the text of Velasco's speech.[66] It also published statements of support, such as that issued by the Comunidad Campesina de Castilla, which reproached "the hacendados that in Piura have usurped the land of the communities" and applauded "the revolutionary military junta for the Law of Agrarian Reform, in what it signifies for the campesinos and communities that should recover the lands that have been snatched from them."[67]

A former SINAMOS employee at the Piura regional office recalled a lack of attention to government activities in the local press, more than outright opposition. There was little coverage, for example, of the 1972 inauguration in Ayabaca of the first agrarian league in the country, according to this employee, who prefers anonymity (communication by letter, 1 April 2013). In order to gain press coverage the government was forced to pay the newspapers to place articles and propaganda. Similarly, SINAMOS bought airtime on two local radio stations, where it broadcast two daily programs: "Movilización Social" (Social Mobilization), which consisted of interviews and news reports, and "Ondas Campesinas" (Peasant Waves), which was produced in collaboration with the Federación Regional Agraria de Piura y Tumbes (Regional Agrarian Federation of Piura and Tumbes). Agrarian league members were trained to be correspondents for their respective valleys and instructed to discuss both the achievements and problems of the various agrarian organizations.

In addition, both the zonal and regional SINAMOS offices produced their own pamphlets, fliers, and posters to promote the government's reforms. These were often made by people who had no prior experience in design or the arts. Edita Herrera, a SINAMOS employee who worked in the communications department of the Piura regional office, described learning how to make stencils for screen printing by hand. Having started work at SINAMOS at the age of 18, she commented that it was "a constant process of learning."[68]

Herrera also worked as a presenter of the radio program "Movilización Social," which had the slogan "a program that rescues from silence the acts and aspirations of the people." The program focused on covering local issues and experiences. Whereas Cusco had a strong history of local radio, the existing stations in Piura had restricted coverage, with most having little reception beyond the departmental capital. As late as 1976, a SINAMOS report observed that the region had "little contact with the mass media such as: magazines, newspapers and all written publications, as well as television" and that it received "systematically alienating information from the radio stations of Colombia and Ecuador."[69] In this context, SINAMOS efforts to promote the campesino voice though the use of rural correspondents represented something genuinely new for the region.

Tacna

Neither of Tacna's newspapers maintained a critical position toward the Velasco government. *La Voz de Tacna* had a reduced circulation throughout the Velasco era for financial and technological reasons. *El Correo* was part of the national news group Empresa Periodística Nacional, and as such it was expropriated in 1974 along with the national newspapers. Even before then, both newspapers were mindful not to draw the attention of government censors. As local historian Oscar Panty Neyra observed, both newspapers responded to the 1968 coup by criticizing the means and not the aims of the change in government, and even these reservations diminished following the declaration of nationalist measures, such as the nationalization of the oilfields.[70] Following the announcement that the International Petroleum Company had been expropriated, *El Correo* responded: "In this line of action, the government will continue to have the support that the country has patriotically given it in this historic hour. And on that path, which is one of dignity and responsibility, *Correo* will provide, as always, its collaboration."[71]

La voz de Tacna greeted the announcement of the agrarian reform with the headline "Now it's true: the reforms have begun!"[72] The scale of the new reform and the speed with which it had been introduced was taken by the newspaper as a positive sign for what the government might go on to do next, commenting, "If the reformist pace accelerates, earlier than we thought . . . the new Water Code may be passed and the reform of the fishing industry. This last one is difficult but not impossible if the military government maintains, and accelerates if possible, the rate of reforms that it has just established with its management of the passage of the new Agrarian Reform Law."[73] The newspaper also printed a selection of readers' letters under the heading: "Majority of Tacna express satisfaction with the radical Agrarian Reform Law."[74]

While backing the need for agrarian reform, the newspaper cautioned that it should be "applied well" and came out in support of those with small and midsize landholdings. An editorial published in May 1971 praised the Minister of Agriculture, General Enrique Valdez, for his assurances that such landholdings would not be expropriated, adding that "the small and medium properties must be recognized by the state for their promotion of its development. It must be understood that the changes to land tenure consecrated by the agrarian reform respond not only to an imperative of agrarian justice, but also, and this does not cease to be transcendent, to the objective of producing more."[75] As I noted in chapter 2, the newspaper drew a sharp distinction between the latifundista economy of the northern departments and Tacna's agriculture, with its predominance of small and midsize farms, and argued that this difference should be taken into account when applying the agrarian reform.

This sense of regional exceptionalism increased following the declaration of an agrarian reform zone in Tacna in February 1975. In a series of articles, the newspaper outlined the case made by the region's small and midsize landholders for repealing the declaration of an agrarian reform zone in Tacna. It highlighted that these landowners had inherited their land from family members who had resisted the Chilean occupation in the early twentieth century: "Therefore, these lands are given a special significance, with deep patriotic content. And because of that and because they are more than productive matter, they want to preserve them, taking care of them with the fervor with which they loved them since childhood, and from a distance when they were expelled from the native land because of their observance of unwavering loyalty to the Homeland."[76]

La voz de Tacna was, however, at pains to differentiate itself from those provincial newspapers that had been labeled "counterrevolutionary" by the government and its allies. In 1974, Guillermo Thorndike, the director of the state-controlled *La Crónica*, denounced a number of provincial newspapers as puppets of the (US-dominated) Inter-American Press Association (SIP in Spanish), the latifundistas, and the counterrevolution, accusing them of undermining the revolutionary process through incomplete reporting, minor errors, and sowing doubts among their readers. Although *La Voz de Tacna* had not been mentioned directly in the article, it had been included in the accompanying photograph and felt compelled to clarify its position:

> La Voz de Tacna is not affiliated or linked to the SIP, neither has it previously had nor does it currently have interest in belonging to that organization. It has not been connected to large landowners or feudal gentlemen, or to any

> group of small or great oligarchs. It understands its independence as its non-dependence upon any group of economic or political power. . . . If we had to give ourselves over to economic power groups to be a great daily newspaper instead of perishing, we would prefer to perish. This is our truth. If it is not accepted, then we stick with it. It is a matter of conscience.[77]

While much of the newspaper's content echoed the government's own rhetoric regarding the "revolutionary process," it defended its autonomy and right to speak on behalf of the region, particularly regarding the rights of those with small and midsize landholdings.

For its part, the government replaced the presenter of state radio in Tacna shortly after the 1968 coup, and subjected the privately owned Radio Tacna to frequent surveillance and temporary closures. The SINAMOS regional office paid for one hour a day of airtime on the stations Radio Nacional and Radio Tacna, which it used to deliver "informative talks" on subjects such as education and agrarian reform. In addition, the regional and zonal offices produced a substantial amount of printed propaganda, often with limited resources. This combined nationally produced iconography with locally produced texts and images. The pamphlet in figure 4.12 is typical; it took the Túpac Amaru logo that had been disseminated throughout national government propaganda and used it to promote Tacna's agrarian federation (FARTAMO).

In evaluating its own performance, the regional SINAMOS office was pessimistic about the impact of its "consciousness raising" activities and identified an absence of creativity in the content and style of its propaganda. In assessing Tacna's contributions to the national Inkari festival—a series of local and national contests designed to select the best examples of folk arts and music—the regional SINAMOS office remarked, "If we wish to evaluate the elevation of the political consciousness of the population, the conclusion is reached that the native culture has been given the value that it merits, the shame of popular culture has been broken, but the objective has not been achieved."[78]

Part of the problem was that the management was unwilling to give its personnel the autonomy enjoyed by those in Piura and Cusco. Fredy Gambetta, who worked at the SINAMOS regional office in Tacna, recalled that it was a "den of intrigues." He was forced to resign from his own position after he was outed as a member of the Tacna Theatre Group (whose director was an Argentinian anarchist) and a friend of Gróver Pango, an APRA party member and a leader of the teachers' union, SUTEP.[79] This was sufficient to label Gambetta as "counterrevolutionary" and unsuitable to occupy his position working with the *pueblos jóvenes*.

Figure 4.12. Logo by the Oficina Regional de Apoyo a la Movilización Social (ORAMS) XI Tacna-Moquegua (ca. 1974). Tacna Regional Archive, Records of the Regional Government of Tacna.

This atmosphere of suspicion and intrigue also led to tactics such as the overnight leafleting of the city of Tacna that spread rumors about the government's opponents. In April 1975, *La Voz de Tacna* reported that in the preceding afternoon and evening there had appeared "a profusion" of leaflets containing "grave accusations" against SUTEP. The accusations included the misuse of public funds, its "ultra" position, and its "counterrevolutionary action."[80]

Yet there are signs that the government's opponents used similar media campaigns. The prefect of Moquegua informed SINAMOS officials that "the existing radio responds to other interests and the population finds itself practically misinformed." He also alleged that there had been an attempt to cut the retransmission of the program "Dialogue with the People" (recently recorded in Tacna) during the part when farmers from Moquegua were participating and that this had been avoided only through his direct intervention.[81] Thus, while it is difficult to ascertain where the government's paranoia ended and concerted opposition began, it is clear that the press and radio became intensely contested ground in Tacna during the Velasco government and that this tension grew steadily worse toward the end of his premiership.

Legacies of the Velasco Government's Use of Mass Media

The Velasco government's innovative use of the mass media to reach rural populations set an important precedent for the development of alternative communication approaches. Whereas the early rural radio stations (beginning in the 1950s) principally played folk music and relayed messages between listeners, in the late 1970s nongovernmental organizations established radio stations that were dedicated to issues of development, political participation, and education. For example, the Centro Peruano de Estudios Sociales (Peruvian Center of Social Studies), founded in Lima in 1976, had a daily radio program called "Tierra Fecunda" (Fertile Land). Similarly in Piura, the nongovernmental organization CIPCA launched in 1983 the radio station Radio Cutivalú. Now one of the region's most popular stations, Radio Cutivalú was set up to provide participative radio that addressed rural issues. In a 2007 interview the director of Radio Cutivalú, Rodolfo Aquino, explained how the station had developed programs in which citizens question the authorities on a given subject. It had become not only a source of information but also a generator of public opinion, with the regional newspapers picking up on items that appeared in Radio Cutivalú's programs.[82]

Of course, a number of social changes since the 1970s have contributed to the growth of participative media, not least the greater accessibility of communications technology. The founders of Radio Cutivalú also cite the El Niño phenomena of 1983 as a motivating factor for the creation of the radio station: the extreme isolation imposed by widespread flooding throughout Piura gave radio communication an immediate importance. Nevertheless, Radio Cutivalú's emphasis on participative communication owes a clear debt to the communications projects of the 1970s, and it is no coincidence that it was founded by CIPCA, an organization that worked closely with the Velasco government (see chapter 3).

A similar legacy can be seen in the work of the Asociación de Comunicadores Sociales (Calandria; Association of Social Communicators), a nongovernmental organization founded in Lima in 1983. The organization is dedicated to promoting the use of communications media to support an active democracy and facilitate political participation. In addition to funding research and publications in this field, the organization carries out practical projects in community-led communications media and produces its own videos and radio programs. Calandria's founder, Rosa María Alfaro, cites her work at the Ministry of Education during the Velasco government as a formative influence on her future interest in communication:

> I traveled through the whole country, and I could see the whole country working in popular communication workshops. That was the first contact that caused me to realize that popular communication was not only a problem of techniques of communication, nor even concepts of production, but of knowing the communication logics of the sectors that had to be attended to. It was not a problem of making a message simple, it was the problem of seeking the culture, the ways of learning and meeting, the truths or information that the people needed and not the other way round, when you go to impart something.[83]

The impact of the Velasco government's use of the mass media is also evident in the increased public presence of peasant leaders. Edita Herrera, cited earlier, described the changes she noticed in those campesinos who participated in SINAMOS radio programs:

> I remember that I looked at them and their rough hands, awkward, with little mobility from the use of the *palana* (hoe). And when they started to write on the typewriters of that time, which were manual, with their fingers: ta ta ta. And later when time passed I saw them writing the editorials. It was exciting for me, to be able to say that it is possible to change. . . . You saw that not only physically with the use of the hands but also their intellectual character began to develop, no? Therefore many people of that era, those campesinos, you could talk with them and it was as if you were in the university. I remember that Calixto Cruz [a peasant leader], once there was a journalist here, Baella, and he interviewed him. And he spoke to him about the international problem of cotton, about the costs, the exploitation, everything! And he was a real authority. And [Baella] asks him: "And what education do you have?" "Second year of primary."[84]

During the Velasco government peasant leaders also began producing their own publications to disseminate the ideas shared at national meetings of the CCP and the CNA. This practice continued beyond the regime change of 1975. César Zapata, a former member and director of the Cooperativa "Abraham Negri Ulloa" in Catacaos, Piura, described his experience of attending the Fifth Congress of the CCP in 1978, where he met peasant leaders from across the country and heard from inspiring figures such as Hugo Blanco and Juan Hipólito Pévez (a founding member of the CCP). On returning to Piura, Zapata decided it was vital to share what he had learned with the local population: "I remember that I spent some fifteen bad nights writing [about] the experience and the program, adapting it to the language of our campesinos."[85] This effort to communicate the CCP's discussions in written form, rather than through public meetings or informal conversation alone, is a reflection of the great importance that was attached to mass communication by both the Velasco government and the CCP in the context of the agrarian reform. It is interesting to note Zapata's particular concern with using "the language of our campesinos." He went on to describe the cultural diversity among Piura's peasants, with the campesinos of Bajo Piura sharing a different (cultural) language to those of Alto Piura, echoing the Velasco government's own strategy of adapting its propaganda to suit different regional audiences.

Conclusion

The Velasco government's promotion of the "campesino voice" created new opportunities for peasant participation in the broadcast media and drew national attention to campesino issues. Government interventions in print propaganda, radio, newspapers, and film drew on international trends of participative media and ideas about the right to communicate. Implemented by young artists and intellectuals excited by the prospect of "socially committed" mass communication, they included the use of "campesino correspondents," radio fora, Quechua language broadcasts and publications, indigenous cultural traditions, and state-sponsored documentaries centered on rural communities. The government's actions also stimulated a good deal of opposition and ferment, as peasants and left-wing groups resisted attempts to co-opt them, and conservative newspapers argued against the approach taken in the agrarian reform and in favor of preserving the status quo.

At the regional level, the degree of opposition from local radio stations and newspapers varied. Antagonism between the government and local radio owners was greatest in Cusco, where the owner of Radio Tuhuantinsuyo proclaimed his station as the "most cusqueño" of Cusco's radio stations and successfully lobbied for its return to private ownership. In Piura and Tacna, local radio was both less extensive in its broadcast range and less central to the articulation of regional identity. On the other hand, Piura's *El Tiempo* newspaper allied itself with the "modern" landowners of the north and maintained a critical position on the agrarian reform. In the aftermath of the expropriation of the national press in 1974, the provincial press were keen to avoid the same fate, but they were nevertheless prepared to criticize the Velasco government where local interests or cultural traditions were seen as being under threat. In engaging with debates on the nature and pace of the agrarian reform, regional media simultaneously commented on the relationship between regional and national politics and defended the right to speak on behalf of their region.

Velasco Alvarado remained unresponsive to such local idiosyncrasies, denouncing all criticism from the press as counterrevolutionary. While the government's rhetoric celebrated the idea that the mass media should provide a democratic space for the expression of multiple opinions and interests, Velasco repeatedly denounced the "oligarchy" for its manipulation of the press and feared that the project to socialize press ownership would be hijacked by "leftist extremists." In an interview with journalist César Hildebrandt in 1977, Velasco was asked why he had not handed the newspapers over to civil associations while he had the opportunity. His response is a telling comment on the government's tense relations with the Left: "We didn't do it simply because there had already been an enormous infiltration of reds in the newspapers, *viejo*. There were communists and [those] of the extreme left. To the extent that to give, let's suppose, *Expreso* to the students was too much, it was pointless, because it was going to fall into the hands of the communists."[86] Although Velasco saw his media reforms as part of a wider process of democratization, his government was ill prepared for the political upheavals that such a process engendered. Following expropriation in July 1974, the newspapers became increasingly subject to government control via the Oficina Central de Información (Central Office of Information). In the absence of private capital the newspapers were underfunded and dependent on advertising revenue, ironically meaning that private, capitalist interests continued to dominate newspaper content.[87]

While policies such as the socialization of the press and state control of TV and radio did not transpire in the way the Velasco government had envisaged, it nevertheless created a window for alternative forms of media and cultural production. The legacies of this moment can be seen in the subsequent development of community radio stations and the increased (though still limited) presence of indigenous culture in the mass media. The public discourse that surrounded the agrarian reform was not contained in a distant rural sphere but rather spilled onto the pages of the national press, and it concerned key questions of national identity and political representation, fundamentally challenging the political order that had prevailed in the years before the agrarian reform. The high profile given to the agrarian reform in the mass media and the ideological terms in which it was portrayed at the time have also helped shape how it is thought about and remembered today.

CHAPTER 5

The Agrarian Reform in Historical Memory

Reflecting on the interviews he conducted in the 1990s and 2000s with people affected by the agrarian reform, Enrique Mayer commented: "In the case of the Peruvian agrarian reform, there is no 'official story,' let alone a 'history' of the reform or of Velasco's military leftist government, that might lay out some guidelines along which people can order their own remembrances."[1] In that respect, Peru differs sharply from Mexico, where the seventy-one–year rule of the PRI (Institutional Revolutionary Party) made the country's agrarian reforms a key part of its revolutionary narrative.[2] In Peru, Velasco's abrupt removal from power in 1975 and the steady shift away from his reformist policies by subsequent regimes has left the agrarian reform an isolated moment in the country's history, about which opinion continues to be extremely divided.

The relationship between history and memory shapes popular understanding of the agrarian reform. Clarifying the meanings of *history* and *memory*, as the following text does, helps set out important theoretical principles for analyzing memory. One way in which the Velasco government actively carved out a place for the agrarian reform in popular consciousness was by positioning it as part of a "people's history" of Peru. In the past five decades, historical memory of the agrarian reform has been affected not only by national events and political developments but also by conscious efforts to influence collective memory through public discourse. Nonetheless, the memory of the agrarian reform remains persistently important for contemporary Peru, both within particular communities and national politics. Whereas in some parts of the world, land reform is remembered as a technocratic process linked to Alliance for Progress notions of economic development, in Peru the agrarian reform remains a central part of debates on the distribution of power and resources.

This chapter departs from the format followed in previous chapters in that it does not focus solely on the regions of Piura, Tacna, and Cusco. Rather, it combines fieldwork (conducted in Chiclayo and Lima as well as the aforementioned regions) with secondary research. This approach compensates for the reluctance of people to talk about their experiences during the agrarian reform and the fact that many of those who were most active during the reform have died or are now quite elderly, and younger generations do not have clear memories of the era. As previous chapters have shown, the agrarian reform was riddled with contradictions and disappointments that left many of its protagonists with ambivalent feelings that in turn make it difficult for them to articulate their thoughts about it. Moreover, complex legacies remain from the internal war between Sendero Luminoso (Shining Path) and the Peruvian state that ravaged the country between 1980 and 2000. Fearful of either stoking the tensions that underpinned the outbreak and spread of violence (some of which originated in land conflicts of the agrarian reform era) or being cast as a "terrorist"—a label often attached to campesino and trade union activists during the war—many individuals choose not to talk about their memories of the agrarian reform; however, this does not mean that the reform has been forgotten. Uncovering the ways in which different and frequently contradictory memories of the reform have been maintained, repressed, constructed, and circulated will elucidate not just the agrarian reform as a historical process but also the nature of contemporary Peruvian society and its relationship with the past.

History and Memory

Within historical research, interest in memory has grown steadily in recent decades, alongside the development of "memory studies" as an interdisciplinary field of study.[3] Kerwin Lee Klein has criticized the tendency to use the word *memory* in academic writing for rhetorical effect, rather than with a clear academic purpose. He argues that many of the issues currently studied through the lens of memory were already being addressed by historians as oral history, commemorative rituals, autobiography, public history, and so on, "without ever pasting them together into something called memory."[4] While it is important to avoid using the term *memory* in evasive or misleading ways, such reservations should not cause us to abandon memory as a field of study. In the case of the Peruvian agrarian reform, studying the politics of memory that surround it can help explain why it continues to hold such symbolic value in Peruvian politics and denaturalize the ways in which different versions of the agrarian reform are formulated and maintained.

In his classic text *The Collective Memory*, Maurice Halbwachs argued that individual memories are always socially framed. Whether or not an event is experienced in the company of others, the individual's ability to recall it is dependent on the connections between that event and a particular social milieu.[5] Whereas the psychoanalytic tradition exemplified by Sigmund Freud approached memory as being contained within the mind of the individual, occasionally making contact with external factors, Halbwachs believed that even the most profoundly personal and apparently unique memories are formulated in relation to the significant social groups in an individual's life and made possible by collectively derived language and concepts.

While Halbwachs emphasized that collective memory evolves with the passing of different generations and can be formed by different groups within a society, he was strongly influenced by Émile Durkheim's ideas about collective consciousness and the structuralist understanding of community. He therefore emphasized coherence rather than conflict in the formation of collective memory.[6] More recent work has explored the tensions between individual and collective memory. In *Anzac Memories: Living with the Legend*, Alistair Thomson showed how Australian veterans of the First World War struggled to formulate their individual memories in ways that accorded with popular myths surrounding the heroic role of the Australian and New Zealand Army Corps (Anzac). He argued that since the so-called Anzac legend is an essential part of Australian national identity, war veterans drew on the tropes of this legend to present a publicly acceptable version of their wartime experiences. Yet they also tried to compose a past that gave them a sense of coherent identity and that tallied with their personal experiences. At times, the inability to make these two versions of the past coincide resulted in "unresolved tension and fragmented, contradictory identities."[7] Work by Thomson and others indicates that, rather than being a natural outcome of a community's evolution, group remembering can be a complex process that requires active negotiation on the part of the group's members.[8]

Historians have also examined the relationship between different group memories, sometimes referred to as "mnemonic communities."[9] As Elizabeth Jelin observes, there can never be a single interpretation of the past shared by a whole society: "One can find moments of historical periods in which the consensus is greater, in which a 'single script' of the past is more accepted or even hegemonic. Normally, this script is what is told by the victors of historical conflicts and battles. There will always be other histories, other memories and alternative interpretations, in the resistance, in the private world, in the 'catacombs.'"[10]

However, these "other histories" may often have to struggle to be heard in public discourse. The silences around dissident memories can be maintained by a dominant state and by the social relations between groups.[11] In the case of Chile, Marian Schlotterbeck argues that the narrative of failure that characterized both left- and right-wing historical accounts of the Allende government (1970–1973) became so hegemonic that the grassroots participants of Allende's revolution ceased talking about it in public, even long after the Pinochet dictatorship ended. Referring to one of her interviewees, Schlotterbeck writes, "The silencing of Chile's recent history, particularly what came before the 1974 military coup, was so complete that Reyes initially had been surprised that I wanted to know about his involvement with the MIR [Movement of the Revolutionary Left]. When the local textile mill closed in 1997, Juan Reyes was the oldest employee—a distinction that earned him a handful of local history interviews. No one had ever asked about his politics."[12]

Such silences have important implications for contemporary society and politics. In their study of post-Franco Spain, Susana Narotzky and Gavin Smith argue that in the rush to consolidate the new democracy, any engagement in political dissent—including talking about past political divisions—was labeled unpatriotic, with profound consequences for the quality of Spain's democracy.[13] The continuing tension regarding the historical legacy of the Spanish Civil War was exemplified by the Valencia regional government's 2014 decision to ban the public display of the tricolor (the flag of the Second Republic).[14]

Judith Butler offers important insights into the mechanisms by which certain viewpoints or memories are silenced within public discourse. She argues that while conventional accounts assume that censorship is an act of power wielded primarily by the state and made in response to speech, it is also possible to think of censorship as an implicit form of control that precedes speech. In this formulation, censorship serves to make certain forms of speech unspeakable, in a process Butler describes as "foreclosure." The distinction between what is speakable and what is unspeakable is not fixed but is continually repeated and reconsolidated: "The subject who speaks within the sphere of the speakable implicitly reinvokes the foreclosure on which it depends."[15]

This concept of foreclosure is useful for thinking about changes in the ways that the agrarian reform is talked about in Peru and the progressive silencing of a radical agrarian reform agenda in recent decades. When I discussed the Peruvian agrarian reform with Fernando Eguren, an expert on the subject, he remarked that on rereading Velasco's speeches some forty years later he had been surprised by the radical tone of his language; such language would be viewed as unacceptable and extremist in present-day Peru. This shift is important, since it has a direct bearing on the kinds of policies that it is possible to discuss and implement in contemporary Peruvian politics, an issue to be considered later in the chapter.

Memory Formation

A prerequisite before considering the current status of the agrarian reform in historical memory is analyzing the ways in which memories of the agrarian reform were constructed at the time. The Velasco government presented its reforms as a revolution and rallied popular support through interventions in local politics, education, and the mass media. The government also dedicated considerable attention to consolidating its place in history. For example, it sponsored the publication of the three-volume *Historia General de los Peruanos* (General history of the Peruvians). The third volume carried the grand title *El Perú: Primera y segunda independencia, 1821 y 1968* (Peru: The first and second independence 1821 and 1968), implying that the start of the Velasco government marked a change of significance equal to that of independence from Spanish colonial rule. Although published in 1972, when the agrarian reform was in the midst of its first phase of implementation, the book dedicates a number of pages to its history and significance:

> The country suffered a jolt: agricultural reform had not only been passed but was already being implemented. Gone forever was the old colonial saying: "The law is revered but not fulfilled." The wheel of history began turning once again in Peru. The implementation of the agrarian reform began precisely in the areas of highest agricultural production on the coast, which the large agricultural interests, in collusion with their proxies in the parliament of the previous regime, had managed to place outside the margins of the reform. From that moment, in Peru and abroad, where the development of the Revolution was followed with great attention, there was the conviction, supported by the facts, that in effect the true liberation of the peasant had begun.[16]

This passage attempts to fix the meaning of a reform that was still very much in process. The text goes on to predict the future outcomes of the agrarian reform: "When the process is completed in the current reform zones, 1,570,000 people, that is, 260 thousand families, will have benefited.

All of Peru, excluding the Selva Baja [Amazonian lowlands], will be a Zone of Agrarian Reform before the end of 1972 and the majority of the land will have been transferred to the adjudicated. At that moment it will be possible to affirm that the latifundio has disappeared from the face of Peru."[17] With one eye firmly on posterity, the author describes the agrarian reform from an imagined future position of success.

By sponsoring historical texts of this kind, the Velasco government sought to shape how its reforms would be remembered in the future. This was particularly important since the government knew that at some point it would have to hand power back to a civilian regime. In an interview with the magazine *Caretas*, SINAMOS director General Rodríguez Figueroa commented: "Only when the structural reforms of the Revolution are truly irreversible and only when there exists the guarantee that the process of transformations cannot be detained but rather consolidated and continued, the Revolution will make the necessary democratic consultation, which, precisely, will have to conform to different principles from the traditional ones."[18] The assertion that the reforms should be "truly irreversible" before any return to electoral democracy reflects the regime's belief that future governments would be unlikely to preserve Velasco's legacy and would, in fact, try to undo the reforms.

As well as sponsoring official histories, the Velasco government used public rallies and ceremonies to commemorate its reforms. The agrarian reform law was announced on a day that already held cultural significance because on it was celebrated both the feast of St. John the Baptist and the Inca festival of Inti Raymi, which marked the end of the winter solstice. In 1930 it had been renamed Día del Indio (Day of the Indian) by President Augusto B. Leguía.[19] The Velasco government capitalized on the cultural associations that the day already carried, while at the same time appropriating them as part of its own political narrative by renaming the festival Day of the Campesino.

At the regional level, commemorations of the anniversary of the agrarian reform law incorporated local and national elements. In Tacna in 1974, for example, the program of events included the official opening of a new building by a campesino; speeches by representatives of an agrarian league, a CAP, and the regional SINAMOS office; musical and theatrical performances by local agronomy students; the formal transfer of land titles; and singing of the Tacna and national anthems.[20] Similarly in Piura, in 1970, the anniversary of the reform was marked by a peasant procession that lasted three hours, with "local color" provided by not only young people wearing typical dress but also members of the Campesino Community of Catacaos arriving on horseback.[21] After the procession, cooperative representative Artidoro Silva gave a speech referring to Manuel Negri Ulloa, a leader of a precursor of the campesino movement in Bajo Piura, and requesting a minute's silence in his memory. A representative from the village of Andanjo (Huancabamba) also recounted "the tragedy that they experienced in 1954 when the hacendados burned down their houses and committed a series of indescribable and inhuman abuses."[22] By linking commemoration of the agrarian reform to regional culture and history, the Velasco government aimed to position the agrarian reform as part of a "people's history." The same tendency is apparent in the naming of the agricultural cooperatives and leagues after locally significant political heroes, for example, the CAP "Negri Ulloa" in Catacaos (Piura) and the Liga Agraria Hugo Blanco in Urcos (Cusco).

Group political identities assumed particular importance during the agrarian reform. Through training and propaganda, the government encouraged SINAMOS employees to think of themselves as the vanguard of the revolution and promoted a national campesino identity that was reinforced through the cooperative and agrarian league structures. Among the government's opponents, radical leftist parties engaged in constant debates about which individuals or groups shared their "political line," and landowners used the national and local press to project their self-image as agriculturalists unfairly victimized by the Velasco regime. These groups formed the context in which individuals' memories of the agrarian reform were formed.

Moreover, many of the group identities established during the agrarian reform continue to exist today. These groups' shared memories of the reform era play an important part in their identity politics. As social psychologist Cristian Tileagă explains, "It is too often (or too hastily) assumed that it is only natural for individuals and groups to have (an) identity(ies) or memory(ies) and too often forgotten that it is through constructing, negotiating or resisting identities that individuals are able to acquire, make sense of and recall their memories."[23] For those who militated for the radical left during the Velasco era, memories of the agrarian reform continue to serve as an important reference point.

In April 2013, I attended a public meeting that was organized in support of Javier Diez Canseco, a highly respected left-wing congressman who at that time was battling cancer (he died in May 2013). The event was a celebration of his life and various political activists were called on to speak about the man and his achievements. These reflections in turn gave way to more general discussion of the political struggles of the past, within which the agrarian reform assumed a central position. A few days after the event, I interviewed former VR coordinator Armando Zapata. He commented:

> You were at that event for Javier. All those people who were there are people who militated on the Left in those years, right? . . . That is a group that is there permanently in the different organizations, right? Proposing things. So I think that we have contributed a level of organization and consciousness [that is] very interesting. That is, we contributed with teams, with people, who continue fighting the fight. I think that if we had not done that at that time, in the case of Piura, it would not be how it is now.[24]

For former (and current) left-wing activists, the group identity forged during the Velasco era still shapes how they remember the agrarian reform and their role in it.

In a similar way, involvement in the agrarian reform was a formative experience for many civil servants. Edita Herrera, a former SINAMOS employee, told me: "I think that for those of us who were in this process it has made a big impression on our lives. It has given us a lot too."[25] She described the young people who joined SINAMOS (herself included) as "dreamers" who did things because they felt committed to the cause, not because they were ordered to.[26] After working for SINAMOS, Herrera was employed by various government agencies before becoming a founding member of the Red Nacional de la Mujer (National Women's Network), a women's rights organization. A number of her colleagues also went on to work for nongovernmental organizations, which experienced a boom in the aftermath of the Velasco government.[27] Former SINAMOS staff have thus developed social and professional networks that reinforce their view of the agrarian reform as an act of social justice. Another former SINAMOS employee who worked in Piura (and wished to remain anonymous) told me in March 2013: "I will never regret having worked in SINAMOS. I was never more aware of the reality of my country. I learned the true meaning of service and to exercise it within an institution." The same interviewee expressed keen interest in knowing what her colleagues had said about the reform process. The SINAMOS group identity therefore seems to play a significant role in individuals' construction and articulation of their memories of the reform.

The strength of these group identities is due in part to the intensity of the propaganda and political arguments that the Velasco government used to promote the agrarian reform at the time. This is particularly apparent in the collective identity of the CNA, which was created by the regime in 1974. At an event in Lima to mark the CNA's thirty-eighth anniversary in 2012, delegates were given a textual summary of the organization's history. The text described the formation of the CNA in the context of the agrarian reform, when "we campesinos could reclaim our lands and leave behind the exploitative condition of our work."[28] Echoing the language used by the Velasco government at the time, the text portrays the CNA as a peasant-led, democratic organization, in contrast to such landowners' associations as the National Agrarian Society, "which were spaces of power and representation only for the large groups of economic power who benefitted from the labor of the farming families."[29] The text goes on to describe how the CNA battled to defend the achievements of the agrarian reform throughout the 1980s and 1990s and emphasizes the organization's determination to "continue struggling in defense of the sacred interests of the country's small agricultural producers, heirs of the agrarian reform, of General Velasco Alvarado."[30]

The CNA thus continues to define itself in relation to the agrarian reform, using key ideas promoted by the regime: rejection of the oligarchy, liberation from servitude, and popular participation. It organizes annual pilgrimages (*romerías*) to visit Velasco's grave in the El Ángel cemetery in Lima. Such events reinforce the organization's ties to the Velasco government and its political legacy. Yet collective memory and collective identity are never fixed; they remain responsive to changes in individuals' immediate circumstances and the wider social context. That contextual responsiveness is apparent in the ways that the historical memory of the agrarian reform has developed in the decades since President Velasco's removal from power.

Paradigm Shifts

Peru's internal armed conflict (IAC), which extended from 1980 until 2000, had a profound effect on perceptions of the agrarian reform and how—and whether—it was spoken about in public. In 1980, the Maoist-inspired Partido Comunista del Perú—Sendero Luminoso (Communist Party of Peru—Shining Path) declared its "popular war" against the Peruvian state and proceeded to target so-called counterrevolutionary individuals, institutions, and communities using an unprecedented degree of violence.[31] Initially centered on isolated rural communities, the war later engulfed much of the country; by 1991 about half of the Peruvian population was living under a state of emergency.[32] Involving widespread human rights violations and massacres carried out by both the Peruvian army and Shining Path, the conflict resulted in the death and disappearance of 69,000 people.[33] As numerous scholars have observed, the war had a catastrophic impact on Peruvian society, and its legacies continue to be keenly felt today.

Occurring immediately after one of the most radical agrarian reforms in Latin America, the IAC seemed to go against the established wisdom that land reform reduced the potential for violent conflict by addressing the demands of poor and marginalized populations. For some, the eruption of violence in rural areas signaled that the agrarian reform had failed in its aim of preempting support for insurgencies.[34] Others argued that the IAC was better understood as a result of the agrarian reform being cut short and unable to realize its full potential, believing that in the absence of any land reform at all the violence would have been even greater and more widespread.[35] This is at least partially confirmed by the geographical distribution of the violence. In coastal agricultural areas, where the agrarian reform was most extensively implemented and the cooperative model had a significant impact (both economically and politically), support for Shining Path was significantly lower than in highland areas where the reform had arrived late or had little effect. Writing in 1983, Cynthia McClintock commented that for Peru's coastal peasants, "their relative prosperity and confidence in the political process are probably key factors in their opposition to Sendero."[36]

On the other hand, scholars have also pointed to the unintended consequences of the reform. Albertus argues that the tendency to focus on implementing the reform in "core" areas within each agrarian reform zone heightened feelings of relative disadvantage, encouraging those who failed to reap any benefit to side with Shining Path. Seligmann points to the reform's myopia toward other sources of social tension in rural areas: "The [agrarian] reform law, because it equated poverty with economic inequities, failed to take account of existing ethnic differences in the countryside based on unequal relations of power and the social construction of cultural identity."[37] By failing to address unequal power dynamics in their wider sense, did the agrarian reform in fact perpetuate long-standing grievances that contributed to the violence? These ongoing debates about the relationship between the reform era and the IAC make it difficult to maintain that the reform was an unequivocally good thing and in many cases reinforce feelings of ambivalence among its protagonists. Moreover, given the suffering and social division experienced during the IAC, many people remain reluctant to talk about the turbulent history of the agrarian reform that preceded it, for fear of stirring up the kinds of feelings and resentments that surged so violently to the surface during the armed conflict.[38]

To further unpack the ways in which the IAC has affected the collective memory of the agrarian reform, it is useful to turn to the theoretical framework proposed by Soifer and Vergara in their volume on the legacies of the conflict. As they point out, "[W]e need a careful temporal framework to distinguish causal chains that originated in the long eighties from factors that emerged thereafter, and also to distinguish the conflict from the longer historical processes of a fragmented society, polarized politics, and weak institutions that long predate it, and that also shape contemporary Peru in fundamental ways."[39] They identify three causal channels through which the effects of Peru's conflict are produced and reproduced: wartime mechanisms, postconflict legacies, and ongoing political struggles over these legacies.[40]

Beginning with the wartime mechanisms (political tendencies and actions introduced during the conflict itself), Shining Path's deliberate targeting of the agricultural cooperatives affected both their viability as institutions and the prospects for consolidating the achievements of the agrarian reform. As Carlos Iván Degregori observed, Shining Path sought total control in the countryside and saw the cooperatives as an impediment to its revolution.[41] The final report of the Truth and Reconciliation Commission, published in August 2003, cited the SAIS Cahuide (Junín) as a representative example of Shining Path's strategy. The largest cooperative enterprise in the country, the SAIS Cahuide covered 270,000 hectares and had 42,000 sheep and 4,500 Brown Swiss cows that allowed it to produce large volumes of milk.[42] Despite its financial success, the SAIS presided over an unequal distribution of benefits among the member cooperatives and communities. Shining Path carried out violent attacks on figures of authority within the cooperative. It also exploited resentments within the SAIS and between different communities in the region to generate support and destroy the SAIS infrastructure, ultimately hastening its dissolution in December 1988.[43] As well as contributing to the breakup of the cooperatives, Shining Path also tried to erase their history: in the case of the SAIS Cahuide, the administrative staff was ordered to burn all of the cooperative's records.[44]

The possibility of interrogation by government forces as part of the internal war also caused a fracturing of civil society organizations, including the cooperatives. The state's counterinsurgency operations were notoriously indiscriminate in their use of repressive violence against rural populations. In 1982, the Belaúnde government declared a state of emergency in Ayacucho (where the conflict began) and sent in a force of fifteen hundred specially trained paramilitaries known as Sinchis. As David Mason writes, "When intelligence was lacking, Sinchi practice was to engage in large-scale search-and-destroy missions in areas thought to be occupied by Sendero. Indiscriminate searches of peasant homes, arbitrary arrests, brutal interrogations of people suspected of having information on Sendero, and the murder or detention of school teachers, students, and leftist political leaders who were considered likely Senderistas became common."[45] César Zapata (former director of the Cooperativa "Negri Ulloa" in Catacaos, Piura) recalled that in the 1980s, the government's counterinsurgency discourse began to place all those engaged in peasant politics under suspicion: "They started to say the cooperatives are also involved here . . . to the extent that at one time they imprisoned me."[46] As a consequence, many individuals stepped back from taking an active role in the cooperatives, fearful of becoming a target of violence or interrogation. This contributed to the decline of individual cooperatives and a wider silencing of historical narratives that celebrated the agrarian reform as a moment of peasant empowerment.

In the postconflict era, mechanisms and social trends developed during the war continued to shape Peruvian society. In April 1992, amid the widespread perception that the Shining Path was reaching a strategic equilibrium with the armed forces, President Alberto Fujimori launched a successful *autogolpe* (self-coup) that allowed him to assume extraordinary powers in the name of prolonged political stability. He then pushed forward a new constitution, passed in 1993, with the argument that constitutional change was essential to ensure the integrity and security of the Peruvian state. The constitution heralded a new political order that has remained in place despite the end of the IAC, Fujimori's dramatic fall from grace in 2000—amid accusations of corruption and human rights abuses—and the return to democracy. Whereas the 1979 constitution enfranchised approximately one million people (by eliminating the literacy restriction on voting), emphasized popular sovereignty, and described the state in interventionist terms, the 1993 constitution removed all references to popular sovereignty, introduced new authoritarian powers to suspend guaranteed rights during a regime of exception, and restricted the role of the state to preventing monopolies and ensuring competition.[47] The IAC thus produced a political crisis that in the short term was exploited by Fujimori to pursue his authoritarian political agenda and in the long term helped marginalize the history of state reformism exemplified by the Velasco government.

Turning to the third element of Soifer and Vergara's framework, ongoing struggles over the legacies of the IAC, collective memory of the agrarian reform has also been shaped by the public discourse and state narratives that developed in the aftermath of the conflict. For example, Isaias Rojas-Perez has shown how, in the wake of the state atrocities uncovered by the Commission of Truth and Reconciliation, the state's handling of the disappeared and their relatives (who overwhelmingly come from highland Quechua communities) paints them as eternal victims rather than political actors in their own right. This is effectively an inversion of the politically engaged campesino citizen promoted by the Velasco government. Through what Rojas-Perez describes as the "necro-governmentality of post conflict," the state "seeks to structure the field of *possible* action and speech of survivors, relatives, and the population."[48] Positioning the survivors as victims limits the space available to them in public discourse and reinforces conservative narratives that characterize agrarian reform beneficiaries as "simple peasants" who were ill prepared to take on the demands of directing an agricultural enterprise.

Similarly, in their analysis of the sustained growth of the Peruvian Right during and after the IAC, Vergara and Encinas note that "the Right has succeeded in vulgarizing and disseminating an interpretation of the conflict in which the Left is linked to the pre-Fujimori economic failure of the country and to the [Shining Path] chaos."[49] In other words, conservative politicians continue to use the specter of the IAC and its associations with left-wing politics to maintain the economically neoliberal and socially conservative status quo. This status quo renders *unspeakable* (to use Judith Butler's term) some of the key questions and ideas that lay at the heart of the agrarian reform process. However, the IAC was not the only political development shaping how the Velasco era was understood and discussed. As mentioned, historical memory of the agrarian reform has also been shaped by the sudden collapse of the Velasco regime and Peru's steady shift toward a neoliberal economic model.

On 29 August 1975, the prime minister and minister of war, General Francisco Morales Bermúdez, seized control of the government through a military coup. This began the so-called second phase of the Revolutionary Government of the Armed Forces. Morales Bermúdez claimed he would continue with the same statutes and objectives as the Velasco regime and that the takeover merely signaled a change in the leadership of the government.[50] In practice, however, the Morales Bermúdez government began to dismantle key aspects of the Velasco government's reforms.

In addition to withdrawing financial support from agricultural cooperatives, Morales Bermúdez agreed to a series of orthodox stabilization measures that involved a reduction in state spending, devaluation of Peruvian currency, and the introduction of policies that were favorable to foreign investors and the private sector.[51] In 1978 the government began paving the way for the breakup, or parcellation, of the cooperatives. The trend toward parcellation was further accelerated under President Belaúnde (1980–1985). Although the agrarian reform law remained on the statute books until 1991, the rate of expropriation and adjudication declined dramatically after Velasco left office, and government support for the cooperatives dwindled.

Beside backtracking on the agrarian reform, Morales Bermúdez engaged in a quite literal destruction of the Velasco government's historical legacy.

The closure of SINAMOS in 1976 was accompanied by deliberate efforts to erase "phase one" from the historical record. Héctor Béjar explains:

> [There was] a commission, with military chiefs, assigned to erase all that had been done, to prepare the transfer to the conservative politicians. . . . But the military officials were very afraid that the professional politicians who were going to return to power were going to use this documentation to accuse them of being communists. And well, they burned absolutely everything. There was nothing left. We were able to rescue a few documents, but not the majority. There were the development plans, no? All the planning. And there were how many zonal offices? SINAMOS had 11 regions. There were at least 400 zonal offices, at least. Well, it was just lost. . . . Today for whatever historical study that would be very valuable documentation, because there is what the people wanted, no? The wishes of the people.[52]

As a former SINAMOS leader, Béjar takes a nostalgic view of what the historical record might have revealed, but he is certainly correct to highlight the loss to history that the destruction of this documentation represents. In the General National Archive there remains a huge amount of material relating to the agrarian reform that has yet to be catalogued and is therefore inaccessible to researchers. While it is difficult to ascertain whether this is due to general financial constraints or a deliberate policy of neglect, it has certainly had an impact on the kind of research that can be conducted.

Discussion of the agrarian reform and its place in history has also been shaped by changes in the Peruvian economic model. In 1980 Fernando Belaúnde Terry was elected as Peru's first democratic president after twelve years of military rule. As Enrique Mayer comments, "Though Belaúnde in his first reign had favored an agrarian reform, he very diplomatically did his best to derail the Velasco reform in his second term in office."[53] Although the land was not directly handed back to the former landowners, as was the case in Pinochet's Chile, Belaúnde passed legislation that gave all cooperatives the right to dissolve. Often heavily indebted and unable to access credit, many cooperatives took up this opportunity. For Belaúnde and his cabinet (many of whom had studied abroad and were strongly influenced by the emerging Washington Consensus), the dissolution of the cooperatives was part of a wider shift in government policy that reduced the role of the state in managing the economy.[54]

During the first presidency of Alan García (1985–1990), there was a brief return to the rhetoric of state-led development, accompanied by large subsidies for agricultural producers and an attempt to breathe new life into the agricultural cooperatives using cash transfers. As Rosemary Thorp observed, García rejected the orthodox economic model embraced by the Belaúnde government and redirected attention toward the rural economy.[55] While García's policies initially achieved moderate success in raising agricultural incomes,[56] his global economic policies ended in financial crisis. The following two governments of Alberto Fujimori (1990–2000) pushed a neoliberal agenda that saw the withdrawal of state subsidies, the formal repeal of the agrarian reform law, closure of the National Agrarian Bank, and the removal of restrictions on foreign investment. Many agricultural cooperatives that had survived the Belaúnde and García governments were forced to dissolve at this point. Characterized by a preference for free markets in place of state regulation, reductions in welfare spending, and a shift toward greater assumption of risk by the individual rather than the state, neoliberalism gained ascendancy across Latin America during the 1990s and early 2000s.[57] Fujimori presided over further decline in peasant activism and a negative shift in popular perceptions of the agrarian reform.[58]

For younger generations, the experience of Fujimori's authoritarian government together with the prevalent conservative narrative of the Velasco government as a one-dimensional, power-hungry dictatorship, had a direct impact on their perception of the Velasco era. In interviews conducted in the early 2000s with two different generational groups, Gonzalo Portocarrero found that those over fifty years old who had lived through the Velasco government tended to have a favorable view of the period. Their memories were framed by the conversations that took place when they got together and discussed old times. By contrast, the younger interviewees were more negative and emphasized the fact that the Velasco government was a dictatorship, an aspect barely mentioned by the older group. The younger group based their opinion of the Velasco era on a disparate set of sources, including their school education, conversations heard at home, and predominantly negative portrayals of Velasco in the mainstream media. According to Portocarrero, the recent jubilant return to democracy had left them with the impression that all dictatorships were necessarily repressive and bloody, and it overshadowed what the Velasco government represented in political terms.[59]

Another key period that helped consolidate conservative narratives of the agrarian reform was Alan García's second presidency (2006–2011), which saw rapid growth in the extractive industries and the reconcentration of agricultural land in the hands of multinational corporations. García's emphasis on free trade, open competition, and capitalist development left little space for discussion of the cooperative model enshrined in the agrarian reform. He actively encouraged the reconcentration of agricultural land in the hands of multinational corporations, as expressed in a polemical article he published in *El Comercio* on 28 October 2007, "El síndrome del perro del hortelano" (The syndrome of the dog in the manger). The title came from the Greek fable about the dog that will not allow the horse to eat the grain in the manger, although he himself cannot eat it. García used the story as a metaphor for the failure to exploit Peru's supposedly "untapped" resources, which he argued was due to the refusal to allow others to do what one could not, or would not, do oneself.[60] According to this logic, the land was no longer to belong to those who worked it but to those who could extract most wealth from it, a complete reversal of the paradigm that underpinned the agrarian reform.

In addition to shifting the terms of the debate on land reform, the rise of neoliberal economics in Peru helped erase the physical legacy of the agrarian reform by reversing its effects on the distribution of land ownership. In April 2010, the Comisión Agraria del Congreso (Congressional Agrarian Commission) approved a proposal for a law to limit land ownership to 40,000 hectares. As Fernando Eguren observed, this apparent restriction far exceeded the size of even the largest latifundios that had existed in Peru before the agrarian reform.[61] Research by María Luisa Burneo de la Rocha shows the extent of the reconcentration of land that has occurred in recent years. In the northern coastal region, an area of 60,000 hectares has been acquired by seven companies across three departments. In Piura, the Romero group—whose vast estates were famously expropriated by the agrarian reform—now owns, in addition to large landholdings in other areas of the country, 10,000 hectares. The transnational enterprise Maple Etanol SRL owns 12,000 hectares, which it uses to grow sugarcane for industries producing bio-combustibles.[62]

The increasingly negative portrayal of the agrarian reform in public discourse was mirrored by the direction of academic research. As was noted in the introduction to this book, the announcement of the reform in 1969 gave rise to a flurry of research by sociologists, anthropologists, and political scientists seeking to understand the reform's social, political, and economic impact. This wave of research continued into the 1980s, but the tone switched from great optimism to increasing pessimism, as a consensus grew that the reform had been a failure, particularly in economic terms. In the 1990s very little research was conducted on the agrarian reform at all. To a large extent this was linked to the danger associated with conducting fieldwork in rural areas in the context of the internal war. Yet, as Elizabeth Jelin reminds us, "there will always be other histories."[63] As the next section will show, even as a relative consensus developed supporting a dominant narrative of failure and the history of the agrarian reform was marginalized in mainstream politics, different social groups mobilized to enforce their own memory of the agrarian reform and articulate its significance for contemporary politics.

Preserving and Controlling Memory

In 1989, on the twentieth anniversary of the passing of the agrarian reform law, conservative newspapers *El Comercio* and *Expreso* and the magazine *Oiga* all published editorials that stressed the reform's economic failings and attacked its model of agricultural cooperatives. The ongoing parcellation of the cooperatives into individual landholdings was, they argued, proof that the cooperatives were untenable. *El Comercio* observed that Peru's agriculture was now less productive than that of Chile and Bolivia, countries that underwent similar agrarian reform processes but with "precise criteria." Its editorial commented: "Our process was not only demagogic but also extremely politicized and abusively executed. For that reason it resulted mostly in plundering and overbearing applications that, [after] directly damaging many and in the end the whole country, did not provide the slightest benefit to the peasantry."[64]

Similarly, *Expreso* argued that the agrarian reform "imposed a collectivist business model that was, from the start, actively or passively rejected by the ex-peons of the haciendas."[65] This editorial went on to describe the cooperative model as one that fostered corruption and immorality, with disastrous social and economic consequences:

> In effect, all over the world collectivist structures are factories of selfishness, of boycott more or less concealed. They incentivize the will to steal, to gain at the cost of others, for a simple reason: because he who works more than the rest knows that his greater effort will not be compensated by a greater income, while he who works less than the rest knows that his lower effort will not be punished with a lower payment. The result is a competition not for who can work or produce most, but for who can work least.[66]

In *Expreso*'s view, the agrarian reform missed the opportunity to consolidate a regime of small and midsize landowners, which, it claimed, "would have been the base for agricultural development and [the] sociological base for authentic democracy."[67] The suggestion is that private ownership is not only a more productive form but also a more moral form of ownership than collectivism.

This perception of the agrarian reform as a socially and economically damaging process was echoed during my interviews with landowners. In Chiclayo (Lambayeque), I interviewed Manfred Zoeger, son of Otto Zoeger, who was president of the National Agricultural Society at the time of the agrarian reform. The family's estate, which comprised some 7,000 hectares and employed 300 families, was expropriated by the agrarian reform. Zoeger commented that the agrarian reform brought forty years of decline for Peruvian agriculture, and he spoke about a golden age in which Peru was an internationally recognized exporter of sugar and cotton. For Zoeger, the economic dominance of Chile in the region was due to the decline in Peru's agriculture and its effective absence from international markets. Without the agrarian reform, he argued in 2013, Peru would equal or exceed Chile's economic achievement.[68]

In addition to criticizing the economic model promoted by the agrarian reform, the conservative press has consistently undermined the political arguments made about peasant participation at the time of the reform by claiming that the agrarian reform entrusted land to peasants who lacked the training or expertise to manage a productive agricultural industry. This narrative is disseminated widely in public discourse. In 2013, Lima art gallery Vértice displayed an exhibition by Peruvian artists Silvana Pestana and Sonia Cunliffe entitled *Desarraigo* (Uprooting). The exhibition's central premise was that upon handing the haciendas over to the peasants, the agrarian reform created a situation analogous to leaving a group of children alone to fend for themselves. This idea was portrayed through a series of photographs that featured the artists' own children playing alone in a casa hacienda. The exhibition description stated: "Using the agrarian reform as a point of departure, the artists propose to represent the uprooting that the paternal absence brings with it. The allegory functions therefore on two levels: the absence of the protective state is also the paternal absence. In this way, the characters discover the darkness, which they cannot confront without the instinctive, primal capacity of the innocent and the wild."[69]

The characterization of agrarian reform beneficiaries as children draws on a long history of racist assumptions about the rural indigenous population's mental and social capacities. The peasants' supposed need for the guidance and intervention of the master provided a central support and justification for the hacienda system well into the twentieth century.[70] It is also a recurring theme of present-day racism in Peru. In his study of video uploads on YouTube relating to the Velasco regime, Paulo Drinot observes that the user comments attached to such videos "converge on the idea that the failure of the reform was a consequence not of Velasco's own failings but of the unpreparedness of those who were given responsibility for making the reform successful: the indigenous peasantry."[71] This interpretation helps perpetuate racialized assumptions about indigenous people and marginalizes the egalitarian agenda that underpinned the agrarian reform. Moreover, it obscures the complex reasons why so many agricultural cooperatives failed (access to credit, market structures, transport infrastructure, price controls, etc.).

This argument was reproduced during my interview with Salvador Aita Germán, the son of another expropriated landowner in Chiclayo. He told me that the agrarian reform was like taking all the arms from the military and giving them to children:

> The child does not know how to use the gun; the child shoots for the sake of shooting, and there are going to be many deaths and injuries among the effects. . . . But *none of them is conscious of what they have been given*. To those people they simply handed a cassette saying that "no more will they rob from your poverty," that no more would the master take advantage of their sweat and labor, . . . [t]hat they were going to be landowners, and it is as if they were, because the lands were handed to them.[72]

The reference to the Velasco government's political propaganda here reflects a wider effort to diminish the ideology that was foundational to the agrarian reform. In May 2014, following a speech by then President Ollanta Humala that alluded to Túpac Amaru, journalist Martha Meier Miró Quesada published an editorial in *El Comercio* entitled "Túpac Mouse." While making brief reference to Humala's speech, Miró Quesada focused on the Velasco government's use of Túpac Amaru as a symbol of its reforms, which she likened to Walt Disney's Mickey Mouse and Fidel Castro's use of Che Guevara: "The dictator Juan 'Chino' Velasco also needed a stamp like Mickey or Che, an image that would communicate the change promised by his 'robolution.'"[73] The article proceeded to debunk the supposed mythology surrounding the historic figure: "Túpac Amaru II was in reality a monied tradesman who dressed elegantly, in the European style, and demanded a title of Inca nobility, despite the fact that, it seems, he was the son of a priest (this according to Alexander von Humboldt, who investigated his rebellion)."[74] The article provoked an instant reaction on Peruvian social media, with historians rushing to defend Túpac Amaru's place in history and to criticize the flimsy basis of Meier Miró Quesada's assertions. While Meier Miró Quesada's views cannot necessarily be taken as representative of the elite, the article is an example of the way in which conservative critics of the agrarian reform seek to belittle the political ideals that lay behind it.

The same sentiment was expressed in my interview with Salvador Aita Germán, cited above. He commented that Velasco was a "resentido social" (someone with a chip on his shoulder), who engineered the agrarian reform out of malice rather than political conviction. He described Velasco as "a soldier of little importance, of little culture and with a lot of anger," whose agrarian reform heralded a disordered process of land grabbing:

> [It was] a government that you couldn't even say was communist or Marxist or Leninist, it wasn't that. The thing that occurred to him was simply to take from those who had and give to those who didn't have, without any control. . . . There was no education, there was no preparation, there was none of that. So, straight up: for every person that had more than 150 hectares of land it was simply taken from them, without rhyme or reason.[75]

This characterization of the reform is perhaps unsurprising from someone whose family was negatively affected by land expropriation, but it draws heavily on arguments that are circulated repeatedly in the conservative media.

As part of their efforts to shape collective memory of the agrarian reform, conservatives have also shifted attention away from the theme of social justice for the peasantry and focused instead on the issue of the agrarian reform bonds, which were issued to expropriated landowners as compensation for their land. The bonds were designed to encourage expropriated landowners to reinvest in industry, which was perceived to be the future engine of economic growth. In practice, very few ex-landowners were prepared to risk investment of any kind; instead, they chose to retain the bonds for their potential future value while seeking employment in the professions and commerce. With the return to democracy, former landowners demanded payment of their bonds, but successive governments have avoided paying. The controversy over the nonpayment of the bonds continues to grab headlines.[76] Such campaigns are strengthened by the growth of neoliberal ideology across Latin America since the mid-1980s, the region having seen the terms of political debate shift toward the so-called blue rights associated with liberalism.[77] Arguments for social justice have been superseded by demands for legal justice and an insistence on the sanctity of contractual obligations.

The right-wing press has thus attacked the agrarian reform and its legacy from multiple angles and painted it with broad strokes as a complete failure.

To a large extent this has become the dominant historical narrative of the agrarian reform, yet at the same time, it continues to be challenged by those who hold alternative perspectives. A CNA executive member, Marcelino Bustamante López, told me:

> If you go to any community and you talk about Velasco among the people in their forties, fifties, sixties, they are going to remember him with a lot of joy. Except the young people from later, those that are in their thirties, forties, sometimes they don't realize, nor have they read the history so they don't know. We as the CNA are doing more to raise awareness of the actions of Juan Velasco Alvarado in terms of the agrarian reform, because without it there would be a lot of servitude even now as there is in many countries still.[78]

In June 2009, on the fortieth anniversary of the agrarian reform, the CNA produced a special edition of its magazine, *Vocero Agrario*. This included a feature that reflected on the legacy of the reform:

> The revolutionary reform adjudicated in favor of the true workers of the countryside, around 11 million hectares. A radical change. . . . But as tends to happen with any historic event, the agrarian reform generates conflicting feelings until today. The powerful continue to criticize it, arguing that the expropriations were unjust and attributing the backwardness of agriculture to the reform. What they do not say is that that law buried forever the Peru of *gamonales* and landlords, of peasants treated like slaves, without access to education or health, and with no hope of development.[79]

In countering the narrative of "the powerful," the CNA emphasizes the agrarian reform's political importance, rather than its consequences for agricultural production. This strategy has also been used by a number of left-of-center newspapers. On the twentieth anniversary of the reform in 1989, both *La República* and the weekly magazine *Sí* stressed the agrarian reform's importance in ending the system of *gamonalismo* and latifundio power. La República commented, "Twenty years after the agrarian reform very few would dispute its historical necessity and the immense transformation that came with the transfer of the land," while José Manuel Mejía began his analysis in the magazine *Sí* by noting, "No agrarian reform in Latin America so affected latifundism as that initiated on 24 June 1969 by General Juan Velasco Alvarado."[80] These newspapers represent a small minority within the Peruvian press, but by focusing on the reform's political achievements they nevertheless try to reframe the terms in which the agrarian reform is evaluated.

Academic researchers have also contested the characterization of the agrarian reform as a failure. Writing in 1982, Bruno Revesz argued that claims that the agrarian reform reduced productivity did not stand up in the case of the Piura cotton industry: "Usually, the current level of production is compared with the maximum production in Peru's history (1963) to conclude that the agrarian reform and the ignorance of the peasantry are the factors [behind] the fall."[81] In reality the decline in cotton production began before the agrarian reform, as a symptom of a more generalized crisis in agrarian capitalism. The production of raw cotton in Piura fell from 101,785 metric tons in 1965 to 44,131 in 1972, when the agrarian reform began to be implemented in the region. There was no rupture in productivity at the time of the transfer of land to the campesinos in 1973, and in fact the average yield for the period 1973–1978 was slightly higher than the average yield for 1965–1972.[82] In recent years nongovernmental organizations such as CEPES and DESCO have organized several public debates and roundtable discussions that aim to generate new perspectives on the agrarian reform and challenge the negative statements made about it in the conservative press.

These negative statements are also contradicted by the memories of agrarian reform beneficiaries. Although critics of the agrarian reform claim that it did nothing to reduce the poverty of the peasantry over the long term, many beneficiaries of the agrarian reform recall a marked improvement in their material conditions. For example, Wenceslao del Rosario, a peasant who worked on one of the Romero Group sugar estates in Piura, told me that in the era of the hacienda the workers were paid just one sol per day (equivalent to approximately four US cents at the time). The number of permanent laborers (who were eligible for certain labor rights and protections) was deliberately limited to 500, with the remaining workforce employed on a temporary basis. With the creation of the CAP Mallares, the number of permanent workers was increased by some 300, and Del Rosario described working conditions as "más descansado" (more relaxed).[83] Similarly, Hilario Pérez, a peasant and former cooperative member from Huyro in Cusco, recalled that his quality of life had improved considerably and remarked that the most important legacy of the agrarian reform was that it "ended the exploitation of man by man."[84]

Mallares and Huyro represent quite different agricultural contexts: Mallares was a large hacienda in the far north of the country that produced mainly rice and sugar for the export market, while Huyro is in the "ceja de selva" (highland jungle region), where tea and coffee estates are predominant. However, comments made by Pérez and Del Rosario indicate certain similarities in their experiences of the agrarian reform. Both men held positions of responsibility within the cooperatives. Del Rosario was elected as a delegate to the Central Cooperativa, the administrative and organizational center that brought together a number of cooperatives in the same region. He told me with evident pride that despite having little education (three years of primary school), he was chosen to represent the cooperative because he was known and respected locally. Within the Central, he was a member of the Administration Committee for three years, during which time he received training from the government and was called upon by the engineers because he could "make the campesinos understand."[85] Hilario Pérez was elected president of the Central de Cooperativas Té Huyro for three years running, during which time he was able to have considerable personal influence over the management of the cooperatives. For both men, the claim that the agrarian reform brought an end to rural exploitation is supported by their own experience of improved financial circumstances and social status.

The memories of individuals such as Pérez and Del Rosario are kept alive by the efforts of the CNA and other similar organizations. In the 2009 special edition of its magazine *Vocero Agrario*, an article entitled "Velasco, a Revolutionary Man" begins as follows:

> Juan Velasco Alvarado's hand never trembled at the moment of taking a decision. Firm in his convictions, he led with lucidity the reforms that changed the face of peasant Peru. . . . His passing caused deep pain. The man of flesh and bones died, but not his ideals, his spirit remaining in all those people who believe in a better Peru, with equality of opportunity for all its inhabitants, whether they be from the sierra, coast, or selva.[86]

This celebration of Velasco as a "people's hero" departs somewhat from the way in which the Velasco government presented itself at the time, when the collective, institutional character of the Revolutionary Government of the Armed Forces was stressed more than Velasco's leadership. The heroic image of Velasco has, to a large extent, developed in the years since he left office.

In the decade following the 1975 coup, Velasco's press secretary and close colleague Augusto Zimmerman Zavala edited a newspaper called *Kausachum Perú* (now discontinued) that celebrated his legacy.[87] A special edition

EDICION EXTRAORDINARIA

ESTA TRISTE POR SU PUEBLO

Y POR SU FUERZA ARMADA

15o ANIVERSARIO DEL
MOVIMIENTO REVOLUCIONARIO
3 DE OCTUBRE

PERU
Kausachum
PROYECTO DE DIARIO DE PARTICIPACION POPULAR

Director: Augusto Zimmermann Zavala Oficinas: Conquistadores 348 San Isidro–Telef.: 41–6884 No. 0065 Impresión: Editora Humboldt Lima, 3 de Octubre de 1983 Precio a Nivel Nacional: 350 Soles

LUNES 3: EL PUEBLO CON VELASCO

Figure 5.1. Front cover of *Kausachum Perú* (3 October 1983), marking the fifteenth anniversary of the Velasco coup.

published on 3 October 1983 celebrated the fifteenth anniversary of the 1968 coup (fig. 5.1). It included articles on Velasco's leadership and achievements and a call to attend a "great march for sovereignty and dignity" in Lima. The event was billed as both a celebration of the Velasco government and an act of protest against the Belaúnde government, which "boldly continues delivering the resources of our people to the voracity of its masters: the transnationals."[88] Thus commemoration of Velasco's legacy has been used both to defend a particular version of history and as a political banner for progressive activists to mobilize behind.

Among peasant communities, the characterization of Velasco as a "people's hero" has become so widespread that even people who opposed the government at the time express respect for him. For example, Demetrio Barrios Moscoso, a member of the Peasant Community of Compone in Anta (Cusco), participated in the *tomas de tierra* against the Cooperativa "Túpac Amaru" that began in 1977 and resulted in the cooperative's formal dissolution in 1979. He commented:

> I would say that, well, Velasco perhaps had—I'm not sure if him, well, him and many of his advisers. He himself, no? He had a sentiment, wishes toward the campesinos, the poor, to want to help us, . . . to get rid of the hacendado who was committing outrages, abuses. He removed them a little. But we thought that with the reform the problem could be totally resolved and the problem was not resolved. That's why I think that some [people] still celebrate him. They recognize Velasco, no? As a leader that felt for the peasantry, for the poor people. [For] me at least, I also think that in his intentions, his wishes were good, to get rid of the hacendado. And he thought that he was giving the land to the great majority of the campesinos but that was not happening.[89]

While conservative histories cast Velasco as a "resentido social" and emphasize the authoritarian nature of the regime, peasants challenge this narrative by celebrating Velasco as a champion of the peasantry and emphasizing that the agrarian reform responded to a genuine need to end exploitation in the countryside. The collectively constructed nature of this historical memory is indicated by Barrios Moscoso's repeated references to what others think. His hesitation suggests a certain degree of tension between this group memory and his own opinions. However, the memory of Velasco as a people's hero serves an important political function in undermining the elite's attempts to diminish the significance of the agrarian reform. Despite those attempts, the ability to mobilize a collective memory of the agrarian reform continues to play a part in the politics of the rural communities.

Ongoing Struggles

Rural Politics

The agrarian reform benefited some individuals substantially more than others; some were granted full cooperative membership while others were not. Disputes also emerged over cooperative management and, later, the decision to maintain or dissolve the cooperative. Rural communities have had to find ways of dealing with different group memories of the agrarian reform in order to avoid social conflict and maintain a cohesive communal identity, especially in the aftermath of the IAC.

In the southern Andean department of Calca (Cusco), anthropologist Ingrid Hall found that despite the profound consequences of the agrarian reform for the people of Llanchu, there was a marked silence on its role in their history. The Comunidad Campesina de Llanchu was officially constituted in 1988, its members drawn from the *ayllu* of Llanchu and the workers of two neighboring haciendas that were expropriated by the agrarian reform. The community was given collective land titles for the *ayllu*'s ancestral land and the former hacienda land, but in practice territorial division was maintained between the hacienda land and the *ayllu*'s land, and cultural divides remained between members of the *ayllu* (*aylluruna*) and the former hacienda workers (*haciendaruna*). These divisions centered on resentments regarding the quality of land available to each group and their respective roles in gaining official recognition of land rights. Hall comments: "One could say that the antagonism inherited from the agrarian reform is what structures communal life. In support of certain events, such as the installation of an irrigation system, the old conflicts reappear, as alive as they are painful. In different ways, the history remains indirectly present. While there is no historiographic discourse, history is inscribed in space and in [the community's] actions."[90] While *comuneros* actively avoid talking about the local history of the agrarian reform, the divisions that it created reemerge in other aspects of community life, such as the organization of work teams or the choice of religious denomination.[91]

In 2009 the Peruvian research group Cholonautas conducted a project entitled "Memorias de la lucha campesina por la tierra en Puno, Cusco y Apurímac" (Memories of the peasant struggle for land in Puno, Cusco and Apurímac). The project revealed how memory of the agrarian reform at the community level has been heavily influenced by the *tomas de tierras* that took place on cooperative lands in the 1970s and 1980s. A number of the interviewees depicted the agrarian reform as a state imposition that exacerbated the situation of the peasant communities and prompted a united response in the form of land occupations. A peasant leader who participated in *tomas* by the Comunidad Huamanrura (Puno) narrated events:

> [W]e continued to be neglected, with our lands cornered in the mountains. There was also a great need to redistribute equitably. We had demanded that and we had organized many campesino schools, many fora, meetings, seminars, and also protest marches, marches of sacrifice. At the legal level we had formulated [our demands] to the president of the republic . . . but they had not listened to us at all, the managers of the forty-four [cooperatives] that existed until then in the department of Puno, they didn't want to give us a little land which the communities had asked for. Around then we decided to take the lands.[92]

This version of events involves an implicit marginalization of community members and other rural workers who worked for the cooperative and/or opposed its dissolution. Similarly in Cusco, Sixto Villavicencio Castillo of the Comunidad Campesina de Tambo Real described those who worked for the cooperative as "engañados" (hoodwinked). When the cooperative got into financial difficulties, he claimed, they took "a little bribe" to keep their mouths shut. Approximately 10 percent of the community did not agree with the plan to take over the cooperative land. When asked what agreements had been reached with these individuals, Villavicencio replied simply that they had been marginalized.[93]

The testimonies of peasants from the Comunidad Campesina de Eqquecco Chacan (Cusco) reveal similar divisions between the *comuneros* who chose to support the cooperative and those who remained outside. For example, Isidoro Franco Pumasupa was part of Hugo Blanco's movement of peasant unionists. He refused to join the cooperative in Eqquecco Chacan and was later a key organizer of the *tomas de tierra* on the cooperative's land. In his account, the community members who supported the cooperative were gullible and "capricious," while those who remained skeptical of Velasco's claims were wise and committed to the "true" peasant struggle:

> Well, brothers, the Agrarian Reform was SINAMOS, and it arrived for us, that's what they said above and below, and they threatened me saying, Isidoro Franco, we are going to take you to the jail. Now, well, there was the first as-

> sembly in the Pampa de Anta, and they told them and offered them everything, that there would be a hospital for peasants. They are going to do it for the people, and the brothers were happy; there is going to be electric light, potable water, and hearing this the men now no longer wanted to have anything to do with us, with Isidoro Franco, for their struggle. . . . I knew what was going to happen, and I told them not to go [to the cooperative] but capricious, they went. I told them, whatever it may be, go as *cargadores* [porters] to Cusco but don't go to the cooperative and they answered me: you go and be a *cargador* in Cusco.[94]

These examples show how different group memories of the agrarian reform continue to divide peasant communities in the sierra.

By contrast, at the former Cooperativa San Isidro–Mamape in Chiclayo, there has been an explicit effort to accommodate different memories of the agrarian reform through local commemoration. In August 2011, two monuments were erected on the lands of the former cooperative: one in honor of President Velasco and another for the former hacendado, Edgardo Seoane Corrales. When I asked former Cooperative President Manuel Céspedes why the former *socios* had chosen to erect the monuments in 2011, he responded:

> Of course, the question is interesting: why [so long] after? Because we got to thinking and we recognize that if not for the revolution that Velasco led we would not have land, that not even our grandparents gave us land; no one left it to us. But thanks to his decision, to apply the agrarian reform law, they did it. For that reason, we said. And we also remember the *hacendado* because those from Mamape, the *serranos*, they have a lot of affection for him, for him we also erected [a monument].[95]

The two monuments were financed separately: the Velasco monument was sponsored by the agriculturalists Genaro Vera Roal Cava and María Damián de Vera in collaboration with the former *socios*, while the Seoane monument was sponsored by his relatives, Carlos Seoane W. and Hilda Segura Delgado. In that respect, they can be seen as distinct commemorative projects. Yet the fact that the monuments were erected simultaneously and only meters apart indicates that they form part of a collective effort to live with the conflicted history of the agrarian reform. Cespedes's comments also reveal a surprisingly personal rationale for creating the monuments: Velasco was celebrated because he gave the *socios* land, not because he altered Peruvian society in a broader sense, while Edgardo Seoane was commemorated because of the affection "the *serranos*" have for him as their former master.

No mention was made (either on the monument itself or in Cespedes' explanation) of the fact that Seoane was vice president of the republic during the first Belaúnde government and a key member of the congressional committee that drafted the 1964 agrarian reform law.

Collective memory of the agrarian reform is invoked in government discourse and in the press as a symbol to advance or resist certain political projects. But for the rural communities that lived through it, the agrarian reform also has a deeply personal significance. This was brought home to me in the comments of Hilario Pérez, former cooperative member in Huyro (Cusco). He told me that although the local *hacendado* left the area soon after his land was expropriated, one of his sons remained:

> He has a small house. He works in tourism and he comes here now. Now we talk; now like civilized people, now there is no rancor, no hatred. Rather we treat him well with respect, he always comes. Even with my son he is not "the *hacendado*'s son," he converses. [Of the sons] of the *hacendado*, none is a professional. Because he liked money. They had money, and they thought that their whole lives they would have money, no? They were not interested in education. That's why they say to my son, they say that "you have studied, I haven't studied," they say. Now they are friends, they converse.[96]

Beyond the ideological struggles of national politics, collective memory of the agrarian reform is thus also shaped by the need for people like Hilario to live alongside those who were once on the opposite side of the political and economic fence.

A Resurgent Memory?

The past two decades have seen renewed scholarly interest in the agrarian reform. Historians and social scientists have begun challenging the narrative of economic failure that dominated accounts of the reform in the 1980s and 1990s. In politics, too, there have been efforts to resurrect the Velasco government's political rhetoric in order to garner popular support among rural communities. In the 2006 and 2011 presidential elections, Ollanta Humala Tasso (a former army officer) presented himself as heir to a tradition of military reformism. Although he did not invoke Velasco's name directly, he redeployed many of the regime's populist slogans. The 2011 election results showed that Humala's support was particularly strong in departments where the rural population was more than 40 percent.[97]

Given that these departments are also characterized by high indices of poverty, this success may be due to the fact that Humala ran a populist campaign that promised to address the needs of the poor and marginalized. However, there are indications that the memory of the agrarian reform also played a role. Vladimiro Valer Delgado, a long-time political activist and former SINAMOS coordinator, argued that the triumph of Humala in the south could not be explained without reference to the agrarian reform: "[T]he South, Cusco among it, has voted for Humala because he offered changes, right? Transformation, etcetera. And that is also a result of the frustration of the agrarian reform."[98] By echoing the slogans of the agrarian reform, Humala raised the expectation that his government would prioritize the needs of the rural poor, in a manner not experienced since the Velasco era.

Once in office, however, Humala pursued a neoliberal agenda and criticized the Velasco government for absorbing wealth rather than promoting opportunity and entrepreneurship. In a 2013 speech, he wraps that message in the rhetoric of the past:

> [O]n 24 June we celebrate the Day of the Campesino, but the Day of the Campesino is a complex issue, because the campesino is the agriculturalist. He is also the man that lives in the countryside, the woman that lives in the countryside, who can dedicate themselves to other activities, because today Peru requires the effort of everyone. For that reason, if 50 years ago it was said to the campesino, they told him that the master will no longer eat from your poverty, today we have a campesino citizen to whom we say that the state will no longer eat from your poverty, because we believe today that what we have to do is eliminate poverty and generate development.[99]

Humala here reappropriates a key slogan of the agrarian reform ("the master will no longer eat from your poverty") to suggest that neoliberal economic policy also corresponds—or better corresponds—to campesino needs and interests. At the same time, he makes a departure from the class-based politics of the 1970s by defining campesinos as simply the men and women who live in the countryside, devoid of any broader collective identity or solidarity. While hoping to tap into nostalgia for the Velasco era and present himself in populist terms, Humala stuck closely to the neoliberal mantras of a small state, entrepreneurship, and support for big business.

Velasco's legacy has been used much more explicitly by his son, Javier Velasco Gonzales, who sought election to the presidency in 2016. In speeches to peasant communities he used the slogans "Campesino, the master will no longer eat from your poverty," and "The land is for those who work it."[100] His political party, "Partido Kausachum Velasquista," echoed the appeal to indigenous culture that characterized the communication strategies used by the Velasco government, and the party's newspaper used images of Velasco and Túpac Amaru in clear allusion to the Velasco era.[101] While Javier Velasco Gonzales occupies a marginal position in Peruvian politics, the fact that he was able to generate support almost entirely on the basis of his father's legacy demonstrates that the ideas and actions of the Velasco government continue to resonate among some sectors of the population.

During the 2016 general election, congressional candidate Marisa Glave provoked controversy by describing the agrarian reform as "an act of justice."[102] The Frente Amplio candidate made the remark in an interview in which she emphasized the need for a more interventionist state, particularly in relation to big business and the extractive industries. It is significant that for left-wing party Frente Amplio, support for the agrarian reform is held to be of a piece with a wider set of social values concerned with social justice, democratic participation, and wealth redistribution. This kind of political rhetoric has gained particular popularity among the urban left, indicating that collective memory of the agrarian reform cuts across urban/rural divides. It should also be noted that from an interview that spanned a diverse range of issues—from the crisis in Venezuela to the role of mining in the Peruvian economy—*El Comercio* chose Glave's brief comment on the agrarian reform as the headline for its article. In this way, references to the agrarian reform continue to function as a kind of shorthand in Peruvian political discourse.

The fiftieth anniversaries of the military coup and the agrarian reform (2018 and 2019, respectively) gave rise to a series of editorials that both celebrated and decried the Velasco regime. The content of these editorials suggests that opinion is more divided than ever and that history of the Velasco era has gained new salience in the battle to define Peru's political future. Writing in the progressive magazine *Otra Mirada*, the sociologist Nicolás Lynch commented:

> Many leftists of my generation opposed—from the Left—the Velasco government. We were wrong. The military character of the process did not let us see that social democratization and nation building are multiple and diverse tasks. Nor did we have an idea of what would come after: the pillage of our resources and the exploitation of the majority like never before in Peruvian

history. . . . The construction of democracy will not come from denying the Velasco government, as the Right insisted throughout the past half-century, but from going beyond it.[103]

For its part, *El Comercio* asserted in its editorial on the anniversary of the agrarian reform, "Half a century should be sufficient to learn to process complex changes like this without dogmatisms or taboos."[104] Yet at the same time, the newspaper remained steadfast in its view that the agrarian reform brought "an agricultural collapse from which the country has still not recovered" and treated landowners unjustly: "an expropriation should never be done without recognizing the rights of those who are the legitimate owners. You do not correct one injustice with another."[105] The right-wing journalist Rosa María Palacios similarly courted controversy on social media: "Universal beliefs after reading about the agrarian reform: a) the landowners were not [landowners]. They were land thieves. b) the peasants were slaves. All of them. Beliefs are not sciences. Absolutes, they do not need data and do not permit evidence against them. Faith is irrefutable. Amen. End."[106] The satirical tone used was a clear attempt to undercut the moral discourse often used in support of the agrarian reform. After being silenced at the height of neoliberalism in the 1990s and 2000s, historical memory of the agrarian reform has become the subject of renewed political debate in Peru.

Conclusion

Like many agricultural cooperatives established during the agrarian reform, the CAP Huando in the Huaral valley (Lima) was dissolved in 1992. In 1994, Charlotte Burenius, the stepdaughter of the former hacendado, who as a child had visited the hacienda at the height of its opulence, recorded the testimony of Zózimo Torres, a life-long trade unionist and former president of the CAP. In a particularly poignant passage of his testimony, Torres laments what is lost:

> That beautiful Huando, that cooperative so beautiful as it was in the first years, is now in the conditions of a true ruin. My ideals and the aims of my struggle were not these. They were preserving and improving Huando as a whole for the workers, the future of their children and the other generations to come, as a privileged place in time, not only as an orange-producing company, but also as a large collective that had to demonstrate before the country

> the workers' potential for management and creation. And since that has not been possible, I maintain, for me, that it is the testimony of a failure, of the failure of what Huando was and what it is now.[107]

Amid Peru's sharp turn toward neoliberalism, the widespread collapse of the cooperatives, and the social divisions that these changes gave rise to, Zózimo struggled to situate his personal memories of the agrarian reform. He recalled the agrarian reform era as a period of euphoric collective action that, at the time, appeared to hold great promise for the future, but this version of events made little sense in the neoliberal context of the 1990s.

As noted at the beginning of this chapter, the sociologist Maurice Halbwachs was among the first to emphasize the collective, socially constructed nature of memory and its articulation. Yet focused as he was on structuralist ideas of memory as a collective resource that contributed to the functioning of community, he did not address at any length the fracturing of collective memory. In examining the opposing versions of the history of the agrarian reform that are maintained by former cooperative members, expropriated landowners, SINAMOS employees, and peasant community members, this chapter has revealed the extent to which collective memory of the reform continues to be deeply divided along ideological lines.

Different collective memories of the agrarian reform are bound up with the political identities that were forged or consolidated during the Velasco era. As previous chapters have shown, state interventions in local politics, education, and the mass media actively encouraged the population to choose sides. They celebrated campesinos, workers, and young people as agents of revolution, while vilifying landowners and "dogmatic" left-wing activists. Through commemorative events and history textbooks, the Velasco regime also inserted the agrarian reform into a broader collective narrative—a people's history—in order to mobilize support for the reform at the time and encourage people to defend it under future governments. The continued efforts of the CNA to support the cooperatives and uphold the agrarian reform throughout the 1980s indicate that this strategy was partly successful. Other ways in which memory of the reform is transmitted include the meetings of left-wing activists who came of age during the Velasco era and the presence of former SINAMOS employees within nongovernmental organizations. The recent resurgence of positive reflections on the agrarian reform among the Peruvian Left—evident in conferences, newspaper articles, and exchanges on social media—demonstrates its continued potency as a political symbol.

Yet, as this chapter has highlighted, some aspects of the history of the agrarian reform do not get transmitted. Ernst van Alphen writes that "experiences and memory are enabled, shaped and structured according to the parameters of available discourses. . . . Memory is not something we have, but something we produce as individuals sharing a culture."[108] Throughout much of the 1980s and 1990s, amid the turmoil of the armed conflict, economic crisis, and the complete restructuring of the economy along neoliberal lines, the political ideals that underpinned the agrarian reform—wealth redistribution, collectivization, popular participation—were widely discredited and silenced within public discourse. The almost complete dissolution of the cooperatives appeared to invalidate the economic model they embodied, and the threat of violence from either the Shining Path or the state caused many campesinos to distance themselves from the politics of the agrarian reform, evidenced in Zózimo Torres's tendency to frame his memories of the agrarian reform as "the testimony of a failure." This narrative of failure was reinforced by deliberate efforts among right-wing politicians, newspapers, and broadcasters to paint the agrarian reform as a misguided policy directed by a malicious, authoritarian regime.

Absent from this narrative were the long histories of social inequality and racial discrimination that preceded the agrarian reform and the significant ways in which the reform tried to address them. This absence of transmission has a significant bearing on the direction of contemporary Peruvian politics. It means that younger generations, who did not experience the reform themselves, are more likely to internalize the conservative narrative circulated in the mainstream media. As Alessandro Portelli notes, historical memory "does not necessarily go down in linear form from generation to generation, from parents to children."[109] For young people, this can give their understanding of the recent past an untethered, possibly incoherent quality: "what prevails is a fluctuating memory on the surface of which formulas caught haphazardly out of common sense float and drift."[110]

Failure to transmit the social history that preceded the agrarian reform also alters the frame of reference within which land rights and wealth distribution are understood. As Fernando Eguren pointed out in 2010, when Peru's Congressional Agrarian Commission approved a proposal to limit land ownership to 40,000 hectares of cultivable land, "For those who have knowledge of the social and economic history of the second half of the last century of Peru and Latin America, the limit of 40,000 hectares is a nonsense."[111] More recently, efforts by progressive politicians, academics, and cultural producers to challenge negative portrayals of the agrarian reform suggest that the taboo surrounding its history is beginning to lift.[112] This in turn raises the prospect of a shift away from the neoliberal consensus and the possibility of a return to state-led social reform.

Yet the struggle to define the agrarian reform's place in history is not just about a battle of opposing ideologies. It also reflects the fact that the agrarian reform was a socially divisive process with which individuals and communities have subsequently had to come to terms. The way in which they choose to do so corresponds closely to the local context. In the case of the former San Isidro–Mamape cooperative in Chiclayo, the former *socios* have done relatively well out of the dissolution of the cooperative, and many continue to farm their plots as small landholdings. While clearly holding enduring significance in the local area, the tensions surrounding the agrarian reform have reduced sufficiently to allow a monument to Velasco and a monument to the former landowner to be erected side by side.

By contrast, the *comuneros* of Llanchu (Cusco) remain reluctant to talk about the agrarian reform, aware that their competing versions of the past might inflame conflict within the community. Such anxieties are heightened by the fact that the ability to attract support from the state and nongovernmental organizations depends to a large extent on the ability to project the idealized image of a traditional peasant community characterized by timeless unity. Whereas the agricultural cooperatives of the north are perceived as ephemeral institutions that have been superseded by new systems of agricultural production, peasant communities in the southern highlands (which were similarly created by legal decree in the context of the agrarian reform) have endured, but they have done so by silencing the agrarian reform's important role in their creation. Similarly, in places where peasant communities engaged in land occupations on cooperative land, opinion continues to be divided between those who supported the cooperative and those who participated in the *tomas de tierra*. The agrarian reform therefore continues to play an important part in both ideological struggles over Peru's future and the identity politics of particular communities.

Conclusion

In announcing the agrarian reform on 24 June 1969, President Velasco described it as "the start of an irreversible process that will lay the foundations of an authentic national greatness . . . cemented in social justice and the real participation of the people in the wealth and destiny of the nation."[1] Prior to the military coup of 1968, large landowners had wielded an extraordinary degree of economic and political power. The semi-servile conditions that characterized the traditional haciendas of the sierra are well documented, but the apparently modern agro-industrial complexes of the northern coast also presided over a system of low wages, poor educational opportunities, entrenched poverty, and racial discrimination. The agrarian reform promised to abolish haciendas and replace them with cooperatives that would give campesinos access to land and political participation, allowing their incorporation into the national economy. According to a slogan of the time, Peru was to become a land without masters (*tierra sin patrones*).

In assessing the political and cultural changes brought by the agrarian reform, this book has looked beyond the success or failure of particular aspects of the reform as an economic, redistributive policy. It has shown the importance of the agrarian reform as an ideological project that fundamentally reoriented the remit and actions of the state and placed the countryside at the heart of nation building. For the Velasco regime, the limited impact of the land reforms introduced in 1961 and 1964 suggested that a more comprehensive overhaul of the political system was required to produce meaningful change in rural areas. The government was also strongly influenced by intellectual currents—prevalent in many parts of the world throughout the 1970s—that identified consciousness (or its absence) as the foundation of social relations. It therefore invested unprecedented resources and intellectual energy in education, grassroots political organization, and mass media campaigns to accompany the agrarian reform and combat its opponents. These interventions shaped how the reform was perceived at the time and have continued to influence how it is remembered and talked about in Peru today.

Comparing the process of agrarian reform in Piura, Tacna, and Cusco has revealed important differences in how the agrarian reform was perceived and experienced. However, in each case there was a consistent thrust toward state expansion and the redefinition of state-society relations. SINAMOS promoters trained in Lima self-consciously carried what they had learnt in the capital to their regions and tried to implement the government plans on the ground. Sociologists and anthropologists employed by the state traveled the country producing detailed assessments on the progress of "ideological training" in each region. Even in Tacna, where the scope and strength of the agrarian reform was limited throughout much of the Velasco era, SINAMOS personnel repeatedly evaluated the impact of their actions and sought new ways to change "peasant mentalities." In all three regions the agrarian reform thus generated significant debates on national identity, popular participation, and the role of the state.

While SINAMOS is frequently referenced in studies of the Velasco era, details of how the organization operated are scarce, and records of the experiences of its staff even more so.[2] The former SINAMOS employees I interviewed described how they were selected on the basis of their "*mística*"—their commitment to the cause. They experienced the agrarian reform as a time when they "discovered" their own country, visiting remote communities and working outside the confines of government offices. In paying attention to the motivations and actions of government functionaries, this book provides a corrective to one-dimensional accounts of SINAMOS as the "steamroller" (*aplanadora*) of the Velasco regime.

The preceding chapters have also shown how the organizational structure of SINAMOS extended the state's presence beyond the traditional administrative centers (provincial and departmental prefectures) and gave state functionaries an explicitly political role: to intervene on behalf of peasant interests and encourage participation in agricultural cooperatives and peasant leagues. The variety of issues that SINAMOS officials became involved in and their widespread presence in rural areas contributed to a growing perception that the state could, and would, intervene on behalf of peasant interests. Beyond hopes of land redistribution, the agrarian reform therefore fostered expectations of fairer and more accountable treatment at the hands of the state.

The agrarian reform also expanded opportunities for political participation. Before the 1968 coup, Peruvian electoral politics were dominated by elite interests, and the majority of the rural population was unable to vote due to the literacy requirement. For many peasants, elections within the agricultural cooperatives (open to all members irrespective of literacy) provided their first experience of voting. The state's efforts to organize the rural population into agrarian leagues, federations, and the CNA fostered a new generation of campesino leaders whose activism extended far beyond local land disputes or workers' rights. The resources and administrative support made available to the leagues and federations allowed them to develop a national network and draw public attention to rural issues.

This push toward popular participation was always in tension with the regime's authoritarian tendencies. Given the strength of anticommunist sentiment within the armed forces and the military's historical antipathy to the Aprista party, the creation of agrarian leagues and federations was motivated at least in part by the government's desire to sideline its political rivals and retain control of the reform process. The political repression used by the military government against those perceived as "ultras" and "saboteurs of the agrarian reform" should not be underestimated.[3] Paradoxically, however, the Velasco regime's drive to bring peasant organizations into its political orbit also helped revitalize the independent CCP, which mobilized to defend its autonomy and assert political control in the countryside through alliances with VR and the MIR. The growth of political participation thus did not necessarily follow the path set out by Velasco's vision of a "social democracy of full participation." But this does not mean that the model should be viewed as incidental to the political developments of the period; the "corporatist" structures introduced by the agrarian reform crucially provided the context in which more autonomous political movements could develop.

The educational initiatives that accompanied the agrarian reform also oriented peasants toward greater political participation. Arguing that the existing education system had maintained privilege and inequality, the 1970 report of the education reform commission called for education that would "achieve a new man in a new society."[4] Drawing on the ideas of "consciousness raising" popularized by Paulo Freire, government education programs not only encouraged peasants to critically examine the inequalities they faced in their daily lives but also presented education as a means to political empowerment. The long-term consequences of these "consciousness raising" activities are captured well in the words of former cooperative member Hilario Pérez: "[T]he hacendado [cannot] return to the countryside. Now the mentality of the people has changed. Now it isn't like before, humiliated. Now they know their law, their rights, they know everything. How is the hacendado going to come back?"[5]

In addition to expanding the state's presence in rural areas and creating new opportunities for political participation, the agrarian reform provided a platform for building a more inclusive national identity. The use of indigenous music and dance in official adjudication ceremonies framed the redistribution of land as part of a broader recognition of rights and culture. Propaganda in the form of posters and pamphlets used images of campesinos from diverse parts of the country and championed Túpac Amaru II—long marginalized by conservative histories of Peru—as a symbol of the "new Peru." Curriculum changes brought by the 1972 education reform encouraged the celebration of indigenous heroes over Spanish or creole ones, and new textbooks used images of workers, peasants, and people of different ethnicities in place of generic, middle-class urban figures.[6] Radio programs produced by SINAMOS used peasant correspondents and targeted a specifically rural audience that had often been overlooked by the mainstream media.

The government's *indigenismo* and celebration of popular culture had lasting consequences for the occupation of public space. Puppeteers Gastón Aramayo and Vicky Morales, who worked for SINAMOS as promoters of the agrarian reform, recalled that in the 1960s one would be unlikely to see a woman wearing the *pollera* (traditional Andean skirts) or a man wearing a *chullo* (Andean hat) in the center of Lima; Andean music was circumscribed to the coliseums, and the Spanish colonial influence was celebrated as part of "*Lima señorial*"—stately Lima. With the leaders of the Velasco government, however, the dominance of the landowning elites was called into question: "they began to propose new concepts," said Aramayo and Morales, "other ways of seeing the world."[7] CNA member Marcelino Bustamente López, originally from the indigenous community of San Pedro de Tapacocha in Ancash, described how, when he visited Lima in the 1950s, he was stopped by the police and prevented from walking down streets that were reserved for "white" Peruvians. He contrasted this experience with visiting the capital again for the 1974 inauguration of the CNA, when campesino delegates were welcomed into the chamber of the Congress of the Republic and the CNA's offices were established close to the main square.[8]

Regional Differences

Although conceived in the center and inspired by global trends in policy making, the agrarian reform had to be implemented in very different social and political contexts in which a range of agricultural models and cultural traditions prevailed. Moreover, the political impact of the agrarian reform varied across the country. In Piura, the agrarian reform was presented primarily as a class struggle against the oligarchy, with workers on the cotton plantations promised better living conditions and the possibility of organizing politically through the cooperatives and agrarian leagues. These openings meant new opportunities for peasant organizations—which had historically been limited—and made the region a hotbed for political struggles involving peasant communities, SINAMOS, and the New Left political parties. Although the model of production cooperatives held little traction in a region more familiar with service cooperatives, those who participated in the cooperatives found ways of adapting the model to suit their own needs and, in the case of the Catacaos peasant community, were able to resist having their communal traditions subsumed into state-controlled cooperatives. Although the region has subsequently experienced an intense reconcentration of land ownership, the agrarian reform left a deep impression on the identity of peasant communities, the vision of left-wing activists, and local approaches to rural development (embodied in the work of CIPCA).

In Cusco, the idea that the agrarian reform was a chance to reclaim indigenous land rights formed a prominent part of government propaganda, alongside the use of Quechua and the incorporation of regional musical and cultural traditions. Popular support for the regime was strong, as indicated by SINAMOS's success in organizing the majority of the peasant population into agrarian leagues within a short period of time. Yet the power of the hacendados was deeply entrenched, and many proved successful at using personal influence to evade the reform or their longstanding personal power to persuade their employees not to participate in the cooperatives. CENCIRA and SINAMOS personnel also encountered difficulties in communicating the government's cooperative ideology; their presentation of collectivized production in moralistic terms bore little relation to local conceptualizations of property and reciprocal labor. Significantly, government promoters appear to have dedicated more attention to "consciousness" and ideological training than to the local ecological conditions that made smaller production units more attractive than collectivized production.

Tacna was not a priority area for the agrarian reform authorities, and their impact there was much lower than in either Piura or Cusco. SINAMOS personnel nevertheless used the reform context to extend the state's presence in rural areas, reorganize peasant communities, and promote cooperative systems. In a region shaped by its frontier location, they presented the agrarian reform as an opportunity to participate in the nation's radical, anti-imperialist revolution. Yet the predominance of minifundism meant that there were few opportunities for major land expropriation, and indigenous communities remained ambivalent about the advantages of official recognition as a peasant community. Promoters complained of indifference among peasants and sustained resistance from conservative parties such as APRA and the Unión Odriísta, whose members denounced them as communist agitators and sought to control the new agrarian leagues and federations. Through systematic comparison of state interventions and local responses in different regions, I have purposefully highlighted the importance of regional politics in shaping the overall outcome of the agrarian reform. This approach is illuminating not only for better understanding past events in Peru but also for interpreting current and future developments.

Land Reform as an Ideological Struggle

While clearly important, the legal mechanisms and economic provisions that underpin any program of land reform can tell only part of the story. Carmen Soliz observed in the case of Bolivia's 1953 agrarian reform that "there was nothing intrinsic in the law that would determine the result of the process. . . . The outcome of the court cases—sometimes very different from one to another—was the result of the particular relations of power and networks that petitioners established within and outside the courts."[9] The debates that occurred beyond courtrooms and government offices played a key role in shaping public perceptions of the reform and informing the narrative that different actors constructed in defending their preferred outcome. This is equally true of the Peruvian case, where peasant cooperatives and communities often used the government's own rhetoric to push for modifications in the application of the agrarian reform as well as to demand its application.

Examining how the Peruvian agrarian reform was represented in newspapers, posters, pamphlets, and film—sources not normally included within studies of agrarian reform—demonstrates the broad cultural impact of the agrarian reform. For example, government efforts to communicate with the peasantry about the agrarian reform via the radio stimulated the development of community radio stations. Oral history interviews allowed access to perceptions of the agrarian reform at the time and showed how these perceptions have evolved over subsequent decades. While anthropologists have long incorporated ethnography into their studies of agrarian reform, historians have relied more heavily on documentary history. Given the high rates of illiteracy in areas across the world where agrarian reform was introduced (particularly during the middle decades of the twentieth century), this has led to an emphasis on the actions of the bureaucracy and legal systems. By contrast, relying on a variety of sources and methodologies, as this book does, allows the rich political debates that state-led agrarian reform produced to be heard again.

Recent research on land reform in other parts of Latin America has demonstrated its importance in reshaping political culture. Examining the cases of Brazil, Chile, and Venezuela, Nancy Lapp found that redistributive land reform coincided with the expansion of suffrage, as politicians used land reform to build their support base, and the push for reform was in turn strengthened by the growth of mass parties.[10] In Chile, Heidi Tinsman found that the successive agrarian reforms of the Frei and Allende governments brought changes to gender roles within rural society, with men being presented as the protagonists of reform and women increasingly sidelined as homemakers and indirect beneficiaries. These gender politics in turn contributed to the wider characteristics of Allende's "road to socialism" and helped define the contours of the Chilean labor movement.[11] In the case of Bolivia, Carmen Soliz has argued that the nationalist paradigm promoted throughout that country's agrarian reform continued to frame Bolivian political debate even after the Movimiento Nacionalista Revolucionario regime was overthrown by a military coup in 1964.[12] By including state interventions in local politics, education, and mass communication within the study of the Peruvian agrarian reform, this book adds to growing efforts to uncover the broad political changes stimulated by agrarian reform across Latin America.

This is important from the perspective of historical completeness because factoring in these other dimensions of the agrarian reform process helps account for its continued significance in Peruvian society. But this approach is also highly relevant to current debates on land use across the globe. Writing in 2006, Michael Courville and Raj Patel argued that in many parts of the world the reorganization of the state along neoliberal lines "forces any current demand for agrarian reform firmly within the parameters of a depoliticized (market-oriented) project" and "avoids addressing the other dimensions of power and historical inequity that in the current agenda have marginalized both the rural sector and the rural poor."[13] Studies of land reform conducted by the World Bank in the 1990s emphasized the need to clarify landholders' legal property and facilitate open competition in land markets. So-called market-led agrarian reform proposed technical and legal solutions for agricultural development in ways that overlooked the entrenched power inequalities that underpinned the distribution of land and people's ability to cultivate it productively. The Peruvian case suggests that significant redistribution of land cannot be achieved without an accompanying political drive to challenge elite power and tackle racial discrimination. The contrasting case of Colombia bears out this assertion: despite agrarian reform emerging on the political agenda in Colombia at roughly the same time as in Peru, state-led agrarian reform there was muted and easily circumvented by major landowners. The absence of significant land reform was a key factor in the country's long-running civil war.[14]

By highlighting the growth of political participation during a military dictatorship, the preceding chapters have also questioned the tendency to interpret Latin America's so-called transitions to democracy in terms of the rise of the human rights agenda and a global break with the statist policies of the 1960s and 1970s. As Greg Grandin satirically observes, this perspective is underpinned by the belief that the free market forms the basis for democracy by fostering the development of the individual, while "mass political movements, including the populist movements Latin America is famous for, work against this process of individuation, functioning something like totalitarian transmission belts, delivering the unmoored self to the absolutist state and its promise of security, justice, and unity."[15] This book challenges such schematic accounts of Latin American politics, demonstrating that voting and other forms of participation in decision-making offered by agricultural cooperatives were an important foundation for modern democratic practices. Moreover, despite extensive government propaganda surrounding the agrarian reform, state interventions in education, local political activity, and mass communication generally increased opportunities for previously underrepresented groups to think, coordinate, and act independently. As a result of the agrarian reform, campesinos understood themselves more fully as citizens, and rural communities found their importance in national politics substantially increased.

Among contemporary social movements, the agrarian reform retains significant political currency. On 5 June 2009, a confrontation between police and protesters in the Amazonian region of Bagua resulted in 33 deaths (23 police officers and 10 civilians).[16] The violence (subsequently referred to as the "baguazo") followed 58 days of tension and 11 days of blockades, as the local populations of Bagua and Utcubamba protested against new legislation that allowed private companies access to the Amazon for oil development.[17] Twenty days after the events in Bagua, *La Revista Agraria* combined its coverage of the violence with a special edition on the fortieth anniversary of the agrarian reform. The front cover featured a split image, with half of a man's face taken from a 1969 photo of an Andean peasant and half taken from a 2009 photo of an Amazonian indigenous man. The headline stated: "40 years after the agrarian reform other indigenous people demand to be citizens."[18] The linking of the agrarian reform to current struggles over resource extraction indicates its continued importance as a political reference point for debates on citizenship, which the Velasco government understood as a series of social rights rather than as a formal legal-political category. This distinction is highly relevant to indigenous communities' contemporary battles to be consulted regarding oil development and its potential destruction of the territory in which they live. Exploring how memory of the agrarian reform has been invoked and reformulated demonstrates just how far agrarian reform is from being a closed chapter in Peru's history.

Notes

Introduction

1. Long and Roberts, "Agrarian Structures," 11:563.

2. Otero, "Agrarian Reform in Mexico."

3. Guerra, *Visions of Power in Cuba*, 59.

4. Tinsman, *Partners in Conflict.*

5. Thiesenhusen, ed., *Searching for Agrarian Reform in Latin America.*

6. Such labor was not always remunerated. For example, *yanaconaje*, a labor practice that had its origins in pre-Hispanic Andean society, consisted of a highly exploitative arrangement between landowner and laborer (*yanacona*). While the landowner supplied access to land, water, machinery, and capital, the *yanacona* received no wages and was required to cultivate the product determined by the landowner and sell the produce exclusively to the landowner. According to José Matos Mar, a modernized version of *yanaconaje* persisted in the Chancay Valley (Lima) well into the 1960s. Matos Mar, *Yanaconaje y reforma agraria en el Perú.*

7. Cleaves and Scurrah, *Agriculture, Bureaucracy, and Military Government in Peru*, 32. This is comparable to the situation in Ecuador, where in 1954, 1 percent of agricultural units controlled 64 percent of agricultural land, while 82 percent of agricultural units had fewer than 5 hectares and made up 11 percent of land. Forster, "*Minifundistas* in Tunguraghua, Ecuador," 93. The dominance of large estates was considerably lower in Argentina where, in 1970, 36.9 percent of land was occupied by latifundios and 3.4 percent by minifundios, leaving 59.7 percent occupied by medium-sized farms. Todaro, *Economic Development in the Third World*, 295.

8. Martha Meier Miró Quesada, "Túpac Mouse, por Martha Meier M.Q.," *El Comercio*, 4 June 2014, http://elcomercio.pe/opinion/columnistas/tupac-mouse-martha-meier-m-q-noticia-1733944.

9. "La Reforma Agraria de 1969," *La Revista Agraria* 108 (2009): 19.

10. Wright, *Latin America in the Era of the Cuban Revolution*, 112.

11. Wright, *Latin America in the Era of the Cuban Revolution*, 112.

12. The Revolutionary Government of the Armed Forces also differed from Peru's previous military governments in that it was an institutional movement rather than one

centered on a single general or charismatic caudillo, as reflected in the title assumed by the government. See North, "Ideological Orientations of Rulers." Although for reasons of style I refer to the regime as the "Velasco government," it should be remembered that General Velasco did not develop the kind of cult of personality adopted by leaders such as Argentina's Juan Perón or Brazil's Getúlio Vargas. For further discussion of the particular characteristics of military reformism in Peru, see Víctor Villanueva, *El CAEM y la revolución de la Fuerza Armada* (Lima: IEP, 1972), and Dirk Kruijt, *Revolution by Decree: Peru 1960–1975* (Purdue, IN: Purdue University Press, 2003).

13. Velasco Alvarado, *Plan Inca*, 1.

14. The Velasco government also pioneered the creation of industrial communities, conceived as a way of reforming capitalist companies to increase the participation of workers in the property, management, and profit of their company. Similar to the imposition of agrarian reform, the creation of industrial communities challenged the power of company owners and proposed a reorganization of the economy according to social objectives rather than capitalist principles. Franco, *Perú: Participación popular*; Knight, "New Forms of Economic Organization in Peru," 350–401.

15. D.L. 17716, Title 1, Article 1.

16. In practice this line was difficult to maintain, as Colin Harding observed in the case of Piura: "In most cases of land occupations—over 80 in Piura by mid-1973—the reform authorities have been forced to accept a fait accompli, expropriate the land very quickly and hand it over to a cooperative of the permanent and temporary labourers, despite the fact that invasions are expressly defined as an act of sabotage against the agrarian reform." Harding, "Agrarian Reform," 13.

17. The sharp shift in policy direction between the Velasco and Morales Bermúdez regimes is highlighted in María del Pilar Tello's in-depth interviews with former members of both governments. Tello, *¿Golpe o revolución?*

18. Economists have generally concluded that the agrarian reform did not have a positive impact on Peru's economic performance. See Caballero, *Agricultura, reforma agraria y pobreza campesina*, and Alvarez, *Política agraria y estancamiento de la agricultura*. However, it is important to note that the agrarian reform's failure to improve productivity has often been used to support the argument that it should never have been carried out, despite the fact that the Velasco government presented the reform primarily as an act of social justice rather than as a plan to raise productivity. See Revesz, *Estado, algodón y productores agrarios*.

19. Cleaves and Scurrah, *Agriculture, Bureaucracy, and Military Government in Peru*; Stepan, *The State and Society*; Lowenthal and McClintock, eds., *The Peruvian Experiment*; Chaplin, ed., *Peruvian Nationalism*; McClintock, *Peasant Cooperatives and Political Change in Peru*.

20. Matos Mar, *Yanaconaje y reforma agraria en el Perú*; Rubín de Celis T., *Las CAPs de Piura*; Eguren López, *Reforma agraria, cooperativazación y lucha campesina*; Harding, "Agrarian Reform"; Deere, *Household and Class Relations*; Arce Espinoza, *La reforma agraria en Piura*.

21. Eguren López, *Reforma agraria, cooperativazación y lucha campesina*; Del Mastro Puccio, *Luchas campesinas*. Fliers produced by peasant organizations were reprinted within appendices in both titles and proved valuable for this book.

22. Eguren López, *Reforma agraria, cooperativización y lucha campesina*.

23. Chaplin, "The Revolutionary Challenge and Peruvian Militarism," 23.

24. Seligmann, *Between Reform and Revolution.*

25. Heilman, *Politics in Rural Ayacucho, 1895–1980.*

26. Rénique, *La batalla por Puno.*

27. To date there has been little comparative research on experiences of the agrarian reform in different regions of Peru. An important exception is Enrique Mayer's *Ugly Stories of the Peruvian Agrarian Reform*, a book that brings together oral histories gathered in the contrasting regions of Lima, Piura, Cusco, and Junín. Through conversations with landowners, peasants, cooperative administrators, and government officials, Mayer provides a vivid picture of how the nature and impact of the agrarian reform varied across social sectors and different areas of the country. Yet place and region are not used as an organizing principle, and the author takes a somewhat eclectic approach to the selection of research sites: "I selected places that I remembered due to their notoriety or because they were emblematic to the reform process, or because I was familiar with the area from previous fieldwork." Mayer, *Ugly Stories*, v.

28. Singh, "The Theoretical Potential of the Within-Nation Comparison," 861–886.

29. Singh, *How Solidarity Works for Welfare.*

30. While *regional* rather than *subnational* is the preferred term within Latin American scholarship, the concept is essentially the same, denoting a region or group within a nation. Examples of regional comparative research on Latin American history include *Exits from the Labyrinth* by Lomnitz-Adler and *Cultural Politics in Revolution* by Vaughan. These studies have strongly informed the approach taken in this book.

31. Bernex de Falen and Revesz, *Atlas regional de Piura*, 8.

32. Bernex de Falen and Revesz, *Atlas regional de Piura*, 44.

33. Arce Espinoza, *La reforma agraria en Piura*, 29.

34. Arce Espinoza, *La reforma agraria en Piura*, 19.

35. Kottek et al., "World Map," 259–263.

36. Hobsbawm, "A Case of Neo-feudalism," 31–50.

37. Encinas Martín, Pérez Casado, and Alonso Ordieres, *Historia social y religiosa del siglo XX.*

38. Neira, *Cuzco: Tierra y muerte*, 12.

39. Nicolás Lynch, "La polémica indigenista," 5–46.

40. Del Mastro Puccio, *Luchas campesinas.*

41. Kottek et al., "World Map."

42. Panty Neyra, *Tacna, economía y sociedad*, 26.

43. Panty Neyra, *Tacna, economía y sociedad*, 30.

44. Panty Neyra, *Tacna, economía y sociedad*, 30.

45. North and Dos Santos, "Orígenes y crecimiento del partido aprista," 175.

46. Panty Neyra, *Tacna, economía y sociedad*, 211.

47. Skuban, *Nationalism and Identity on the Peruvian-Chilean Frontier.*

48. Héctor Béjar, a former SINAMOS official, interviewed by the author in Lima, 12 April 2010.

49. The most extensive and well-preserved cinema archive is the Filmoteca de Lima, now housed at the Pontifical Catholic University of Peru.

50. Stoler, "Colonial Archives and the Arts of Governance," 87–109.

51. Mayer, *Ugly Stories*, xviii.

52. This did not mean that they were immune to government influence, however, as discussed in chapter 4.

53. These assessments were consulted at the Peruvian National Library, Pontifical Catholic University of Peru, and CEDEP (a nongovernmental organization) in Lima, and in local archives in the regions of Piura, Tacna, and Cusco.

54. Portelli, "Uchronic Dreams," 46–55; Summerfield, "Culture and Composure," 65–93; Thomson, *Anzac Memories*.

55. For a detailed analysis of the posters of the agrarian reform, see Cant, "'Land for Those Who Work It,'" 1–37.

Chapter 1: The History of the Land Question in Peru

1. For pre-Columbian systems of reciprocity and trade, see Bauer, *The Development of the Inca State*; Harris, Larson, and Tandeter, eds., *Ethnicity, Markets, and Migration in the Andes*; and Sammells, "Production, Trade, Reciprocity, and Markets," 251–265.

2. Keith, *Conquest and Agrarian Change*.

3. For a history of colonial haciendas in Peru, see Cushner, *Lords of the Land*; Davies, *Landowners in Colonial Peru*; and Spalding, *Huarochirí*.

4. The term *ayllu* actually encompasses a variety of social ties, including kinship, territory, religious practice, language use, and occupation. See Sammells, "Production, Trade, Reciprocity, and Markets," 252.

5. Keith, *Conquest and Agrarian Change*, chapter 5.

6. Klaren, *Peru: Society and Nationhood in the Andes*, 69–98.

7. Mar and Mejía, *La reforma agraria en el Perú*, 19.

8. Cumpa and Alfaro, *Capitalismo y formación regional*, 21.

9. Peloso and Tenenbaum, *Liberals, Politics, and Power*.

10. Piel, *El capitalismo agrario en el Perú*.

11. A number of authors have underscored the importance of the nineteenth century, with the breakthrough of liberal ideas about land and changes to the global economy, in deepening existing land inequality. In the case of highland Bolivia, Erwin Peter Grieshaber argues that hacienda-community coexistence remained in balance (in terms of the size of the land controlled) until the late nineteenth century. In Peru, the power of the latifundistas was strengthened considerably following the war with Chile (1879–1884), as their participation in global markets increased and both foreign and national investment in export agriculture and mining grew. According to Heraclio Bonilla, this led to "an assault on the adjacent peasant communities." See Grieshaber, *Survival of Indian Communities in Nineteenth-Century Bolivia*; Bonilla, "Comunidades de indígenas y estado nación en el Perú," 35–51. For more recent research on this trend in the highland border region between Peru and Bolivia, see Cottyn, "Renegotiating Communal Autonomy," https://biblio.ugent.be/publication/4432196.

12. Contreras, "El centralismo peruano en su perspectiva histórica," 81–82.

13. Mar, *Yanaconaje y reforma agraria en el Perú*.

14. The presence of indigenous communities varied substantially across Peru. In 1928, just 0.32 percent of indigenous communities were located in the northern coastal department of Lambayeque. The number of communities in the northern departments as a whole comprised 12.23 percent of the total, whereas indigenous communities in the southern departments comprised 73.24 percent. See Gómez Cumpa and Bazán Alfaro, *Capitalismo y formación regional*, 21.

15. Gómez Cumpa and Bazán Alfaro, *Capitalismo y formación regional*, 21.
16. Klaren, *Formación de las haciendas azucareras.*
17. Matos Mar and Mejía, *La reforma agraria en el Perú*, 24.
18. Varese, "Social Justice and Cultural Rights in the Peruvian Amazon," 60–79.
19. Matos Mar and Mejía, *La reforma agraria en el Perú*, 114.
20. Klaren, *Formación de las haciendas azucareras.*
21. Matos Mar and Mejía, *La reforma agraria en el Perú*, 22.
22. Kapsoli Escudero, *Los movimientos campesinos en el Perú.*
23. Kapsoli Escudero, *Los movimientos campesinos en el Perú*, 126.
24. During peasant protests in La Mar province (Ayacucho) in 1923, for example, more than 60 peasants were killed when they challenged the landowners' abusive demands. Kapsoli Escudero, *Los movimientos campesinos en el Perú*, 65–67.
25. Flores Galindo, "Movimientos campesinos en el Perú."
26. Flores Galindo, "Movimientos campesinos en el Perú."
27. Klaren, *Formación de las haciendas azucareras*, 71–100.
28. Hobsbawm, "A Case of Neo-feudalism," 31.
29. Hobsbawm, "A Case of Neo-feudalism," 45.
30. For a detailed account of the protests in La Convención, see Rolando Rojas, *La revolución de los arrendires.*
31. Neira, *Cuzco: Tierra y muerte.*
32. "La reforma agraria es urgente," *La Prensa*, 9 May 1962.
33. Mariátegui, *Siete ensayos de interpretación de la realidad peruana*, 32.
34. North and Dos Santos, "Orígenes y crecimiento del partido aprista," 165.
35. Klaren, *Formación de las haciendas azucareras.*
36. Klaren, *Formación de las haciendas azucareras.*
37. Contreras and Cueto, *Historia del Perú contemporáneo*, 314–324.
38. Malpica, *Los dueños del Perú*, 68.
39. Malpica, *Los dueños del Perú*, 92–96.
40. Béjar, *Peru 1965*, 46–59.
41. Kapsoli Escudero, *Los movimientos campesinos en el Perú*, 104.
42. Béjar, *Peru 1965.*
43. Caballero, "From Belaúnde to Belaúnde," 8.
44. Guardia Mayorga, *La reforma agraria en el Perú*, 41–47.
45. Sklar and Hagen, comps., Inter-American relations.
46. Matos Mar and Mejía, *La reforma agraria en el Perú*, 86–90.
47. Matos Mar and Mejía, *La reforma agraria en el Perú*, 91–93.
48. Mayer, *Ugly Stories*, 17–19.
49. Ministerio de Agricultura, *Exposición de la Oficina Nacional de Reforma y Promoción Agraria*, 1.
50. Matos Mar and Mejía, *La reforma agraria en el Perú*, 94–104.
51. Matos Mar and Mejía, *La reforma agraria en el Perú*, 103.
52. Kruijt, *La revolución por decreto*, 94.
53. Kruijt, *La revolución por decreto*, 97.
54. Stepan, *The State and Society.*
55. McClintock, "Velasco, Officers, and Citizens, 280.
56. Alberto Ruiz Eldredge, unpublished interview by María del Pilar Tello, conducted in Lima about 1981. I am indebted to María del Pilar Tello for allowing access

in Lima to the unpublished transcripts of her interviews with senior figures of the Velasco government.

57. See, for example, Matos Mar, *Las actuales comunidades de indígenas* and *Dominación y cambios en el Perú rural*, and Bourricaud, *Cambios en Puno: Estudios de sociología andina*.

58. Revesz, "Necesidad de una nueva interpretación de la reforma agraria y sus efectos," 87–121.

59. Benjamín Semanez Concha, unpublished interview by María del Pilar Tello conducted in Lima about 1981.

60. Semanez Concha, unpublished interview.

61. De la Peña, "Rural Mobilizations in Latin America Since c. 1920," 6:459–460.

62. Agrarian reform zones were created gradually across the country following the passage of D.L. 17716. However, they were based directly on the agrarian zones first created by the Agrarian Research and Promotion Service in 1960 to promote agricultural development. These same zonal divisions were retained by the Velasco government for both pragmatic and political reasons. See Michael Albertus, "Land Reform and Civil Conflict."

63. The limit was two hundred hectares on the coast and between five and fifty hectares in the sierra. See D.L. 17716, Title 3, chapter 1.

64. The agrarian reform bonds later became a highly contentious political issue, as subsequent governments refused to pay out. See Seoane, *La deuda secreta del Perú*.

65. Seligmann, *Between Reform and Revolution*, 93–104.

66. Seligmann, *Between Reform and Revolution*, 62–69.

67. Seligmann, *Between Reform and Revolution*, 59.

68. For discussion of the internal differentiation among the peasantry created by the reform and the problem of underemployment in the Piura region, see Van der Ploeg, *El futuro robado*.

69. D.L. 17716, Title 10, Article 119.

70. D.L. 17716, Title 6, Article 77, and Title 10, Article 117.

71. Martín Sánchez, "Indigenismo bifronte en el gobierno peruano de Velasco Alvarado," 191–250.

72. Alvarez and Caballero, *Aspectos cuantitativos de la reforma agraria*, 25. Note that this figure refers to all types of land and does not take into account different types of land, degrees of irrigation, etc.

73. D.L. 17716, Title 7, Article 91, stated: "The order of priority will be the following: Cooperatives, Peasant Communities, Agricultural Social Interest Societies, small and medium awardees."

74. For the impact of the restructuring process on peasant communities, see Rosa Elvira Huayre Cochachin, "Reforma agraria y comunidades campesinas (Perú, 1969–1975): Aproximación al proceso de reestructuración comunal," *Heraldos* (CEHIS [Centro de Estudiantes de Historia]-UNMSM [Universidad Nacional Mayor de San Marcos]), 1, no. 1 (2012): 104–114.

75. Chu, "The Answer Was Cooperative."

76. Chu, "The Answer Was Cooperative," 36.

77. McClintock, "Velasco, Officers, and Citizens."

78. McClintock, "Velasco, Officers, and Citizens,

79. North and Korovkin, *The Peruvian Revolution and the Officers in Power*, 90.

80. Jorge del Prado (speech to the International Conference of Communist Parties and Workers, Moscow, June 5–17, 1969), https://www.marxists.org/espanol/delprado/1969/junio/17.htm.

81. The Partido Comunista del Perú—Sendero Luminoso, which would later initiate war against the state in 1980, also emerged during this period; however, it did not attract serious attention until the 1970s. Even then it was considered a minor faction of little concern by the police and government authorities. See Letts, *La izquierda peruana*.

82. Dorais, "La crítica maoísta peruana frente a la reforma agraria de Velasco."

83. Armando Zapata, interviewed by the author in Piura, 16 April 2013.

84. Letts, *La izquierda peruana*.

85. Dorais, "La crítica maoísta peruana."

86. Vanguardia Revolucionaria, "Aplastemos a los hacendados, expulsemos a los yanquis."

87. Dorais, "La crítica maoísta peruana."

88. Juan Velasco Alvarado, "Mensaje a la nación del Presidente del Perú, General de División EP Juan Velasco Alvarado, el 28 de julio de 1973," http://www.congreso.gob.pe/participacion/museo/congreso/mensajes/mensaje_nacion_congreso_28_julio_1973.

89. CENPLA/SINAMOS, *Grupos Maoistas*, 9.

Chapter 2: SINAMOS

1. Kruijt, *La revolución por decreto*.

2. Following the military coup of 3 October 1968, the National Congress was suspended. Under military rule all legislation was passed by legal decree.

3. Aldana Rivera, "Pensando la región," 27.

4. See, for example, Lowenthal, ed., *The Peruvian Experiment* (1975); Martín Sánchez, *La revolución peruana* (2002); Tello, *Golpe o revolución?* (1983); Franco, ed., *El Perú de Velasco*, 3 vols. (1986).

5. Carlos Delgado, a close advisor to Velasco and one of the architects of SINAMOS, wrote: "The System was actually created in April 1972. But the idea of SINAMOS emerged much earlier. In other words, long before those decrees were formulated and approved, the revolutionary leadership gained full consciousness of the problem that SINAMOS would be destined to solve. In effect, at the end of June 1969 . . . among the political leadership of the revolution the problem of participation in the development of the process was clearly stated as the principal problem of the revolution. From then on this question was debated and analyzed on numerous occasions by the leaders of the government." Delgado, "SINAMOS," 22–23.

6. Lomnitz-Adler, *Exits from the Labyrinth*.

7. Contreras, "El centralismo peruano en su perspectiva histórica," 28. As Contreras notes, the tension between central and departmental layers of government has been recurrent throughout Peru's republican history, with the central government in Lima typically promising decentralization and greater regional autonomy during times of plenty and taking back control during moments of financial crisis.

8. Mesclier, "De la complementariedad a la voluntad de aplanar los Andes," 541–562.

9. The Velasco regime was a government of the armed forces, with major govern-

ment departments distributed among the army, navy, and air force. However, Velasco and the majority of his advisory council (Comité de Asesoramiento de la Presidencia) were soldiers by training, and the army exerted greater influence on the policies and direction of the government than either the navy or the air force. What follows deals primarily with perceptions within the army of regional territory.

10. Kruijt, *La revolución por decreto*, 87.

11. Koonings and Kruijt, *Political Armies*, 1.

12. Masterson, *Militarism and Politics in Latin America*, 19.

13. "Nueva mentalidad militar," 12–15, 31.

14. "Nueva mentalidad militar," 12–15, 31.

15. "El ejército educa," vi–vii.

16. "El campesino y la reforma agraria," 39.

17. Méndez G., "Las paradojas del autoritarismo," 18.

18. Méndez G., "Las paradojas del autoritarismo," 29.

19. "El ejército educa," vi–vii.

20. Masterson, *Militarism and Politics in Latin America*, 228.

21. "Me siento feliz de retornar a Piura dijo el Presidente a los periodistas," *El Tiempo*, 9 October 1969, 4.

22. "Me siento feliz de retornar a Piura dijo el Presidente a los periodistas," *El Tiempo*, 9 October 1969, 4.

23. Francisco Guerra García, interviewed by the author in Lima, 27 August 2012.

24. For details on the early propaganda efforts of the Velasco government, see Cant, "'Land for Those Who Work It,'" 1–37.

25. Pedro Morote (former director of communications at the Ministry of Agriculture), interviewed by the author in Lima, 2 October 2012.

26. D.L. 18896, Article 1.

27. D.L. 18896, Article 2.

28. Delgado, "SINAMOS," 6–25.

29. D.L. 18896, Article 1.

30. Docafe, "La nueva historia del Perú," 442. Presented as a general history textbook, *Historia general de los peruanos*, in fact, dedicated a considerable proportion of its third volume to the achievements of "the Revolution" and is therefore an important source for how the regime understood and portrayed its actions at the time.

31. As well as expressing the government's ideological desire to serve the people, the organizational structure of SINAMOS can be read as an attempt to bypass the established bureaucracy. Resistance to the government's reforms from within the bureaucracy was a matter of constant concern to the Velasco government.

32. SINAMOS, *Movilización social: ¿De quién? ¿Para qué?*, 6.

33. Hugo Herrera, interviewed by the author in Piura, 9 April 2014.

34. Former SINAMOS Piura regional communications office employee who requested anonymity, interviewed by the author in Lima, 7 May 2013.

35. Former SINAMOS Piura regional communications office employee who requested anonymity, interviewed by the author in Lima, 7 May 2013.

36. Armando Zapata (former VR activist), interviewed by the author in Piura, 16 April 2013.

37. "Memorandum 067-75-DDR" (8 July 1975), legajo 07-0027, SINAMOS, ORAMS XI, Gobierno Regional de Tacna (GRT), Archivo Regional de Tacna (ART).

38. Former SINAMOS Piura regional communications office employee who requested anonymity, interviewed by the author in Lima, 7 May 2013.

39. Carlos Franco, in an unpublished interview by Maria del Pilar Tello in Lima, ca. 1981.

40. North and Korovkin, *The Peruvian Revolution and the Officers in Power*, 49. The authors note that divisions within the regime became more severe as the class and sectoral conflicts unleashed by its reforms accelerated.

41. Apel, *De la hacienda a la comunidad*, 77–89.

42. Revesz, "El campesino piurano en la escena regional," 113.

43. Zona Agraria I (Piura), *Catacaos*.

44. Panamericana, *Videoteca histórica de la televisión pionera en el Perú*, DVD 1, Reforma Agraria (Abancay: Biblioteca Nacional del Peru, Mediateca). The *marinera*, a Peruvian coastal dance, is particularly associated with the north of the country.

45. Arce Espinoza, *La reforma agraria en Piura*, 44.

46. Andrés Luna Vargas (a native of Piura and leader of the CCP during the Velasco years), interviewed by the author in Lima, 8 October 2012.

47. Van der Ploeg, *El futuro robado*.

48. Van der Ploeg, *El futuro robado*, 83.

49. Van der Ploeg, *El futuro robado*, 72.

50. Armando Zapata, interviewed by the author in Piura, 16 April 2013.

51. Armando Zapata, interviewed by the author in Piura, 16 April 2013.

52. García Sayán, *Tomas de tierras en el Perú*, 19–71.

53. Diez, "Gobierno comunal," 127. The Ministry of Agriculture had originally proposed adjudicating the land to a macrocommunity made up of the peasant communities of Catacaos, Sechura, and Castilla, an option rejected by the *comuneros* because it would mean paying for the land and creating a supracommunal organization. SINAMOS proposed instead the creation of independent companies that would essentially have meant bypassing the communities altogether. By contrast, the UCP model allowed all community members access to the land through usufruct, with production and marketing coordinated by a cooperative center.

54. Diez, "Gobierno comunal," 127.

55. Harding, "Agrarian Reform," 13.

56. Harding, "Agrarian Reform," 17.

57. "Lista Celeste," Federación Departamental de Campesinos de Piura (FEDECAP), Confederación Campesina del Perú, Central Archive, ca. 1974.

58. Apel, *De la hacienda a la comunidad*, 89.

59. Nelson Peñaherrera, interviewed by the author in Sullana, 11 April 2013.

60. Of the 37 peasant communities officially recognized in the Sierra of Piura before the agrarian reform, only eight received land through the reform. Apel, *De la hacienda a la comunidad*, 81.

61. Hugo Herrera, interviewed by the author in Piura, 9 April 2014.

62. Gramsci, *Selections from the Prison Notebooks*, 131–161.

63. Edita Herrera, interviewed by the author in Lima, 11 May 2013.

64. Florencia Mallon argues that such assumptions have formed the basis of orthodox thinking on state formation and national politics in Peru: "In Peru the lack of a successful national-bourgeois revolution was articulated to the perception that the

Indian majority had been unable to comprehend, much less creatively engage, concepts of nation and nationalism." Mallon, *Peasant and Nation*, 4.

65. Nelson Peñaherrera, interview by the author in Sullana, 11 April 2013.

66. Arce Espinoza, *La reforma agraria en Piura*, 103.

67. Arce Espinoza, *La reforma agraria en Piura*, 103.

68. Hugo Herrera, interviewed by the author in Piura, 9 April 2013.

69. Division de Capacitación ORAMS I, "Diagnóstico de capacitación SINAMOS," ca. 1975 (CIPCA).

70. Hugo Herrera, interviewed by the author in Piura, 9 April 2013.

71. Rénique, *Los sueños de La Sierra*, 249.

72. Rénique, *Los sueños de La Sierra*, 249.

73. "Reforma agraria," *Videoteca histórica de la televisión pionera en el Perú*, DVD 1 (Lima: Panamericana Television, n.d.), Biblioteca Nacional del Peru (Abancay), Mediateca, Lima.

74. Poole, "Corriendo riesgos," 83–100.

75. Articles 30–34 of D.L. 17716 set out a series of conditions under which an area of land could be declared exempt from the reform, or "*inafectable*," provided it was farmed directly by the landowner. The size of this allowance could be extended if the landowner demonstrated compliance with certain financial and labor requirements.

76. Mayer, *Ugly Stories*, 41–74. Mayer notes that the community of Arín in particular adopted a combative position toward the hacienda and was experienced in union organizing, since a number of its members had spent time in La Convención, the center of Hugo Blanco's peasant movement.

77. The film, *Kuntur Wachana* (1977), was produced in collaboration with the agricultural cooperative and featured campesinos from Huarán in leading roles. For a discussion of the nature of this collaboration and the problems that emerged from it, see Mayer, *Ugly Stories*, 41–74.

78. Uzátegui was simultaneously the head of the military region, ORAMS VII, and the decentralized Organismo de Desarrollo y Cooperación (Organization of Regional Development of the Southeast), giving him an extraordinary degree of power. Rénique, *Los sueños de la sierra*, 269.

79. Vladimiro Valer Delgado (former SINAMOS coordinator), interviewed by the author in Cusco, 28 May 2013. El Sepa was an infamous penal colony in the remote Amazonian jungle of Loreto. In the early 1960s, Valer was arrested for his political activities and sent to El Sepa, along with numerous other associates of protest leader Hugo Blanco.

80. Hilario Pérez Jaro, interviewed by the author in Huyro (Cusco), 31 May 2013.

81. Mendoza Salazar, "Los programas en quechua en la radiodifusión peruana," 11.

82. This spelling of the word was predominant in government publications of the time, although *Kausachun* or *Kausachum* has now become the standard form. During the Velasco era, particularly following the declaration of Quechua as an official language, there was wide variation in Quechua orthography and considerable debate about how Quechua should/could be written for education purposes. See Coronel-Molina, *Language Ideology, Policy and Planning in Peru*. The powerful use of Quechua language radio avoided many of these issues. See chapter 4.

83. Anthropologist Penelope Harvey, in "Language and the Power of History," has

argued that among bilingual populations, the use of Quechua and Spanish reflects conscious efforts to define particular power relations, rather than a set of given language domains. Although not extensive, the Velasco government's use of Quechua crossed the boundary that had historically been maintained between Spanish as the language of power and officialdom and Quechua as the language of home life in rural communities.

84. SINAMOS communications officer (who requested anonymity), interviewed by the author in Lima, 7 May 2013.

85. While it does not designate a fixed category, the term *gamonales* is used here to mean "cruel or abusive landlords."

86. The film is entitled *Causachu* (a Quechua term roughly equivalent to the Spanish word *viva*).

87. The Túpac Amaru rebellion was itself part of a larger tradition of indigenous revolt that included the Taqi Onqoy uprising of the 1560s, the insurrection led by Juan Santos Atahualpa in 1742, and the Katarista revolt led by Túpac and Tomás Katari. For a detailed account of the Túpac Amaru rebellion, see Walker, *The Túpac Amaru Rebellion*. The figure of Túpac Amaru was later invoked during the 1980s by the guerrilla organization Movimiento Revolucionario Túpac Amaru (Túpac Amaru Revolutionary Movement).

88. Asensio, *El apóstol de los Andes*.

89. Turino, *Moving Away from Silence*, 143 (Turino's translation). Interestingly, the interviewee here conflates the terms *Indian* and *campesino*, suggesting overlap in their meaning and usage. Although the Velasco government insisted on using the term *campesino* as a more neutral and dignified social category than *Indian*, it continued to use *indigenista* tropes in its portrayal of the campesino.

90. Asensio, *El apóstol de los Andes*, 80–81.

91. SINAMOS, *"General Ollanta" de la provincia de Urubamba*.

92. SINAMOS, *"General Ollanta" de la provincia de Urubamba*.

93. SINAMOS, *"General Ollanta" de la provincia de Urubamba*. For more on the relationship between the Catholic Church and the Velasco government, see Klaiber, *La iglesia en el Perú*, especially chapter 9 (pp. 393–428).

94. Del Mastro Puccio, *Luchas campesinas*.

95. Rénique, *Los sueños de la sierra*, 247.

96. Del Mastro Puccio, *Luchas campesinas*, 49.

97. SINAMOS, *Informe de los promotores Luis Urquizo i Guillermo Guzmán*, 23 January 1974, Centro Bartolomé de las Casas (CBC), in Cusco.

98. SINAMOS, *Informe de los promotores Luis Urquizo i Guillermo Guzmán*.

99. SINAMOS, *Informe del promoter Luis Urquizo al jefe de la UPO*.

100. Juan de Mata Segovia Sosaya, interviewed by the author in Maras, Cusco, 24 May 2013.

101. *El Sol de Cusco*, 22 January 1973, 5.

102. *El Sol de Cusco*, 22 January 1973, 30.

103. Expedientes, Records of the Dirección Regional de Agricultura (DRAT), ART.

104. "Informe No. 7," Expediente VII 0906-72, DRAT, ART.

105. *La Voz de Tacna*, 1 October 1971, 3.

106. *La Voz de Tacna*, 1 October 1971, 3.

107. "Plan de actividades de la FARTAMO, 1975–76," caja 1, legajo 07-0001, GRT, ART.
108. Legajo 07-0042, GRT, ART.
109. *La voz de Tacna*, 17 May 1972, 1.
110. Fredy Gambetta, "Confesión de parte" (Personal testimony), *Peruan-Ità* (2001–2004), n.d., http://www.peruan-ita.org/personaggi/gambetta/confesion.htm.
111. SINAMOS ORAMS XI, "Análisis socio-económico de las cooperativas agrarias en Tacna y Moquegua" (1973), caja 3, legajo 07-0007, GRT, ART.
112. SINAMOS ORAMS XI, "Análisis socio-económico" (1973).
113. "Reunión de trabajo sobre guía de reflexión el carácter político del SINAMOS" (1 August 1974), legajo 07-0042, GRT, ART.
114. "Acta sesión de trabajo grupo N. 1–1er piso" (20 June 1974), legajo 07-0042, GRT, ART.
115. SINAMOS, "Informe 01: Desarrollo de cursillo de capacitación para dirigentes de comunidades campesinas" (20 August 1975), caja 1, legajo 07-001, GRT, ART.
116. Felipe Ramos Pacci to Jefe de Departamento de Registro, Reclamos y Conciliaciones de Comunidades Campesinas de Zona Agraria VII, 22 June 1971, Comunidades Campesinas, DRAT, ART.
117. Ramos to Jefe de Departamento de Registro, 22 June 1971.
118. Ramos to Jefe de Departamento de Registro, 22 June 1971.
119. Ramos to Jefe de Departamento de Registro, 22 June 1971.
120. "Informe referente a acciones realizadas en la Comunidad Campesina de Huanuara," 24 December 1974, Comunidades Campesinas, DRAT, ART.
121. Oficio No S/N-75, Letter from the President of the Community of Huanuara to SINAMOS, 23 August 1975, Comunidades Campesinas, DRAT, ART.
122. Oficio No S/N-75, Letter from the President of the Community of Huanuara to SINAMOS.
123. Jefe del Dpto. De Registro, Reclamos y Conciliaciones, Tacna-Moquegua al Jefe de la División de Comunidades, 21 December 1970, Comunidades Campesinas, DRAT, ART.
124. SINAMOS, "Evaluación situación socio-política zonal—Tacna" (January 1975), legajo 07-0027, GRT, ART.
125. SINAMOS, "Informe final: Evento de evaluación y programación correspondiente al IV trimestre del bienio en curso" (January 1976), caja 2, legajo 07-0003, GRT, ART. APRA-UNO refers to the right-wing coalition formed between APRA and UNO between 1963 and 1968.
126. FARTAMO, "Plan de actividades de la FARTAMO, 1975–76," caja 1, legajo 07-0001, GRT, ART.
127. Franco, in an unpublished interview by Maria del Pilar Tello in Lima, ca. 1981.

Chapter 3: Education for Social Change

1. Oficina Nacional de Difusión del SINAMOS, *Velasco, la voz de la revolución*, 40.
2. Velasco Alvarado, "Discurso en la Manifestación Popular de la Plaza de Armas, Lambayeque" (11 de octubre de 1969), in "Separata de la Revista Participación," no. 2, 112, cited in Taller Nacional sobre Educación de Adultos en Areas Rurales, *Educación*

de adultos en areas rurales: Lineamientos técnicos y metodológicos (Lima: Ministerio de Educación, Ministerio de Agricultura, SINAMOS, Instituto Interamericano de Ciencias Agrícolas, 1975), 38.

3. Rodríguez Figueroa, in an interview that appeared in *Caretas* (15 April 1972), extracted and reproduced in SINAMOS, "Sesenta y cuatro preguntas y respuestas" (Lima: SINAMOS, ca. 1972), 4, in box 2, K320 pamphlets, ISA Pamphlets, Senate House Library (SHLISAP), London.

4. Merkel-Hess, "Reading the Rural Modern," 44–54.

5. El Colegio de México, *Historia de la lectura en México*, 249.

6. El Colegio de México, *Historia de la lectura en México*, 259.

7. Abendroth, *Rebel Literacy*.

8. Comisión Nacional de Alfabetización, *Alfabeticemos*.

9. Stites and Semali, "Adult Literacy for Social Equality or Economic Growth?," 44–75.

10. Stites and Semali, "Adult Literacy for Social Equality or Economic Growth?," 44–75.

11. Wilson, *Citizenship and Political Violence*, 44.

12. Wilson, *Citizenship and Political Violence*, 44.

13. Degregori, *Qué difícil es ser Dios*, 237.

14. Freire, *Pedagogy of the Oppressed*.

15. Freire, *Pedagogy of the Oppressed*.

16. Salomon and Niño-Murcia, *The Lettered Mountain*, 292–293.

17. Ragas, "Leer, escribir, votar," 108.

18. The term *colonial pact* was first used by Tristan Platt for the case of Bolivia, where indigenous caciques retained access to land in return for tribute paid to the colonial authorities. Tristan Platt, *Estado boliviano y ayllu andino*.

19. Águila, "Historia del sufragio en el Perú, 23.

20. Águila, "Historia del sufragio en el Perú, 23.

21. Salomon and Niño-Murcia, *The Lettered Mountain*, 1.

22. Salomon and Niño-Murcia, *The Lettered Mountain*, 71–123.

23. De la Cadena, *Indigenous Mestizos*, 90.

24. "El Tawantinsuyu" (28 July 1921), quoted in De la Cadena, *Indigenous Mestizos*, 90, quoting Kapsoli Escudero, *Ayllus del sol*, 251.

25. De la Cadena, *Indigenous Mestizos*, 97.

26. Mariátegui, *Siete ensayos de interpretación de la realidad peruana*, 133.

27. De la Cadena, *Indigenous Mestizos*.

28. L.D. 006-69, introduced in March 1969, required secondary school students to pay for any course they had failed and needed to repeat. Designed as a cost-cutting measure, the law met with huge protests that only began to subside after the announcement of the agrarian reform law on 24 June 1969, which for many signaled the government's intention to introduce meaningful change for the peasantry. See Heilman, *Before the Shining Path*, 148–172.

29. *El Comercio*, 24 June 1969, 4.

30. Ministerio de Educación, *Reforma de la educación peruana*, in Patricia Oliart, *Educación en tiempos de cambio*, 85–119.

31. Velasco, message to the nation on 28 July 1970, cited in Bizot, *Educational Reform in Peru*, 17.

32. Oliart, *Educación en tiempos de cambio*, 10.

33. Oliart, *Educación en tiempos de cambio*, 24.

34. Ministerio de Educación, *Reforma de la educación peruana*, 111.

35. Ministerio de Educación, *Reforma de la educación peruana*, 112.

36. *Núcleos educativos rurales* were first introduced by Luis Valcárcel when he served as minister of education during the government of José Luis Bustamante y Rivero (1945–1948). See Ministerio de Educación, *Reforma de la educación peruana*, 62.

37. Taller Nacional sobre Educación de Adultos en Areas Rurales, *Educación de adultos en areas rurales.*

38. Paloma Valdeavellano, *Lograr la participación: Reto del extensionista*, documento 2 (Lima: Ministerio de Educación, 1974), cited in Bizot, *Educational Reform in Peru*, 36.

39. Churchill, *The Peruvian Model of Innovation*. It is important to recognize, however, that the Escuelas Superiores de Educación Profesional were relatively short-lived, since they were abolished during the second Belaúnde administration (1980–1985). According to José Rivero, Belaúnde's education policy reversed all efforts to build links between formal and nonformal education. See Rivero, *Educación*, 405.

40. Churchill, *The Peruvian Model of Innovation*, 29.

41. Chiappo, "La liberación de la educación," 28–29.

42. Chiappo, "La liberación de la educación," 28–29. It should be noted, however, that the education reform—and the Velasco regime in general—was ambivalent regarding the role of indigenous languages in modern Peru. While it recommended the use of the vernacular language "where necessary," it did so on a pragmatic basis and largely rejected the broader belief systems of indigenous cultures. See Oliart, "Politicizing Education," 134–135.

43. Patricia Oliart, "State Reform and Resilient Powers," 73.

44. D.L. 19326, Title XIX, Special Programs (21 March 1972).

45. Taller Nacional sobre Educación de Adultos en Areas Rurales, *Educación de adultos en areas rurales*, 3.

46. Taller Nacional sobre Educación de Adultos en Areas Rurales, *Educación de adultos en areas rurales*, 93.

47. Taller Nacional sobre Educación de Adultos en Areas Rurales, *Educación de adultos en areas rurales*, 94.

48. CENCIRA, "El proceso electoral en la Cooperativa Agraria de Producción Casagrande."

49. "CAPS: En torno a una capacitación," *Sinamos informa* 1, no. 5 (1972): 15–16.

50. "Vicos: A Virtual Tour from 1952 to the Present," Cornell University, https://courses.cit.cornell.edu/vicosperu/vicos-site/cornellperu_page_2.htm.

51. *El Peruano* [Suplemento extraordinario], 3 October 1969, 12.

52. In some cases training programs were delivered in advance of full adjudication, but these were later abandoned because of the high level of interference and obstruction encountered from landowners.

53. Tinsman, *Partners in Conflict*, 139.

54. SINAMOS OZAMS Moquegua, "Empresas Campesinas," caja 1, legajo 07-0001, GRT, ART.

55. Gastón Aramayo and Victoria Morales, interviewed by the author in Lima, 7 September 2012.

56. Salomon, interviewed by the author in Lima, 5 September 2012.
57. Instituto Nacional de Estadística, ed., *Compendio de estadísticas sociales 1991.*
58. Rivero, *Educación*, 392.
59. Dirección General de Educación Básica Laboral y Calificación, *Guía metodológica ALFIN.*
60. Burton, "The Submerged and the Seers," 236.
61. Vaughan, *Cultural Politics in Revolution*, 6.
62. Prawda, "Desarrollo del sistema educativo mexicano," 71.
63. Franco, *La iglesia y la educación.*
64. Franco, *La iglesia y la educación.*
65. Franco, *La iglesia y la educación*, 388–389.
66. Vom Hau, "Unpacking the School," 147.
67. Vom Hau, "Unpacking the School," 147.
68. Wilson, "Transcending Race?," 728.
69. Rivero, *Educación*, 386–387.
70. Oliart, *Educación en tiempos de cambio*, 20.
71. Oliart, *Educación en tiempos de cambio*, 20.
72. Rivero, *Educación*, 366.
73. Salomon, interview.
74. Alvarez Calderón, "Reflexiones," 303.
75. Burton, "The Submerged and the Seers," 244.
76. Rivero, *Educación*, 392.
77. "Primer congreso provincial de campesinos de Calca, del 27 al 30 enero 1972," Dirección Regional de Agricultura, Cusco (DRAC).
78. "Primer congreso provincial de campesinos de Calca, del 27 al 30 enero 1972," DRAC.
79. "Primer congreso provincial de campesinos de Calca, del 27 al 30 enero 1972," DRAC.
80. The Konrad-Adenauer-Stiftung (KAS), a German political foundation of Christian-Democrat orientation, has had offices in Peru for more than forty years. I thank Hilario Pérez Jaro, former president of the Central de Cooperativas Té Huyro, for facilitating access to the Central's annual reports.
81. Hilario Pérez Jaro, interviewed by the author in Huyro (Cusco), 31 May 2013.
82. Pérez Jaro, interview.
83. Pérez Jaro, interview.
84. Pérez Jaro, interview.
85. CENCIRA, "Central de Cooperativas Agrarias 'Té Huyro Ltda.,'" no. 43, documentos relacionados con la asamblea general ordinaria de delegados del día 31 de marzo de 1974.
86. CENCIRA, "Central de Cooperativas Agrarias 'Té Huyro Ltda.,'" no. 43 documento de trabajo, La Convención-Cuzco, 1972, 3–4 (emphasis in original), in CBC, Cusco.
87. CENCIRA, "Central de Cooperativas Agrarias 'Té Huyro Ltda.,'" 3–4, CBC, Cusco.
88. CENCIRA, "Cooperativa Agraria de Producción [CAP] Lauramarca Ltda.," no. 56, Quispicanchi-Cusco (Lima: CENCIRA, 1972), 68.
89. CENCIRA, "Central de Cooperativas Agrarias 'Té Huyro Ltda.,'" no. 43, 65.

90. Nor was there a clear equivalence to the traditional Andean forms of reciprocal labor, known as *ayni* and *mink'a*. See Sallnow, "Cooperation and Contradiction," 241–257.

91. CENCIRA, "CAP Lauramarca," 65.

92. CENCIRA, "CAP Lauramarca," 65. The Quechua word *misti* refers to a white, mestizo, or "non-Indian" person. Among indigenous communities it signifies both otherness and superior social status. See De la Cadena, *Indigenous Mestizos*.

93. CENCIRA, "CAP Lauramarca," 66.

94. CENCIRA, "CAP Lauramarca," 86.

95. CENCIRA, "CAP Lauramarca," 67.

96. Del Mastro Puccio, *Luchas campesinas*, 80–81.

97. CENCIRA, "CAP Lauramarca," 57.

98. "Conclusiones de la II Convención de Delegados de la Liga Agraria 'Eugenio Flores Q.,'" August 1975, caja 1, legajo 07-001, GRT, ART.

99. "Conclusiones de la II Convención de Delegados de la Liga Agraria 'José Carlos Mariátegui,'" August 1975, caja 1, legajo 07-001, GRT, ART.

100. Tacna's SUTE was the regional affiliate of the national SUTEP.

101. *La voz de Tacna*, 20 July 1975, 3.

102. SINAMOS, "Informe socio-político OZAMS—Tacna 1973-Nov 1974," legajo 07-0027, GRT, ART.

103. SINAMOS, "Informe socio-político OZAMS—Tacna 1973-Nov 1974," legajo 07-0027, GRT, ART.

104. SINAMOS, "Evaluación situación socio-política zonal—Tacna (enero 1975)," legajo 07-0027, GRT, ART.

105. SINAMOS, "Evaluación situación socio-política zonal—Tacna (enero 1975)," legajo 07-0027, GRT, ART.

106. *Correo*, 24 June 1973, 7.

107. *Correo*, 24 June 1973, 7.

108. SINAMOS, "Informe No. 100-74-UAT-AJA-ORAMS XI," 06 November 1974, Legajo 07-0027, GRT, ART.

109. SINAMOS, "Informe No. 100-74-UAT-AJA-ORAMS XI," 06 November 1974, Legajo 07-0027, GRT, ART.

110. SINAMOS, "Informe de trabajo: Asistencia técnica a Cooperativas Agrarias de la zona CAP 135," 7 November 1973, legajo 07-0027, GRT, ART.

111. *La voz de Tacna*, 16 May 1975, 8.

112. "Sistema nacional de Capacitación de la Confederación Nacional Agraria. Comités de capacitación. 1975," p. 22, caja 1, legajo 07-001, GRT, ART.

113. "Sistema nacional de Capacitación de la Confederación Nacional Agraria. Comités de capacitación. 1975," p. 22, caja 1, legajo 07-001, GRT, ART.

114. Lauer and Cevallos, "Reforma agraria," 36.

115. Miguel Zegarra, interviewed by the author in Piura, 14 March 2013.

116. Menacho Jaramillo, "El Congreso Nacional Agrario y la operación ALFIN," 314.

117. Menacho Jaramillo, "El Congreso Nacional Agrario y la operación ALFIN," 306–318.

118. Santuc, "CIPCA: Un proyecto en Piura, análisis de algunas acciones."

119. Santuc, "CIPCA: Un proyecto en Piura, análisis de algunas acciones," 9–10.

120. Otero and Revesz, "Educación popular y alfabetización en CIPCA," 30.

121. Otero and Revesz, "Educación popular y alfabetización en CIPCA," 30.
122. Juan Hernández Astudillo, interviewed by the author in Piura, 16 April 2013.
123. Santuc, "CIPCA: Un proyecto en Piura, análisis de algunas acciones," 21.
124. Mariano Fiestas Chunga, interviewed by the author in Piura, 17 April 2013.
125. Fiestas Chunga, interview.
126. Zegarra, interview.
127. Fiestas Chunga, interview.
128. Fiestas Chunga, interview.
129. Revesz, "El campesinado piurano en la escena regional," 117.
130. César Zapata, interviewed by the author in Catacaos (Piura), 19 April 2013.
131. Robespierre Bayona, interviewed by the author in Piura, 19 April 2013.
132. Plaza-J., "Campesinado, analfabetismo y el problema del voto en el Perú," 82.

Chapter 4: The Agrarian Reform in Public Discourse

1. Jesús Ruiz Durand, interviewed by the author in Lima, 30 March 2010.

2. In August 1975, 28 people including journalists, political activists, and trade union leaders were expelled from the country. According to *La Voz de Tacna*, the journalists were charged with publishing "insulting articles against the government of Chile," while the other two groups were accused of "subversive and counterrevolutionary actions related to land invasions, strikes, stoppages etc." "Puntos de vista sobre la deportación de periodistas, dirigentes sindicales y políticos," *La Voz de Tacna*, 9 August 1975.

3. SINAMOS produced 6,356,464 leaflets and documents for dissemination between 1973 and 1976. Guerra García, "SINAMOS y la promoción de la participación," 705.

4. DPDRA, *A los yanaconas, aparceros, arrendires*, 10, K320 Pam Box 3, SHLISAP, London.

5. DPDRA, *ABC de la reforma agraria peruana*, K320 Pam Box 3, SHLISAP, London.

6. DPDRA, *Al hombre de la ciudad peruana*, K320 Pam Box 3, SHLISAP, London.

7. *El Comercio*, 8 October 1969, 19.

8. Hugo Neira, interviewed by the author by telephone, 26 September 2012.

9. Héctor Béjar, interviewed by the author in Lima, 26 September 2012.

10. This tradition was most pronounced in Mexico. See Mraz, *Looking for Mexico*.

11. "La participación comenzó por casa," *Sinamos informa* 1, no. 2 (1972):25.

12. "La participación comenzó por casa," 25.

13. Juan Gargurevich, *Prensa, radio y tv: Historia crítica* (Lima: Editorial Horizonte, 1987), 206.

14. Gargurevich, *Prensa, radio y tv*, 211.

15. Rosas Paravicino, "Tentativa de socialización de los diarios de circulación nacional en el Perú."

16. Richard Cott, "Giving the Press to the People," *Guardian* (UK edition), 4 December 1974, 14.

17. Germán E. Ornes, chairman of the Inter-American Press Association Committee on Freedom of the Press and Information, cited in Jerry W. Knudson, *Roots of Revo-*

lution: The Press and Social Change in Latin America (Lanham, MD: University Press of America, 2009), 131.

18. Jaworski, "Democracia y 'socialización,'" 3:771.

19. UNESCO, *Communication Policies and Planning*, 3.

20. Masmoudi, *The New World Information Order*, 1–2.

21. Middents, *Film Journals and Film Culture in Peru*, 150.

22. This kind of collaboration was not without its tensions, however. While *Runan Caycu* privileged the role of peasant action in achieving social change—a key aspect of the Velasco government's rhetoric—the film was initially censored due to its unfavorable representation of the military's role in repressing the 1963–1964 peasant uprisings.

23. Rosas Paravicino, "Tentativa de socialización de los diarios de circulación nacional en el Perú," 81.

24. *Cronicawan* 9:7. I am grateful to Odi Gonzales of New York University for providing Spanish translations of the Quechua texts. In Quechua, the language is known as Runa Simi, meaning "language of the people."

25. This change appears to have been made in order to encourage readers to use the newspaper to learn Quechua, as indicated by the inclusion of illustrated lists of Quechua vocabulary.

26. *Cronicawan* 12:5.

27. CENCIRA, *Los boletines en las empresas campesinas*.

28. Mikael Wiström to Anna Cant, 24 October 2013.

29. The "agrarian debt" was the payment that cooperatives were required to pay to the state toward the costs of expropriating the land that had been adjudicated to them.

30. "Informe presentado al II Congreso Nacional Extraordinaria de la Confederación del Perú (CCP), Querecotillo, Piura, Julio 1975 por la Federación del Valle de Huaral, Chancay y Aucallama," file 82, Koos Koster archive, International Institute of Social History, Amsterdam.

31. Vanguardia Revolucionaria, "Circular No. 2—18.6.75. Propagandizar la alianza obrero-campesina el 24 de Junio," item APP3/VR 98, Archivo de Partidos Políticos, PUCP, Lima.

32. Vanguardia Revolucionaria, "Circular No. 2—18.6.75."

33. *Informativo agrario* 3, August 1973, item 33.0038, Archivo de Partidos Políticos, PUCP, Lima.

34. "Algunos dispositivos desalentarán la producción—dice presidente de SNA," *La Crónica*, 27 June 1969, 5.

35. "Invocación al gobierno," *La Prensa*, 22 June 1969, 15.

36. "Dos aspectos de la reforma agraria," *La Prensa*, 29 June 1969, 17.

37. "Dos aspectos de la reforma agraria," 17.

38. "La nueva ley de reforma agraria," *La Crónica*, 27 June 1969, 4.

39. "Reforma agraria: Nueva etapa para el Perú," *Dominical* (Sunday supplement of *El Comercio*), 4.

40. "Trujillo presenció el mitin más grande de su historia," *Dominical*, 12 October 1969, 1.

41. "Trujillo presenció el mitin más grande de su historia," 3.

42. "Trujillo presenció el mitin más grande de su historia," 3.

43. In July 1973 the company published a notice entitled (in translation) "*El Comer-*

cio to the country," in which it denounced strikes by its workers as a pretext for expropriating the company. *Última Hora*, 31 July 1973.

44. Sindicato de Trabajadores y Campesinos de la CAP Tambo Real Ltda. 154, Comunicado de Prensa, 12 March 1973, cited in Padrón Castillo and Pease García, *Planificación rural, reforma agraria y organización campesina*, 440. Capitalization as in original.

45. Padrón Castillo and Pease García, *Planificación rural, reforma agraria y organización campesina*, 441.

46. Guido Guevara Ugarte, interviewed by the author in Cusco, 22 September 2012.

47. Guevara Ugarte, interview. The group's namesake was a well-known poet and activist who was shot dead in 1963 as he participated in the Ejército de Liberación Nacional guerrilla insurgency. Following the collapse of the group, many of its members were integrated into SINAMOS, where they continued to work on cultural activities.

48. *El Sol*, 9 May 1973, 6.

49. "Se forma cooperativa de campesinos sin ninguna clase de ayuda," *El Sol*, 18 January 1973; "Mujeres campesinas formaron Asociación. No seremos serviles dice Presidenta," *El Sol*, 1 February 1973.

50. Asensio, *El apóstol de los Andes*, 108.

51. Mendoza Michilot, "Gestión de las empresas periodísticas regionales," 77.

52. "Tratan de enfrentar a Sinamos contra empresa," *El Sol*, 22 May 1973; "Trabajadores rechazan maniobra contra El Sol. Amplio respaldo a la dirección," *El Sol*, 24 May 1973.

53. "Cusco, dpto. Con mayor numero de transistores: Perú," *El Comercio*, 22 June 1970, 1.

54. Mujica Escalante, *Una vida y un rumbo*, 9–13.

55. Francisco León Farfán, interviewed by the author in Cusco, 22 May 2013.

56. Mujica Escalante, *Una vida y un rumbo*, 35–36.

57. Mujica Escalante, *Una vida y un rumbo*, 35–36.

58. Francisco León Farfán, interviewed by the author in Cusco, 22 May 2013. Pachakutiq was the ninth ruler of the Kingdom of Cusco and later the Emperor of the Inca Empire.

59. León, interview.

60. "El golpe militar de ayer," *El Tiempo*, 4 October 1968.

61. "Por la libertad de prensa en el país," *El Tiempo*, 2 November 1968.

62. *El Tiempo*, 8 October 1969.

63. "Bienvenido Presidente," *El Tiempo*, 8 October 1969.

64. *El Tiempo*, 18 October 1969, 6.

65. "Liga Agrícola pide que distribución de tierras por RA llene su cometido," *El Tiempo*, 7 November 1969, 4.

66. *La Industria*, 25 June 1969, 1.

67. "Comunidad Campesina de Castilla: Comunicado," *La Industria*, 27 June 1969.

68. Edita Herrera Calle, interviewed by the author in Lima, 11 May 2013.

69. ORAMS Piura, "Diagnóstico preliminar de capacitación," 1976, CIPCA, Piura.

70. Panty Neyra, *Historia de la prensa escrita en Tacna*, 106.

71. *El Correo*, 12 October 1968, cited in Panty Neyra, *Historia de la prensa escrita en Tacna*, 106.

72. "Ahora sí es cierto: Empezaron las reformas!" *La voz de Tacna*, 26 June 1969.

73. "Ahora sí es cierto: Empezaron las reformas!" *La voz de Tacna*, 26 June 1969.

74. "Mayoría Tacneña expresa satisfacción por radical Ley de Reforma Agraria," *La voz de Tacna*, 26 June 1969.

75. "La pequeña y mediana propiedad agraria," *La voz de Tacna*, 21 May 1972.

76. "Proceden excepciones en la reforma agraria?," *La voz de Tacna*, 3 April 1975.

77. "Los diarios de provincias al servicio de la SIP y la contrarevolución," *La voz de Tacna*, 15 June 1975.

78. "Informe socio-político OZAMS-Tacna 1973–November 1974," legajo 07-0027, GRT, ART.

79. Fredy Gambeta, "Confesión de parte" (3 parte), http://www.peruan-ita.org/personaggi/gambetta/top-gambetta.htm.

80. "Volantes contra el SUTEP," *La Voz de Tacna*, 18 May 1975.

81. "Informe No. 12—75—CAP," legajo 07-0042, GRT, ART.

82. Rodolfo Aquino, director of Radio Cutivalú, interviewed October 2007. See AMARC Perú, "La experiencia de Radio Cutivalú," https://www.youtube.com/watch?v=Hn8knmo1qUs.

83. Rosa María Alfaro, founder of Calandria, interviewed by Jair Vega and Rafael Obregón, 16 September 2003. See "Entrevista con Rosa Maria Alfaro," by the Communication Initiative Network, http://www.comminit.com/democracy-governance/node/67296.

84. Herrera Calle, interview.

85. César Zapata, interviewed by the author in Catacaos (Piura), 19 April 2013.

86. Hildebrandt, *Cambio de palabras*, 83.

87. The same could be said for the state's interventions in television and radio; the innovative programs referred to earlier in this chapter represented a minority of content throughout this period. See Rosas Paravicino, "Tentativa de socialización de los diarios de circulación nacional en el Perú."

Chapter 5: The Agrarian Reform in Historical Memory

1. Mayer, *Ugly Stories*, xix.

2. On the construction of official narratives of the Mexican Revolution, see Knight, "The Myth of the Mexican Revolution," 223–273.

3. Sturken, "Memory, Consumerism and Media," 73–78.

4. Klein, "On the Emergence of Memory in Historical Discourse," 128.

5. Halbwachs, *The Collective Memory.*

6. Halbwachs, *The Collective Memory*, especially 50–87.

7. Thomson, *Anzac Memories*, 10.

8. See also Dawson, *Soldier Heroes*; Summerfield, "Culture and Composure"; Olick and Robbins, "Social Memory Studies"; Zerubavel, *Time Maps*; Andrews, *Shaping History.*

9. Andrews, *Shaping History.*

10. Jelin, *Los trabajos de la memoria*, 6.

11. Jelin, *Los trabajos de la memoria*, 6.

12. Schlotterbeck, *Beyond the Vanguard*, 1. The Chilean MIR was a movement contemporary but unconnected to Peru's Movimiento de la Izquierda Revolucionaria.

13. Narotzky and Smith, "'Being Político' in Spain."

14. "EL PP ordena retirar las banderas republicanas de las instituciones," *El País*, 5 June 2014.

15. Butler, "Vocabularies of the Censor," 256.

16. Docafe, "La nueva historia del Perú," 366. The book was a collaborative project that included the work of known Velasco supporters, including C. D. Valcarcel, alongside such conservative historians as José Agustín de la Puente Candamo.

17. Docafe, "La nueva historia del Perú," 366.

18. General Leonidas Rodríguez, in an interview conducted and published by *Caretas*, reproduced in part in SINAMOS, *Sesenta y cuatro preguntas y respuestas*, 4, Pam Box 2, K320, SHLISAP, London.

19. "Origen del Día del Campesino en el Perú," *RPP Noticias*, 24 June 2011, http://www.rpp.com.pe/2011-06-24-origen-del-dia-del-campesino-en-el-peru-noticia_378473.html.

20. "Culmina mañana programa de celebraciones," *La voz de Tacna*, 23 June 1974, 5.

21. "Desfile tres horas de campesinos en apoyo a Reforma," *La Industria*, 25 June 1970, 1.

22. "Desfile tres horas de campesinos en apoyo a Reforma," *La Industria*, 25 June 1970, 1.

23. Tileagă, *Political Psychology: Critical Perspectives*, 112.

24. Armando Zapata, interviewed by the author in Piura, 16 April 2013.

25. Edita Herrera Calle, interviewed by the author in Lima, 11 May 2013.

26. Herrera Calle, interview.

27. CEDEP in Lima and the Centro de Estudios Sociales Solidaridad (Solidarity Center of Social Studies) in Chiclayo were both founded by former SINAMOS staff and currently pursue research agendas that to a large extent reflect the aims of the Velasco government.

28. CNA, "Nuestra historia: Agricultura para la vida" (unpublished text), distributed at the thirty-eighth anniversary celebration of the CNA, Lima, 3 October 2012. The fact that the CNA was founded on 3 October, the anniversary of the 1968 coup, provides a further example of the government's self-memorialization.

29. "Nuestra historia."

30. "Nuestra historia."

31. In 1984 the Cuban-inspired leftist organization Movimiento Revolucionario Túpac Amaru (Túpac Amaru Revolutionary Movement) launched its own armed uprising against the Peruvian state, but the principal conflict in terms of scale and number of people affected remained that waged by Shining Path.

32. Soifer and Vergara, "Leaving the Path Behind," 4. The term *conflicto armado interno* (internal armed conflict) was introduced by Peru's Comisión de la Verdad y Reconciliación, whose 2003 report, *Informe final*, is a constant point of reference for researchers working on the topic.

33. Comisión de la Verdad y Reconciliación, *Informe final*.

34. Mason, "Take Two Acres," 199–230.

35. Neira, *Cuzco: Tierra y muerte*, 17–18.

36. McClintock, "Why Peasants Rebel," 83.

37. Albertus, "Land Reform and Civil Conflict," 1–19; Seligmann, "Civil War in Peru," 124.

38. Seligmann, "Civil War in Peru."

39. Soifer and Vergara, "Leaving the Path Behind," 8.

40. Soifer and Vergara, "Leaving the Path Behind," 13.

41. Degregori, *El conflicto armado interno en el Perú*, 247.

42. Comisión de la Verdad y Reconciliación, *Informe final*, 182.

43. Comisión de la Verdad y Reconciliación, *Informe final*, 183–196.

44. Mayer, *Ugly Stories*, 211.

45. Mason, "Take Two Acres," 222.

46. César Zapata, interview with the author in Catacaos (Piura), 19 April 2013.

47. Cameron, "From Oligarchic Domination," 91–92.

48. Rojas-Perez, *Mourning Remains*, 49.

49. Vergara and Encinas, "From a Partisan Right to the Conservative Archipelago," 243.

50. "General Morales B. preside Gobierno Revolucionario de La Fuerza Armada," *La Voz de Tacna*, 30 August 1975, 3.

51. Thorp, "The Stabilisation Crisis in Peru 1975–8," 121–122.

52. Héctor Béjar, interviewed by the author in Lima, 12 April 2010.

53. Mayer, *Ugly Stories*, 28.

54. Contreras and Cueto, *Historia del Perú contemporáneo*, 366–370.

55. Thorp, "The APRA Alternative in Peru," 167.

56. Hopkins, "Política agraria," 9–19.

57. Conaghan, Malloy, and Wolfson, "Democracia y neoliberalismo en Perú, Ecuador y Bolivia," 867–890.

58. Portocarrero, "Memorias del velasquismo," 229–256.

59. Portocarrero, "Memorias del velasquismo," 229–256.

60. Alan García Pérez, "El síndrome del perro del hortelano," *El Comercio*, 28 October 2007.

61. Eguren, "40 mil hectáreas ¿Es poco o mucho?," *La República*, 29 April 2010.

62. María Luisa Burneo de la Rocha, "'Los hacendados están de vuelta': Dinámicas alrededor de la tierra en una comunidad de la costa norte peruana, 45 años después de la reforma agraria" (paper presented at the Latin American Studies Association Congress, Chicago, 21–24 May 2014), 6, https://members.lasaweb.org/prot/congress-papers/Past/lasa2014/files/42594.pdf.

63. Jelin, *Los trabajos de la memoria*, 6.

64. "Veinte años de reforma agraria," *El Comercio*, 28 June 1989, in *A veinte años de la reforma agraria: dossier regional 5*, compiled by CIPCA (Piura: CIPCA, 1989), 14.

65. "Veinte años perdidos," *Expreso*, 29 June 1989, in *A veinte años de la reforma agraria: Dossier regional 5*, compiled by CIPCA (Piura: CIPCA, 1989), 16.

66. "Veinte años perdidos," *Expreso*.

67. "Veinte años perdidos," *Expreso*.

68. Manfred Zoeger Navarro, interviewed by the author in Chiclayo, 24 April 2013.

69. *Desarraigo*, presented in Lima, 4 April to 3 May 2013.

70. De la Cadena, *Indigenous Mestizos*.

71. Drinot, "Remembering Velasco," 96.

72. Salvador Aita Germán, interviewed by the author in Chiclayo, 22 April 2013. Emphasis added.

73. Martha Meier Miró Quesada, "Túpac Mouse," *El Comercio*, 4 June 2014, http://elcomercio.pe/opinion/columnistas/tupac-mouse-martha-meier-m-q-noticia-1733944.

74. "Túpac Mouse," *El Comercio*.

75. Salvador Aita Germán, interviewed by the author in Chiclayo, 22 April 2013.

76. "Bonos agrarios: ¿De qué trata la denuncia por el pago de la deuda agraria?," *El Comercio*, 17 December 2018, https://elcomercio.pe/economia/peru/bonos-agrarios-trata-denuncia-pago-deuda-agraria-nndc-noticia-588598.

77. Lazar, "Education for Credit," 107.

78. Marcelino Bustamante López, interviewed by the author in Lima, 5 October 2012.

79. Taboada and Lopez, "La reforma agraria 40 años después," 13.

80. José Manuel Mejía, "La neo reforma agraria," *Sí*, 122, in *A veinte años de la reforma agraria: Dossier regional 5*, compiled by CIPCA, 15, 28.

81. Revesz, *Estado, algodón y productores agrarios*, 67.

82. Revesz, *Estado, algodón y productores agrarios*, 67.

83. Wenceslao del Rosario Ponce, interviewed by the author in Sullana (Piura), 26 April 2013.

84. Hilario Pérez Jaro, interviewed by the author in Huyro (Cusco), 31 May 2013.

85. Del Rosario Ponce, interview.

86. "Velasco, un hombre revolucionario," *Vocero Agrario* 4, no. 10 (2009): 17.

87. *Kausachum Perú* carried the tagline "newspaper project of popular participation," echoing the Velasco government's ideas about participative media.

88. *Kausachum Perú*, 3 October 1983, 13.

89. Demetrio Barrios Moscoso, Cooperativa Túpac Amaru, Pampa de Anta (Cusco), interviewed and recorded by Cholonautas (Instituto de Estudios Peruanos) for the project "Memorias de la lucha campesina por la tierra en Puno, Cusco y Apurímac" (Memories of the peasant struggle for land in Puno, Cusco and Apurímac), https://www.youtube.com/watch?v=Hvn6JgMMeF4. The project studied the period from the agrarian reform until around 2012 and focused in particular on those who led or participated in *tomas de tierra* on former cooperative lands in the late 1970s and 1980s.

90. Hall, "La reforma agraria," 122.

91. Hall, "La reforma agraria," 122. For Hall, this desire to avoid confronting the recent past goes hand in hand with the perception, common among nongovernmental organizations and government administrators, that "legitimate" peasant communities are those that are "ancestral" and can trace their origins to the pre-Hispanic era, a perception that in turn shapes how communities represent themselves and their history.

92. Clemente Condori Espilla of Comunidad Campesina de Huamanrura (Puno), interviewed and recorded by Cholonautas (Instituto de Estudios Peruanos) for the project "Memorias de la lucha campesina por la tierra en Puno, Cusco y Apurímac."

93. Sixto Villavicencio Castillo of Comunidad Campesina de Tambo Real (Cusco), interviewed by the Centro Andino de Educación y Promoción José María Arguedas, http://www.ivoox.com/audios-cholonautas_sa_f231555_p2_1.html?o=all.

94. Testimony of Isidoro Franco Pumasupa, spoken in Quechua and transcribed

in Spanish, in *Testimonio campesino*, transcribed and published by CENCIRA, 6. *Cargadores* are manual laborers who are employed—particularly in the towns and cities of the southern highlands—to carry large loads of agricultural produce, construction materials, or other heavy materials on their backs in return for an extremely low wage. The strenuous nature of the job makes it an option of last resort for those unable to maintain subsistence in the countryside. For detailed insight on the life of a *cargador* in mid-twentieth century Cusco, see Valderrama Fernandez and Escalante Gutierrez, eds., *Andean Lives*.

95. Manuel Céspedes Zamora, interviewed by the author in Ferreñafe (Lambayeque), 23 April 2013. The term *serranos* here refers to the cooperative workers who came from or were descendants of people from the northern highlands.

96. Hilario Pérez Jaro, interview.

97. Jungbluth Melgar, "El voto rural en la segunda vuelta," 4–5.

98. Vladimiro Valer Delgado, interviewed by the author in Cusco, 28 May 2013.

99. Speech by President Ollanta Humala Tasso at the ceremony for Day of the Campesino, Grau (Apurímac), 24 June 2013, https://www.youtube.com/watch?v=WZmGKw-MWfs.

100. "Hijo de ex presidente Juan Velasco Alvarado busca firmas en la Región Puno," *Diario Los Andes*, 4 June 2014.

101. *Kausachum Velasco* 4 (2014).

102. "Glave: 'Creo que la reforma agraria fue un acto de justicia,'" *El Comercio*, 28 March 2016, https://elcomercio.pe/politica/elecciones/glave-creo-reforma-agraria-acto-justicia-394206-noticia/.

103. Nicolás Lynch, "Hace 50 años: ¡Velasco revolución!," *Otra Mirada*, 4 October 2018, http://www.otramirada.pe/hace-50-a%C3%B1os-%C2%A1velasco-revoluci%C3%B3n.

104. "Editorial: La reforma agraria," *El Comercio*, 23 June 2019, https://elcomercio.pe/opinion/editorial/editorial-reforma-agria-agraria-velasco-alvarado-agricultura-noticia-ecpm-648284.

105. "Reforma agraria: ¿Un acto de justicia?, por Fernando Cáceres Freyre," *El Comercio*, 2 July 2019, https://elcomercio.pe/opinion/rincon-del-autor/reforma-agraria-expropiacion-propiedad-privada-acto-justicia-fernando-caceres-freyre-noticia-ecpm-651343.

106. Rosa María Palacios (@rmapalacios), "Universal Beliefs," Twitter, 25 June 2019, https://twitter.com/rmapalacios/status/1143542707656282112.

107. Burenius, *Testimonio de un fracaso*, 192.

108. Van Alphen, "Symptoms of Discursivity," 37–38.

109. Portelli, *The Order Has Been Carried Out*, 286.

110. Portelli, *The Order Has Been Carried Out*, 287.

111. Fernando Eguren López, "40 mil hectáreas ¿Es poco o mucho?," *La República*, 29 April 2010, https://larepublica.pe/economia/460940-40-mil-hectareas-es-poco-o-mucho/.

112. See, for example, the proliferation of Velasco-inspired memes on social media and the documentary *La revolución y la tierra*, directed by Gonzalo Benavente Secco and produced by Carolina Denegri and Autocinema, Animalita and Bebeto Films SAC (2019).

Conclusion

1. Oficina Nacional de Difusión del SINAMOS, *Velasco, la voz de la revolución*, 38.

2. To my knowledge, there has been no dedicated research on the history of SINAMOS. The most comprehensive accounts of the organization's structure and political impact are provided by Béjar in *La revolución en la trampa* and Franco and Ames, eds., in *El Perú de Velasco*. This lacuna is starting to be addressed by a new generation of Peruvian scholars, including Mijail Mitrovic, Mercedes Crisóstomo, Javier Puente, and Adrián Lerner Patrón.

3. Andrés Luna Vargas (former president of the Confederación Campesina del Perú), was interviewed by the author in Lima, 8 August 2012. Luna Vargas was not subjected to political violence or torture, but on several occasions he was captured by the authorities and imprisoned without trial. Such repression became more frequent toward the end of the Velasco regime, as its popularity diminished and left-wing resistance grew stronger.

4. Ministerio de Educación, Comisión de Reforma de la Educación, *Reforma de la educación peruana, informe general* (Lima: Ministerio de Educación, Comisión de Reforma de la Educación, 1970), referenced in Oliart, *Educación en tiempos de cambio*, 111.

5. Hilario Pérez Jaro, interviewed by the author in Huyro (Cusco), 31 May 2013.

6. Oliart, *Educación en tiempos de cambio*, 31.

7. Gastón Aramayo and Vicky Morales, interviewed by the author in Lima, 7 September 2012.

8. Marcelino Bustamante López, interviewed by the author in Lima, 5 October 2012.

9. Soliz, "Politics of Agrarian Reform in Bolivia," 361.

10. Lapp, *Representation and Land Reform*.

11. Tinsman, *Partners in Conflict*.

12. Soliz, "Politics of Agrarian Reform in Bolivia," 348.

13. Michael Courville and Raj Patel, introduction and overview to *Promised Land: Competing Visions of Agrarian Reform*, ed. Rossett, Patel, and Courville, 8.

14. Centro Nacional de Memoria Histórica, *La política de reforma agraria y tierras en Colombia*.

15. Grandin, *The Last Colonial Massacre*, xv.

16. "A tres años del 'baguazo' la justicia aún no señala a los culpables," *El Comercio*, 5 June 2012, http://elcomercio.pe/peru/lima/tres-anos-baguazo-justicia-aun-no-senala-culpables-noticia-1424118?ref=flujo_tags_106144&ft=nota_36&e=titulo.

17. "A tres años del 'baguazo' la justicia aún no señala a los culpables," *El Comercio*, 5 June 2012.

18. See *La Revista Agraria* 108 (June 2009): 3, 15–24, https://larevistagraria.files.wordpress.com/2019/05/lra-108_completo.pdf. Centro Peruano de Estudios Sociales is the publisher.

Selected Bibliography

This listing of resources is divided into three parts: manuscript and archival sources, primary sources, and secondary sources. Some resources, including interviews conducted by the author, reports in newspapers, and information from similar sources are cited in full in the notes; otherwise, notes bear short titles.

Manuscript and Archival Sources

Archivo General de la Nación, Lima.

Archivo Regional de Tacna (Intermedio) (ART). Records of the Gobierno Regional de Tacna (GRT).

Biblioteca Nacional del Perú (BNP), Lima. Publications of Sistema Nacional de Apoyo a la Movilización Social (SINAMOS).

Centro de Estudios Histórico—Militares del Perú, Lima.

Centro de Estudios para el Desarrollo y la Participación (CEDEP), Lima. Publications of SINAMOS.

Centro de Investigación y Promoción del Campesinado (CIPCA), Piura. Records of the Oficina Regional de Apoyo a la Movilización Social (ORAMS) I, SINAMOS.

Confederación Campesina del Perú (CCP), Central Archive, Lima.

Dirección Regional de Agricultura, Cusco (DRAC).

Dirección Regional de Agricultura, Tacna (DRAT).

International Institute of Social History, Amsterdam. Archive of Koos Koster and papers of Dirk Kruijt.

Pontificia Universidad Católica del Perú (PUCP), Lima. Archivo de Partidos Políticos and publications and reports of Centro Nacional de Capacitación y Investigación para la Reforma Agraria (CENCIRA) and SINAMOS.

Princeton University Library, Princeton, New Jersey. Records of Peruvian agrarian issues, 1955–1987; *Cronicawan*.

Senate House Library, London. ISA Pamphlets (SHLISAP).

Primary Sources

CENCIRA. "Central de Cooperativas Agrarias 'Té Huyro Ltda.'" Documento de trabajo no. 43, La Convención–Cusco, 1972, Centro Bartolomé de las Casas (CBC), Cusco.

———. "Cooperativa Agraria de Producción Lauramarca Ltda." No. 56, Quispicanchi-Cusco. Lima: CENCIRA, 1972.

———. "El proceso electoral en la Cooperativa Agraria de Producción Casagrande." Documento de trabajo 32. Lima: CENCIRA, 1972.

———. *Los boletines en las empresas campesinas: Propósitos de los boletines, su preparación e impresión*. Lima: CENCIRA, 1975.

———. *Objetivos y acciones del comité de educación de las empresas campesinas*. Lima: CENCIRA, 1975.

———. *Primer conversatorio de dirigentes campesinos de Sociedades Agrícolas de Interés Social, Cooperativas Agrarias de Producción, comités profesionales de administración y comisiones de adjudicación provisional. Informe del conversatorio*. Lima: CENCIRA, 1972.

———. *Radio forum*. Lima: CENCIRA, n.d.

———. *Testimonio campesino sobre las áreas asociativas en las comunidades campesinas de la micro región de Anta*. Lima: CENCIRA, 1981.

CENPLA/SINAMOS. *Grupos Maoistas: Primera parte, Bandera Roja*. Lima: CENPLA/SINAMOS, ca. 1975.

Chiappo, Leopoldo. "La liberación de la educación en la revolución peruana." *Participación* 2, no. 2 (1973): 26–37.

Comisión Nacional de Alfabetización, Ministerio de Educación. *Alfabeticemos: Manual para el alfabetizador*. Havana: Comisión Nacional de Alfabetización, 1961.

Confederación Campesina del Perú. *Manifiesto de la CCP: Por la unidad clasista del campesinado*. Lima: Confederación Campesina del Perú, 1974.

Delgado, Carlos. "SINAMOS, la participación popular en la revolución peruana." *Participación* 2, no. 2 (1973): 22–23.

Dirección de Promoción y Difusión de la Reforma Agraria (DPDRA). *ABC de la reforma agraria Peruana*. Lima: DPDRA, 1969.

———. *Al hombre de la ciudad: ¿Cómo ayudar a la reforma agraria?* Lima: DPDRA, 1969.

———. *A los campesinos de las zonas a las cuales todavía no ha llegado la reforma agraria: Sobre parcelación*. Lima: DPDRA, ca. 1971.

———. *A los yanaconas, aparceros, arrendires . . .* Lima: DPDRA, 1969.

———. *¡A los yanaconas, aparceros, arrendires, allegados, colonos, mejoreros, precarios, huacchilleros así como a los demás tipos de feudatarios y los pequeños arrendatarios y sub-arrendatarios: Ustedes tienen derecho preferencial a la tierra que ocupan!* Lima: DPDRA, 1969.

———. *Del latifundio a la cooperativa*. Lima: DPDRA, ca. 1970.

———. *Educación de adultos en el contexto de la revolución peruana*. Lima: Dirección General de Educación Básica Laboral y Calificación, 1975.

Dirección General de Educación Básica Laboral y Calificación. *Guía metodológica ALFIN*. Lima: Dirección General de Educación Básica Laboral y Calificación, 1973.

Docafe, Enrique. "La nueva historia del Perú: La revolución peruana de 1968 o segunda independencia nacional." In *El Perú: Primera y segunda independencia, 1821 y 1968*, edited by C. D. Valcárcel, 294–446. Vol. 3 of *Historia general de los peruanos*. Lima: Ediciones Peisa, 1973.

Ejército del Perú. "El campesino y la reforma agraria." *Actualidad Militar* 153 (July 1970): 39–40.

———. "El ejército educa." Suplemento, *Actualidad Militar* 134 (Dec. 1968): vi–vii.

———. "Nueva mentalidad militar." *Actualidad Militar* 157 (Nov. 1970): 12–15, 31.

Lauer, Mirko, and Leonidas Cevallos. "Reforma agraria: Las dos educaciones." *Educación: La revista del maestro peruano* 1, no. 2 (Oct. 1970): 34–39.

Masmoudi, Mustapha. *The New World Information Order*. International Commission for the Study of Communication Problems Document 31. Paris: UNESCO, 1978.

Mejía, Percy. *Comunicación y educación de adultos, CENCIRA documento de trabajo*. Lima: CENCIRA, 1972.

Oficina Nacional de Difusión del SINAMOS. *Velasco, la voz de la revolución: Discursos del presidente de la república, General de Division Juan Velasco Alvarado, 1968-1970*. Lima: Oficina Nacional de Difusión del SINAMOS, 1972.

SINAMOS (ONAMS). *¿Adónde vamos? Una explicación de la política nacional de SINAMOS*. Lima: SINAMOS, ca. 1972.

———. *Comunidades campesinas del Perú: Información censal población y vivienda 1972*. Vol. 2. Lima: SINAMOS, 1977.

———. *Cuatro años de revolución*. Lima: SINAMOS, 1972.

———. "Hermanos! Una mañana del mes de noviembre de 1781, y luego de la transitoria derrota de Túpac Amaru, apareció en bandos públicos diseminados a lo largo del Cuzco la siguiente sentencia contra el pueblo." Lima: SINAMOS, 1973.

———. *La singularidad de nuestro proceso revolucionario*. Series 2, no. 3. Lima: SINAMOS, ca. 1972.

———. *Logros de la revolución peruana*. Series 2, no. 2. Lima: SINAMOS, ca. 1972.

———. *Los promotores y la participación popular*. Series 3, no. 2. Lima: SINAMOS, 1974.

———. *Movilización social: ¿De quién? ¿Para qué?* Lima: SINAMOS, ca. 1972.

———. *Movilización social y SINAMOS*. Series 3, no. 1. Lima: SINAMOS, ca. 1972.

———. *Ocho preguntas a la revolución peruana: Nociones elementales de política*. Lima: SINAMOS, 1973.

———. *¿Por qué se ataca al SINAMOS?* Lima: SINAMOS, ca. 1973.

———. *Sesenta y cuatro preguntas y respuestas*. Lima: SINAMOS, ca. 1972.

———. *Subdesarrollo y dominación*. Series 1, no. 1. Lima: SINAMOS, ca. 1974.

———. *Teatro y escuela de títeres*. Lima: SINAMOS, ca. 1972.

SINAMOS (ORAMS VII). "Diagnóstico socio político evaluativo de la Liga Agraria 'General Ollanta' de la provincia de Urubamba." Cusco: ORAMS VII, n.d.

Sociedad Agrícola de Interés Social (SAIS). "Cahuide Ltda." *Jatari* no. 6 (mimeographed publication). Huancayo: SAIS, División de Desarrollo, 1972.

Taller Nacional sobre Educación de Adultos en Areas Rurales. *Educación de adultos en areas rurales: Lineamientos técnicos y metodológicos*. Lima: Ministerio de Educación, Ministerio de Agricultura, SINAMOS, Instituto Interamericano de Ciencias Agrícolas, 1975.

UNESCO [United Nations Educational, Scientific and Cultural Organization]. *Report of the Meeting of Experts on Communication Policies and Planning.* Paris: UNESCO, 1972.

UNESCO, Regional Office for Education in Latin America and the Caribbean. *Evolución reciente de la educación en América Latina*, vol. 1: *Progresos, escollos y soluciones*. Mexico, 1976.

Valcárcel, C. D., ed. *El Perú: Primera y segunda independencia, 1821 y 1968*. Vol. 3 of *Historia general de los peruanos*. Lima: Ediciones Peisa, 1973.

Vanguardia Revolucionaria. *Aplastemos a los hacendados, expulsemos a los yanquis*. Declaración de Vanguardia Revolucionaria, 7 July 1969. Contemporary Archive on Latin America, Senate House Library, London.

———. *Contra la alianza reaccionaria unirse por la revolución popular. Manifiesto de Vanguardia Revolucionaria*. 11 July 1975. ISA Pamphlets, Senate House Library, London.

Velasco Alvarado, Juan. *Plan Inca o plan de gobierno revolucionario de la Fuerza Armada del Perú*. Lima: Ed. C. L. Cabrera V., 1974.

Zona Agraria I (Piura). *Catacaos: Veinticuatro de junio de 1973, día histórico para el campesino piurano*. Piura: Zona Agraria I, 1973.

Secondary Sources

Abendroth, Mark. *Rebel Literacy: Cuba's National Literacy Campaign and Critical Global Citizenship*. Duluth, MN: Litwin Books, 2009.

Abrams, Philip. "Notes on the Difficulty of Studying the State." *Journal of Historical Sociology* 1, no. 1 (1988): 58–89.

Albertus, Michael. *Autocracy and Redistribution: The Politics of Land Redistribution*. Cambridge: Cambridge University Press, 2015.

———. "Land Reform and Civil Conflict: Theory and Evidence from Peru." *American Journal of Political Science* (2019): 1–19.

Aldana Rivera, Susana. "Pensando la región: Una reflexión en torno al cambio y a la diversidad, al todo y a las partes." *Revista Interdisciplinaria de Historia y Ciencias Sociales* 1 (2012): 23–36.

Alvarez, Elena. *Política agraria y estancamiento de la agricultura, 1969–1977*. Lima: Instituto de Estudios Peruanos, 1980.

Alvarez, Elena, and José María Caballero. *Aspectos cuantitativos de la reforma agraria (1969–1979)*. Lima: Instituto de Estudios Peruanos, 1980.

Alvarez Calderón, Carlos. "Reflexiones sobre la operación de alfabetización integral." In *Educación de adultos en el contexto de la revolución peruana*, ed. Dirección General de Educación Básica Laboral y Calificación, 292–305. Lima: Dirección General de Educación Básica Laboral y Calificación, 1975.

Andrews, M. *Shaping History: Narratives of Political Change*. Cambridge: Cambridge University Press, 2007.

Apel, Karin. *De la hacienda a la comunidad: La Sierra de Piura 1934–1990*. Lima: IEP, IFEA, 1996.

Arce Espinoza, Elmer. *La reforma agraria en Piura: 1969–1977*. Lima: CEDEP, 1983.

Asensio, Raúl. *El apóstol de los Andes: El culto a Túpac Amaru en Cusco durante la revolución velasquista (1968–1975)*. Lima: IEP, 2017.

Bauer, B. S. *The Development of the Inca State*. Austin: University of Texas Press, 1996.

Béjar, Héctor. *Peru 1965: Notes on a Guerrilla Experience*. Translated by William Rose. New York: Monthly Review Press, 1970.

———. *La revolución en la trampa*. Lima: Ediciones socialismo y participación, 1976.

Bernex de Falen, Nicole, and Bruno Revesz. *Atlas regional de Piura*. Lima: CIPCA, 1988.

Bizot, Judithe. *Educational Reform in Peru: A Study Prepared for the International Educational Reporting Service*. Paris: UNESCO, 1975.

Bonilla, Heraclio. "Comunidades de indígenas y estado nación en el Perú." *Histórica* 6, no. 1 (1982): 35–51.

Bonnell, Victoria E. *Iconography of Power: Soviet Political Posters under Lenin and Stalin*. Berkeley: University of California Press, 1997.

Booth, John A. "The Revolution in Nicaragua: Through a Frontier of History." In *Revolution and Counterrevolution in Central America and the Caribbean*, edited by Donald E. Schulz and Douglas H. Graham, 301–330. Boulder, CO: Westview, 1984.

Bourricaud, François. *Cambios en Puno: Estudios de sociología andina*. Mexico City: Instituto Indigenista Interamericano, 1967.

Brouillete, Sarah. "UNESCO and the Book in the Developing World." *Representations* 127, no. 1 (2014): 33–54.

Burenius, Charlotte. *Testimonio de un fracaso. Huando: Habla el sindicalista Zózimo Torres*. Lima: IEP, 2001.

Burton, Anthony. "The Submerged and the Seers: Adult Literacy in Peru, 1973–1974." *Anthropology and Education Quarterly* 11, no. 4 (1980): 235–253.

Butler, Judith. "Ruled Out: Vocabularies of the Censor." In *Censorship and Silencing: Practices of Cultural Regulation*, edited by Robert C. Post, 247–259. Los Angeles: Getty Research Institute for the History of Art and the Humanities, 1998.

Caballero, José María. *Agricultura, reforma agraria y pobreza campesina*. Lima: IEP, 1980.

———. "From Belaúnde to Belaúnde: Peru's Military Experiment in Third-Roadism." Centre of Latin American Studies Working Paper 36, University of Cambridge, Cambridge, 1981.

Cameron, Maxwell A. "From Oligarchic Domination to Neoliberal Governance: The Shining Path and the Transformation of Peru's Constitutional Order." In *Politics after Violence: Legacies of the Shining Path Conflict in Peru*, edited by Hillel David Soifer and Alberto Vergara, 79–108. Austin: University of Texas Press, 2019.

Cant, Anna. "'Land for Those Who Work It': A Visual Analysis of Agrarian Reform Posters in Velasco's Peru." *Journal of Latin American Studies* 44, no. 1 (2012): 1–37.

Cardó Franco, Andrés. *La iglesia y la educación en el Perú*. Arequipa: Universidad Católica San Pablo, 2005.

Carr, Raymond. "Mexican Agrarian Reform 1910–1960." In *Agrarian Change and Economic Development: The Historical Problems*, edited by E. L. Jones and S. J. Woolf, 151–168. London: Methuen, 1969. Reprinted Abingdon, UK: Routledge, 2006.

CENCIRA. *Testimonio campesino sobre las áreas asociativas en las comunidades campesinas de la micro región de Anta*. Lima: CENCIRA, 1981.

Centro Nacional de Memoria Histórica. *La política de reforma agraria y tierras en Colombia: Esbozo de una memoria institucional*. Bogotá: Imprenta Nacional, 2013.

Centro Peruano de Estudios Sociales (CEPES). "Especial: Reforma agraria, a los 40 años." *La Revista Agraria* 108 (June 2009): 15–24, https://larevistagraria.files.wordpress.com/2019/05/lra-108_completo.pdf.

Chaplin, David, ed. *Peruvian Nationalism: A Corporatist Revolution*. New Brunswick, NJ: Transaction Books, 1976.

———. "The Revolutionary Challenge and Peruvian Militarism." In *Peruvian Nationalism: A Corporatist Revolution*, edited by David Chaplin, 3–34. New Brunswick, NJ: Transaction Books, 1976.

Chirinos Soto, Enrique, and Guido Chirinos Lizares. *El septenato 1968–75*. Lima: Editorial Alfa, 1977.

Chu, Ying-Ying. "The Answer Was Cooperative: How Anthropologists in Peru Redefined the 'National Problem,' 1948–1975." PhD diss., State University of New York at Stony Brook, 2016.

Churchill, Stacey. *The Peruvian Model of Innovation: The Reform of Basic Education, a Study Prepared for the International Educational Reporting Service*. Paris: UNESCO, 1976.

CIPCA, comp. *A veinte años de la reforma agraria: Dossier regional 5*. Piura: CIPCA, 1989.

Cleaves, Peter S., and Martín J. Scurrah. *Agriculture, Bureaucracy, and Military Government in Peru*. Ithaca, NY: Cornell University Press, 1980.

El Colegio de México. *Historia de la lectura en México*. Seminario de historia de la educación en México. México, DF: Ediciones del Ermitaño, 1988.

Comisión de la Verdad y Reconciliación. *Informe final*. Lima: Comisión de la Verdad y Reconciliación, 2003.

Conaghan, Catherine M., James M. Malloy, and Leandro Wolfson. "Democracia y neoliberalismo en Perú, Ecuador y Bolivia." *Desarrollo Económico* 36, no. 144 (1997): 867–890.

Contreras, Carlos. "El centralismo peruano en su perspectiva histórica." IEP documento de trabajo 127. Lima: IEP, 2002.

Contreras, Carlos, and Marcos Cueto. *Historia del Perú contemporáneo*. 4th ed. Lima: IEP, Pontificia Universidad Católica del Perú, and Universidad del Pacífico, 2010.

Coronel-Molina, Serafin M. *Language Ideology, Policy and Planning in Peru*. Bristol, UK: Multilingual Matters, 2015.

Correa, Martín, Raúl Molina, and Nancy Yáñez. *La reforma agraria y las tierras mapuches: Chile 1962–1975*. Santiago: LOM Ediciones, 2005.

Cotler, Julio. "The Mechanics of Internal Domination and Social Change in Peru." In *Peruvian Nationalism: A Corporatist Revolution*, edited by David Chaplin, 35–71. New Brunswick, NJ: Transaction Books, 1976.

Cottyn, Hanne. "Renegotiating Communal Autonomy: Communal Land Rights and Liberal Land Reform on the Bolivian Altiplano: Carangas, 1860–1930." PhD diss., University of Ghent, 2014. https://biblio.ugent.be/publication/4432196.

Courville, Michael, and Raj Patel. "Introduction and Overview: The Resurgence of Agrarian Reform in the Twenty-first Century." In *Promised Land: Competing Visions of Agrarian Reform*, edited by Peter Rosset, Raj Patel, and Michael Courville, 3–22. Oakland, CA: Food First Books, 2006.

Craven, David. *Art and Revolution in Latin America 1910–1990*. New Haven, CT: Yale University Press, 2002.

Cushner, Nicholas P. *Lords of the Land: Sugar, Wine, and Jesuit Estates of Coastal Peru, 1600–1767.* Albany: State University of New York Press, 1980.

Das, Veena, and Deborah Poole, eds. *Anthropology in the Margins of the State.* Santa Fe, NM: School of American Research Press, 2004.

Davies, Keith A. *Landowners in Colonial Peru.* Austin: University of Texas Press, 1984.

Dávila, Jerry. *Dictatorship in South America.* Chichester, UK: Wiley-Blackwell, 2013.

Dawson, Graham. *Soldier Heroes: British Adventure, Empire and the Imagining of Masculinities.* London: Routledge, 1994.

Deere, Carmen. *Household and Class Relations: Peasants and Landlords in Northern Peru.* Berkeley: University of California Press, 1990.

Degregori, Carlos Iván. *Qué difícil es ser Dios: El Partido Comunista del Perú, Sendero Luminoso y el conflicto armado interno en el Perú: 1980–1999.* Lima: IEP, 2010.

De la Cadena, Marisol. *Indigenous Mestizos: The Politics of Race and Culture in Cuzco, Peru, 1919–1991.* Durham, NC: Duke University Press, 2000.

———. "Silent Racism and Intellectual Superiority in Peru." *Bulletin of Latin American Research* 17, no. 2 (1998): 143–164.

Del Águila, Alicia. "Historia del sufragio en el Perú, s. XIX–XX: Una lectura desde la ciudadanía y la participación indígena." In *Participación electoral indígena y cuota nativa en el Perú: Aportes para el debate*, edited by Alicia del Águila and Milagros Suito, 17–35. Lima: Idea, 2012.

De la Peña, Guillermo. "Rural Mobilizations in Latin America Since c. 1920." In *Latin America since 1930: Economy, Society and Politics*, 379–482. Vol. 6 of *The Cambridge History of Latin America*, edited by Leslie Bethell. Cambridge: Cambridge University Press, 1994.

Del Mastro Puccio, Marco. *Luchas campesinas: Cuzco 1968–1978.* Lima: CEPES, 1979.

Diez, Alejandro. "Gobierno comunal: Entre la propiedad y el control territorial, el caso de la Comunidad de Catacaos." *Sepia* 14, no. 1 (2012): 115–148.

Dorais, Geneviéve. "La crítica maoísta peruana frente a la reforma agraria de Velasco (1969–1980)." IEP Documento de Trabajo 167, Lima, 2012.

Drinot, Paulo. "Remembering Velasco: Contested Memories of the Revolutionary Government of the Armed Forces." In *The Peculiar Revolution: Rethinking the Peruvian Experiment under Military Rule*, edited by Carlos Aguirre and Paulo Drinot, 95–119. Austin: University of Texas Press, 2017.

Durston, Alan. "Native-Language Literacy in Colonial Peru: The Question of Mundane Quechua Writing Revisited." *Hispanic American Historical Review* 88, no. 1 (2008): 41–70.

———. "Quechua for the *Patria Nueva*: Indigenous-Language Propaganda in 1920s Peru." Unpublished manuscript, 2013.

Eguren López, Fernando. *Reforma agraria, cooperativazación y lucha campesina: El valle Chancay-Huaral.* Lima: DESCO [Centro de Estudios y Promocion del Desarrollo], 1975.

Encinas Martín, Alfredo, Ángel Pérez Casado, and Rafael Alonso Ordieres. *Historia social y religiosa del siglo XX, historia de la provincia de La Convención.* Vol. 2. Lima: Centro Cultural José Pío Aza, 2008.

Escobar Ohmstede, Antonio, and Matthew Butler, eds. *México y sus transiciones: Reconsideraciones sobre la historia agraria mexicana, siglos XIX y XX.* Mexico, DF:

CIESAS [Centro de Investigaciones y Estudios Superiores en Antropología Social], 2013.

Espinoza, César, and Olga Egúsquiza Pereda. "El sistema de hacienda en el valle del alto Chira: El régimen de propiedad y posesión de la tierra en Poechos, San Francisco y Chocán (Siglos XVI–XX)." In *El problema agrario en el valle del Chira, Piura*, edited by Marika López et al., 193–240. Lima: UNMSM [Universidad Nacional Mayor de San Marcos], 1982.

Fernández Montenegro, Blanca. "Reforma agraria y condición socio-económica de la mujer: El caso de dos cooperativas agrarias de producción peruana." In *Debate sobre la mujer en América Latina y el Caribe: Discusión acerca de la unidad producción-reproducción*, edited by Magdalena León, 261–276. Bogota: Asociacion Colombiana para el Estudio de la Poblacion, 1982.

Flores Galindo, Alberto. "Movimientos campesinos en el Perú: Balance y esquema." *Cuaderno Rural* 18 (ca. 1977).

Forster, Nancy R. "*Minifundistas* in Tunguraghua, Ecuador: Survival on the Agricultural Ladder." In *Searching for Agrarian Reform in Latin America*, edited by William C. Thiesenhusen, 92–126. Boston: Unwin Hyman, 1989.

Franco, Carlos, and Rolando Ames, eds. *El Perú de Velasco*. 3 vols. Lima: CEDEP, 1983.

———. *Perú: Participación popular*. Lima: Ediciones CEDEP, 1979.

Freire, Paulo. *Pedagogy of the Oppressed*. 30th anniversary ed. London: Bloomsbury, 2000.

García Sayán, Diego. *Tomas de tierras en el Perú*. Lima: DESCO, 1982.

Gargurevich, Juan. *Prensa, radio y tv: Historia crítica*. Lima: Editorial Horizonte, 1987.

Giraudo, Laura, and Juan Martín-Sánchez, eds. *La ambivalente historia del indigenismo: Campo interamericano y trayectorias nacionales 1940–1970*. Lima: IEP, 2011.

Gómez Cumpa, José, and Inés Bazán Alfaro, eds. *Capitalismo y formación regional: Chiclayo entre los siglos XIX y XX*. Chiclayo: Población y Desarrollo Instituto de Investigación y Capacitación, 1989.

Gorriti Ellenbogen, Gustavo. *The Shining Path: A History of the Millenarian War in Peru*. Chapel Hill: University of North Carolina Press, 1999.

Gotkowitz, Laura. *A Revolution for Our Rights: Indigenous Struggles for Land and Justice in Bolivia, 1880–1952*. Durham, NC: Duke University Press, 2007.

Gramsci, Antonio. *Selections from the Prison Notebooks*. Edited by Quentin Hoare and Geoffrey Nowell Smith. London: ElecBook, 2001.

Grandin, Greg. *The Last Colonial Massacre: Latin America in the Cold War*. Chicago: University of Chicago Press, 2011.

Grieshaber, Erwin Peter. *Survival of Indian Communities in Nineteenth-Century Bolivia*. Chapel Hill: University of North Carolina Press, 1977.

Guardia Mayorga, César. *La reforma agraria en el Perú*. 2nd ed. Lima: Minerva, 1962.

Guerra, Lillian. *Visions of Power in Cuba: Revolution, Redemption, and Resistance, 1959–1971*. Chapel Hill: University of North Carolina Press, 2012.

Guerra García, Francisco. "SINAMOS y la promoción de la participación." In *El Perú de Velasco*, vol. 3, edited by Carlos Franco and Rolando Ames, 681–708. Lima: CEDEP, 1983.

Halbwachs, Maurice. *The Collective Memory*. New York: Harper and Row, 1980.

Hall, Ingrid. "La reforma agraria, entre memoria y olvido (Andes Sur peruanos)." *Anthropologica* 31 (2013): 101–125.

Harding, Colin. "Agrarian Reform and Agrarian Struggles in Peru." Centre of Latin American Studies Working Paper 15, Cambridge University, Cambridge, 1974.

Harris, O., B. Larson, and E. Tandeter, eds. *Ethnicity, Markets, and Migration in the Andes: At the Crossroads of History and Anthropology*. Durham, NC: Duke University Press, 1995.

Harvey, Penelope M. "Language and the Power of History: A Study of Bilinguals in Ocongate (Southern Peru)." PhD diss., London School of Economics, 1987.

Heilman, Jaymie Patricia. *Before the Shining Path: Politics in Rural Ayacucho, 1895-1980*. Stanford, CA: Stanford University Press, 2010.

Hildebrandt, César. *Cambio de palabras: Veintiseis entrevistas*. Lima: Mosca Azul, 1981.

Hinajosa, Iván. "On Poor Relations and the Nouveau Riche: Shining Path and the Radical Peruvian Left." In *Shining and Other Paths: War and Society in Peru, 1980-1995*, edited by Steve J. Stern, 60–83. Durham, NC: Duke University Press, 1998.

Hobsbawm, E. J. E. "A Case of Neo-Feudalism: La Convención, Peru." *Journal of Latin American Studies* 1, no. 1 (1969): 31–50.

Holston, James. *Insurgent Citizenship: Disjunctions of Democracy and Modernity in Brazil*. Princeton, NJ: Princeton University Press, 2008.

Hopkins, Raúl. "Política agraria: Entre el discurso y los desafíos de la realidad." *Debate Agrario: Análisis y Alternativas* 1 (1987): 9–19.

Huayre Cochachin, Rosa Elvira. "Reforma agraria y comunidades campesinas (Perú, 1969–1975): Aproximación al proceso de reestructuración comunal." *Heraldos* [Centro de Estudiantes de Historia-Universidad Nacional Mayor de San Marcos] 1, no. 1 (2012): 104–114.

Instituto Nacional de Estadística, ed. *Compendio de estadísticas sociales 1991*. Lima: Instituto Nacional de Estadística, 1992.

Jaworski, Helán. "Democracia y 'socialización' en los medios de comunicación." In *El Perú de Velasco*, vol. 3, edited by Carlos Franco and Rolando Ames, 767–807. Lima: CEDEP, 1983.

Jelin, Elizabeth. *Los trabajos de la memoria*. Madrid: Siglo XXI de España Editores/ Social Science Research Council, 2002.

Joseph, Gilbert M. "Rethinking Mexican Revolutionary Mobilization: Yucatán's Seasons of Upheaval, 1909–1915." In *Everyday Forms of State Formation: Revolution and the Negotiation of Rule in Modern Mexico*, edited by Gilbert M. Joseph and Daniel Nugent, 135–169. Durham, NC: Duke University Press, 1994.

Jungbluth Melgar, Werner. "El voto rural en la segunda vuelta." *La Revista Agraria* 130 (2011): 4–5.

Kapsoli Escudero, Wilfredo. *Ayllus del sol: Anarquismo y utopía andina*. Lima: Tarea, 1984.

———. *Los movimientos campesinos en el Perú, 1879-1965*. 2nd ed. Lima: Ediciones Atusparia, 1982.

Keith, Robert G. *Conquest and Agrarian Change: The Emergence of the Hacienda System on the Peruvian Coast*. Cambridge, MA: Harvard University Press, 1976.

Kirkendall, Andrew J. *Paulo Freire and the Cold War Politics of Literacy*. Chapel Hill: University of North Carolina Press, 2010.

Klaiber, Jeffrey. *La iglesia en el Perú: Su historia social desde la Independencia*. 3rd ed. Lima: Pontificia Universidad Católica del Perú, 1996.

———. "The Popular Universities and the Origins of Aprismo, 1921–1924." *Hispanic American Historical Review* 55, no. 4 (1975): 693–715.

Klaren, Peter F. *Formación de las haciendas azucareras y orígenes del APRA* [Alianza Popular Revolucionaria Americana]. 2nd ed. Lima: IEP, 1976.

———. *Peru: Society and Nationhood in the Andes*. New York: Oxford, 2000.

Klein, Kerwin Lee. "On the Emergence of Memory in Historical Discourse." *Representations* 69 (Winter 2000): 127–150.

Knight, Alan. "The Myth of the Mexican Revolution." *Past and Present* 209 (2010): 223–273.

———. "Populism and Neo-Populism in Latin America, especially Mexico." *Journal of Latin American Studies* 30, no. 2 (1998): 223–248.

Knight, Peter. "New Forms of Organization in Peru: Toward Workers' Self-Management." In *The Peruvian Experiment: Continuity and Change under Military Rule*, edited by Abraham Lowenthal, 350–401. Princeton, NJ: Princeton University Press, 1975.

Knudson, Jerry W. *Roots of Revolution: The Press and Social Change in Latin America*. Lanham, MD: University Press of America, 2009.

Koonings, Kees, and Dirk Kruijt. *Political Armies: The Military and Nation Building in the Age of Democracy*. London: Zed Books, 2002.

Kottek, Markus, Jürgen Grieser, Christoph Beck, Bruno Rudolf, and Franz Rubel. "World Map of the Köppen-Geiger Climate Classification Updated." *Meteorologische Zeitschrift* 15, no. 3 (2006): 259–263.

Kruijt, Dirk. *La revolución por decreto: Perú durante el gobierno militar*. Translated by R. B. Smith. San José, Costa Rica: Facultad Latinoamericana de Ciencias Sociales, 1991.

Lapp, Nancy D. *Landing Votes: Representation and Land Reform in Latin America*. London: Palgrave Macmillan, 2004.

Lazar, Sian, ed. *The Anthropology of Citizenship: A Reader*. Hoboken, NJ: Wiley, 2013.

———. "Education for Credit: Development as Citizenship Project in Bolivia, 2004." In *The Anthropology of Citizenship: A Reader*, edited by Sian Lazar, 107–119. Hoboken, NJ: Wiley, 2013.

Letts, Ricardo. *La izquierda peruana: Organizaciones y tendencias*. Lima: Mozca Azul, 1981.

Lomnitz-Adler, Claudio. *Exits from the Labyrinth: Culture and Ideology in the Mexican National Space*. Berkeley, CA: University of California Press, 1992.

Long, Norman, and Bryan Roberts. "Agrarian Structures." In *The Cambridge History of Latin America*, edited by Leslie Bethell, 11:556–568. Cambridge: Cambridge University Press, 1995.

Lowenthal, Abraham F., ed. *The Peruvian Experiment: Continuity and Change under Military Rule*. Princeton, NJ: Princeton University Press, 1975.

Lynch, Nicolás. "La polémica indigenista y los origenes del comunismo en el Cusco." *Crítica Andina* no. 3 (1979): 5–46.

Mallon, Florencia E. *Peasant and Nation: The Making of Postcolonial Mexico and Peru*. Berkeley: University of California Press, 1995.

Malpica, Carlos. *Los dueños del Perú*. 3rd ed. Lima: Ensayos Sociales, 1968.

Mariátegui, José Carlos. *Siete ensayos de interpretación de la realidad peruana*. Caracas: Biblioteca Ayacucho, 2007.

Marshall, T. H. *Citizenship and Social Class and Other Essays*. Cambridge: Cambridge University Press, 1950.

Martín Sánchez, Juan. "Indigenismo bifronte en el gobierno peruano de Velasco Alvarado: Continuidad y alternativa, sierra y selva." In *La ambivalente historia del indigenismo: Campo interamericano y trayectorias nacionales 1940–1970*, edited by Laura Giraudo and Juan Martín Sánchez, 191–250. Lima: IEP, 2011.

———. *La revolución peruana: Ideología y práctica política de un gobierno militar 1968–1975*. Sevilla: Universidad de Sevilla, 2002.

Mason, T. David. "'Take Two Acres and Call Me in the Morning': Is Land Reform a Prescription for Peasant Unrest?" *Journal of Politics* 60, no. 1 (1998): 199–230.

Masterson, Daniel M. *Militarism and Politics in Latin America: Peru from Sánchez Cerro to Sendero Luminoso*. Westport, CT: Greenwood, 1991.

Matos Mar, José. *Las actuales comunidades de indígenas: Huarochirí en 1955*. Lima: UNMSM, 1958.

———. *Dominación y cambios en el Perú rural: La micro-región del valle de Chancay*. Lima: IEP, 1969.

———. *Yanaconaje y reforma agraria en el Perú: El caso del valle de Chancay*. Lima: IEP, 1976.

Matos Mar, José, and José Manuel Mejía. *La reforma agraria en el Perú*. Lima: Instituto de Estudios Peruanos, 1980.

Mayer, Enrique. *Ugly Stories of the Peruvian Agrarian Reform*. Durham, NC: Duke University Press, 2009.

Mayorga, César Guardia. *La reforma agaria en el Perú*. 2nd ed. Lima: Minerva, 1963.

McClintock, Cynthia. *Peasant Cooperatives and Political Change in Peru*. Princeton, NJ: Princeton University Press, 1981.

———. "Velasco, Officers, and Citizens: The Politics of Stealth." In *The Peruvian Experiment Reconsidered*, edited by Cynthia McClintock and Abraham F. Lowenthal, 275–308. Princeton, NJ: Princeton University Press, 1983.

———. "Why Peasants Rebel: The Case of Peru's Sendero Luminoso." *World Politics* 37, no. 1 (1984): 48–84.

Menacho Jaramillo, Rafael. "El Congreso Nacional Agrario y la operación ALFIN." In *Educación de adultos en el contexto de la revolución peruana*, edited by Dirección General de Educación Básica Laboral y Calificación, 306–318. Lima: Dirección General de Educación Básica Laboral y Calificación, 1975.

Méndez G., Cecilia. "Las paradojas del autoritarismo: Ejército, campesinado y etnicidad en el perú, siglos XIX al XX." *Iconos: Revista de Ciencias Sociales* 26 (2006): 17–34.

Mendoza Michilot, María. "Gestión de las empresas periodísticas regionales: El Sol, de Cusco; El Tiempo, de Piura e Ímpetu, de Ucayali." *Revista de Comunicación* 14 (2015): 70–99.

Mendoza Salazar, Felícitas. "Los programas en quechua en la radiodifusión peruana." Undergraduate thesis, Pontificia Universidad Católica del Perú, 1974.

Merkel-Hess, Kate. "Reading the Rural Modern: Literacy and Morality in Republican China." *History Compass* 7, no. 1 (2009): 44–54.

Mesclier, Evelyne. "De la complementariedad a la voluntad de aplanar los Andes: Representaciones de la naturaleza y pensamiento económico y político en el Perú del siglo XX." *Bulletin de l'Institut Français d'Études Andines* 30, no. 3 (2001): 541–562.

Middents, Jeffrey. *Writing National Cinema: Film Journals and Film Culture in Peru.* Hanover, NH: Dartmouth College Press, 2009.

Ministerio de Agricultura. *Exposición de la Oficina Nacional de Reforma y Promoción Agraria.* Lima: Ministerio de Agriculture, 1963.

Mitchell, T. "The Limits of the State: Beyond Statist Approaches and Their Critics." *American Political Science Review* 85, no. 1 (1991): 77–96.

Mitchell, W. J. T. *Iconology: Image, Text, Ideology.* Chicago: University of Chicago Press, 1987.

Montoya, Rodrigo. *Capitalismo y no capitalismo en el Perú: Un estudio histórico de su articulación en un eje regional.* Lima: Mosca Azul Editores, 1980.

Mraz, John. *Looking for Mexico: Modern Visual Culture and National Identity.* Durham, NC: Duke University Press, 2009.

Mujica Escalante, Abel Fernando. *Una vida y un rumbo: Cincuenta años de cusqueñismo, Radio Tahuantinsuyo y Raúl Montesinos Espejo.* Cusco: El Diario del Cusco, ca. 1998.

Narotzky, Susana, and Gavin Smith. "'Being Político' in Spain: An Ethnographic Account of Memories, Silences and Public Politics." *History and Memory* 14, no. 1–2 (2002): 189–228.

Neira, Hugo. *Cuzco: Tierra y muerte.* Lima: Editorial Herética, 2008.

North, Liisa L. "Ideological Orientations of Rulers." In *The Peruvian Experiment Reconsidered*, edited by Cynthia McClintock and Abraham F. Lowenthal, 245–274. Princeton, NJ: Princeton University Press, 1983.

North, Liisa L., and Mario Dos Santos. "Orígenes y crecimiento del partido aprista y el cambio socioeconómico en el Perú." *Desarrollo Económico* 10, no. 38 (1970): 63–214.

North, Liisa L., and Tanya Korovkin. *The Peruvian Revolution and the Officers in Power, 1967–1976.* Montreal: Centre for Developing-Area Studies, McGill University, 1981.

Nugent, Daniel, and Ana María Alonso. "Multiple Selective Traditions in Agrarian Reform and Agrarian Struggle: Popular Culture and State Formation in the Ejido of Namiquipa Chihuahua." In *Everyday Forms of State Formation: Revolution and the Negotiation of Rule in Modern Mexico*, edited by Gilbert M. Joseph and Daniel Nugent, 209–246. Durham, NC: Duke University Press, 1994.

Nugent, Guillermo. *El laberinto de la choledad.* 2nd ed. Lima: Universidad Peruana de Ciencias Aplicadas, 2013.

Oliart, Patricia. *Educación en tiempos de cambio, 1968–1975.* Lima: Derrama Magisterial, 2013.

———. "Education for Social Change: Peru 1972–1975." *Journal of Social Science Education* 12, no. 3 (2013): 8–18.

———. "Politicizing Education: The 1972 Reform in Peru." In *The Peculiar Revolution: Rethinking the Peruvian Experiment under Military Rule*, edited by Carlos Aguirre and Paulo Drinot, 123–148. Austin: University of Texas Press, 2017.

———. "State Reform and Resilient Powers: Teachers, School Culture and the Neoliberal Education Reform in Peru." PhD diss., Newcastle University, 2007.

Olick, J., and J. Robbins. "Social Memory Studies: From 'Collective Memory' to the Historical Sociology of Mnemonic Practices." *Annual Review of Sociology* 24 (1998): 105–140.

Otero, Gerardo. "Agrarian Reform in Mexico: Capitalism and the State." In *Searching for Agrarian Reform in Latin America*, edited by William C. Thiesenhusen, 276–304. Boston: Blackwell, 1989.

Otero, Pedro, and Bruno Revesz. "Educación popular y alfabetización en el Centro de Investigación y Promoción del Campesinado (CIPCA)." In *Formación de promotores para la alfabetización, informe final*, edited by Oficina Regional de Educación para America Latina y el Caribe, 26–30. Santiago: Oficina Regional de Educación para America Latina y el Caribe, 1982.

Padrón Castillo, Mario, and Henry Pease García. *Planificación rural, reforma agraria y organización campesina: Programa de promoción campesina en el Valle del Santa 1971–1973*. Lima: DESCO, 1974.

Panty Neyra, Oscar. *Historia de la prensa escrita en Tacna*. Tacna: Javier Flore Arocutipa, 1999.

———. *Tacna, economía y sociedad: Introducción al periodo reformista-desarrollista, 1970–1980*. Tacna: Ediciones Liberación, 1980.

Peloso, Vincent C., and Barbara A. Tenenbaum. *Liberals, Politics, and Power: State Formation in Nineteenth-Century Latin America*. Athens: University of Georgia Press, 1996.

Philip, George. *Oil and Politics in Latin America: Nationalist Movements and State Companies*. Cambridge: Cambridge University Press, 1982.

Piel, Jan. *El capitalismo agrario en el Perú*. Lima: Institut français d'études andines, Universidad Nacional de Salta, 1995.

Platt, Tristán. *Estado boliviano y ayllu andino: Tierra y tributo en el norte de Potosí*. Lima: IEP, 1982.

Plaza-J., Orlando. "Campesinado, analfabetismo y el problema del voto en el Perú." *Nueva Sociedad* 41 (Mar.–Apr. 1979): 71–82.

Poole, Deborah. "Corriendo riesgos: Normas, ley y participación en el Estado neoliberal." *Anthropologica* 30 (2012): 83–100.

Poole, Deborah, and Gerardo Rénique. *Peru: Time of Fear*. London: Latin American Bureau, 1992.

Portelli, Alessandro. *The Order Has Been Carried Out: History, Memory, and Meaning of a Nazi Massacre in Rome*. New York: Palgrave Macmillan, 2003.

———. "Uchronic Dreams: Working Class Memory and Possible Worlds." *Oral History Journal* 16, no. 2 (1988): 46–55.

Portocarrero, Gonzalo. "Memorias del velasquismo." In *Batallas por la memoria: Antagonismos de la promesa peruana*, edited by Marita Hamann et al., 229–256. Lima: Pontificia Universidad Católica del Perú, Universidad del Pacífico, Instituto de Estudios Peruanos, 2003.

Pulgar Vidal, Javier. *Geografía del Perú: Las ocho regiones naturales, la regionalización transversal, la sabiduría ecológica tradicional*. Lima: Peisa, 1996.

Ragas, José. "Leer, escribir, votar: Literacidad y cultura política en el Perú (1810–1900)." *Histórica* 31, no. 1 (2007): 107–134.

Rénique, José Luis. *La batalla por Puno: Conflicto agrario y nación en los Andes peruanos 1866–1995*. Lima: IEP, 2004.

———. *Los sueños de La Sierra: Cusco en el siglo XX*. Lima: CEPES, 1991.

Revesz, Bruno. "El campesino piurano en la escena regional (1978–1983)." *Socialismo y participación* 28 (Dec. 1984): 111–122.

———. "Catacaos: Una comunidad en la modernidad." *Debate agrario: Análisis y alternativas* 14 (June–Sept. 1992): 75–105.

———. *Estado, algodón y productores agrarios*. Piura: CIPCA, 1982.

———. "Necesidad de una nueva interpretación de la reforma agraria y sus efectos." In "Peru: El problema agario en debate," a special issue of *SEPIA* 1, no. 1 (1985): 87–121.

Rivero, José. *Educación, docencia y clase política en el Perú*. Lima: Ayuda en Acción/ Tarea Asociación de Publicaciones Educativas, 2007.

Rojas, Rolando. *La revolución de los arrendires: Una historia personal de la reforma agraria*. Lima: IEP, 2019.

Rojas-Perez, Isaias. *Mourning Remains: State Atrocity, Exhumations, and Governing the Disappeared in Peru's Postwar Andes*. Stanford, CA: Stanford University Press, 2019.

Rosas Paravicino, Enrique. "Tentativa de socialización de los diarios de circulación nacional en el Perú." Undergraduate thesis, Universidad Nacional de San Antonio Abad del Cusco, 1978.

Rosset, Peter, Raj Patel, and Michael Courville, eds. *Promised Land: Competing Visions of Agrarian Reform*. Oakland, CA: First Food Books, 2006.

Rubín de Celis T., Emma. *Las CAPs de Piura y sus contradicciones*. Piura: CIPCA, 1977.

———. *¿Qué piensa el campesino de la reforma agraria?: Caso Piura*. Piura: CIPCA, 1978.

Sallnow, M. "Cooperation and Contradiction: The Dialectics of Everyday Practice." *Dialectical Anthropology* 14 (1989): 241–257.

Salomon, Frank, and Mercedes Niño-Murcia. *The Lettered Mountain: A Peruvian Village's Way with Writing*. Durham, NC: Duke University Press, 2011.

Sammels, Clare A. "Production, Trade, Reciprocity, and Markets." In *The Andean World*, edited by Linda J. Seligmann and Kathleen S. Fine-Dare, 251–265. London: Routledge, 2019.

Sánchez Enríquez, Rodrigo. *Toma de tierras y conciencia política campesina*. Lima: IEP, 1981.

Santuc, Vicente. *CIPCA: Un proyecto en Piura. Análisis de algunas acciones*. 2nd ed. Piura: CIPCA, 1983.

Schlotterbeck, Marian E. *Beyond the Vanguard: Everyday Revolutionaries in Allende's Chile*. Berkeley: University of California Press, 2018.

Seligmann, Linda J. *Between Reform and Revolution: Political Struggles in the Peruvian Andes, 1969–1991*. Stanford, CA: Stanford University Press, 1995.

———. "Civil War in Peru: Culture and Violence in Historical Perspective." In *The State, Identity and Violence: Political Disintegration in the Post-Cold War World*, edited by R. Brian Ferguson, 117–148. London: Routledge, 2002.

Seligmann, Linda J., and Kathleen S. Fine-Dare, eds. *The Andean World*. London: Routledge, 2019.

Seoane, Mario. *La deuda secreta del Perú: Los bonos de la reforma agraria*. Lima: Grijley, 2011.

Silva, Patricio. "Doing Politics in a Depoliticised Society: Social Change and Political Deactivation in Chile." *Bulletin of Latin American Research* 23, no. 1 (2004): 63–78.

Singh, Prerna. *How Solidarity Works for Welfare: Subnationalism and Social Development in India*. Cambridge: Cambridge University Press, 2016.

———. "The Theoretical Potential of the Within-Nation Comparison: How Sub-

National Analyses Can Enrich Our Understandings of the National Welfare State." *American Behavioral Scientist* 61, no. 8 (2017): 861–886.

Sklar, Barry, and Virginia M. Hagen, comps. *Inter-American Relations: Collection of Documents, Legislation, Descriptions of Inter-American Organizations, and Other Material Pertaining to Inter-American Affairs*. Washington, DC: U.S. Government Printing Office, 1972. http://avalon.law.yale.edu/20th_century/intam15.asp.

Skuban, William E. *Lines in the Sand: Nationalism and Identity on the Peruvian-Chilean Frontier*. Albuquerque: University of New Mexico Press, 2007.

Soifer, Hillel David, and Alberto Vergara. "Introduction: Leaving the Path Behind." In *Politics after Violence: Legacies of the Shining Path Conflict in Peru*, edited by Hillel David Soifer and Alberto Vergara, 1–16. Austin: University of Texas Press, 2019.

———, eds. *Politics after Violence: Legacies of the Shining Path Conflict in Peru*. Austin: University of Texas Press, 2019.

Soliz, Carmen. "Fields of Revolution: The Politics of Agrarian Reform in Bolivia, 1935–1971." PhD diss., New York University, 2014.

Spalding, Karen. *Huarochirí: An Andean Society under Inca and Spanish Rule*. Stanford, CA: Stanford University Press, 1984.

Stepan, Alfred C. *The State and Society: Peru in Comparative Perspective*. Princeton, NJ: Princeton University Press, 1978.

Stites, Regie, and Ladislaus Semali. "Adult Literacy for Social Equality or Economic Growth? Changing Agendas for Mass Literacy in China and Tanzania." *Comparative Education Review* 35, no. 1 (1991): 44–75.

Stoler, Ann Laura. "Colonial Archives and the Arts of Governance." *Archival Science* 2 (2002): 87–109.

Sturken, Marita. "Memory, Consumerism and Media: Reflections on the Emergence of the Field." *Memory Studies* 1, no. 73 (2008): 73–78.

Summerfield, Penny. "Culture and Composure: Creating Narratives of the Gendered Self in Oral History Interviews." *Cultural and Social History* 1 (2004): 65–93.

Taboada, Nila, and Gustavo Lopez. "La reforma agraria 40 años después." *Vocero Agrario* 4, no. 10 (2009): 13–16.

Taylor, Philip M. *Munitions of the Mind: A History of Propaganda from the Ancient World to the Present Era*. Manchester, UK: Manchester University Press, 1995.

Tello, María del Pilar. *¿Golpe o revolución? Hablan los militares del 68*. 2nd ed. 2 vols. Lima: SAGSA, 1983.

Thiesenhusen, William C., ed.. *Searching for Agrarian Reform in Latin America*. Boston: Unwin Hyman, 1989.

Thomson, Alistair. *Anzac Memories: Living with the Legend*. Melbourne: Oxford University Press, 1994.

Thorp, Rosemary. "The APRA Alternative in Peru: Preliminary Evaluation of García's Economic Policies." *Bulletin of Latin American Research* 6, no. 2 (1987): 163–182.

———. "The Stabilisation Crisis in Peru 1975–8." In *Inflation and Stabilisation in Latin America*, edited by Rosemary Thorp and Laurence Whitehead, 110–143. London: Palgrave Macmillan, 1979.

Tileagă, Cristian. *Political Psychology: Critical Perspectives*. Cambridge: Cambridge University Press, 2013.

Tinsman, Heidi. *Partners in Conflict: The Politics of Gender, Sexuality, and Labor in the Chilean Agrarian Reform, 1950–1973*. Durham, NC: Duke University Press, 2002.

Todaro, Michael. *Economic Development in the Third World*. 2nd ed. London: Longman, 1985.

Turino, Thomas. *Moving Away from Silence: Music of the Peruvian Altiplano and the Experience of Urban Migration*. Chicago: University of Chicago Press, 1993.

———. "Nationalism and Latin American Music: Selected Case Studies and Theoretical Considerations." *Latin American Music Review* 24, no. 2 (2003): 169–209.

UNESCO, Regional Office for Education in Latin America and the Caribbean. *Progresos, escollos y soluciones*. Vol. 1 of *Evolución reciente de la educación en América Latina*. Mexico, DF: UNESCO and Secretaria de Educación Pública, 1976.

Valderrama Fernandez, Ricardo, and Carmen Escalante Gutierrez, eds. *Andean Lives: Gregorio Condori Mamani and Asunta Quispe Huamán*. Translated by Paul Gelles and Gabriela Escobar. Austin: University of Texas Press, 1996.

Van Alphen, Ernst. "Symptoms of Discursivity: Experience, Memory, and Trauma." In *Acts of Memory: Cultural Recall in the Present*, edited by Mieke Bal, Jonathan Crewe, and Leo Spitzer, 24–38. Hanover, NH: University Press of New England, 1999.

Van der Ploeg, Jan Douwe. *El futuro robado: Tierra, agua y lucha campesina*. Lima: IEP/WALIR [Water Law and Indigenous Rights], 2006.

Varese, Stefano. *Salt of the Mountain: Campa Asháninka History and Resistance in the Peruvian Jungle*. Translated by Susan Giersbach Rascón. Norman: University of Oklahoma Press, 2002.

———. "Social Justice and Cultural Rights in the Peruvian Amazon." In *Witness to Sovereignty: Essays on the Indian Movement in Latin America*, edited by Stefano Varese and Alberto Chirif, 60–79. Copenhagen: International Work Group for Indigenous Affairs, 2006.

Vaughan, Mary Kay. *Cultural Politics in Revolution: Teachers, Peasants, and Schools in Mexico, 1930–1940*. Tucson: University of Arizona Press, 1997.

Vergara, Alberto, and Daniel Encinas. "From a Partisan Right to the Conservative Archipelago: Political Violence and the Transformation of the Right-Wing Spectrum in Contemporary Peru." In *Politics after Violence: Legacies of the Shining Path Conflict in Peru*, edited by Hillel David Soifer and Alberto Vergara, 226–249. Austin: University of Texas Press, 2019.

Vom Hau, Matthias. "Unpacking the School: Textbooks, Teachers, and the Construction of Nationhood in Mexico, Argentina, and Peru." *Latin American Research Review* 44, no. 3 (2009): 127–154.

Walker, Charles. *The Túpac Amaru Rebellion*. Cambridge, MA: Harvard University Press, 2014.

Wilson, Fiona. *Citizenship and Political Violence in Peru: An Andean Town, 1870s–1970s*. Basingstoke, UK: Palgrave Macmillan, 2013.

———. "Transcending Race? Schoolteachers and Political Militancy in Andean Peru, 1970–2000." *Journal of Latin American Studies* 39 (2007): 719–746.

Wright, Thomas C. *Latin America in the Era of the Cuban Revolution*. Westport, CT: Greenwood, 2000.

Zerubavel, E. *Time Maps: Collective Memory and the Social Shape of the Past*. Chicago: University of Chicago Press, 2004.

Index

Note: Page numbers in *italics* refer to figures.